Father India

Father India

Father India

How Encounters with an Ancient Culture
Transformed the Modern West

Jeffery Paine

HarperCollins*Publishers*

HarperCollins books may be purchased for educational, business, or sales promotional use. For information please write: Special Markets Department, HarperCollins Publishers, Inc., 10 East 53rd Street, New York, NY 10022.

FIRST EDITION

Designed by Elina D. Nudelman

Library of Congress Cataloging-in-Publication Data

Paine, Jeffery, 1944–

    Father India : how encounters with an ancient culture transformed the modern west / Jeffery Paine. — 1st ed.

      p.   cm.

    Includes bibliographical references and index.

    ISBN 0-06-017303-3

    1. India—Description and travel. 2. Travelers—India.

    3. Europeans—Travel—India. 4. India—Civilization. I. Title.

    DS413.P28   1998

    954—dc21   98-12590

---

98 99 00 01 02 ❖/RRD 10 9 8 7 6 5 4 3 2 1

To the Magnificent Eight
whose friendship was sustenance to me during the years of writing
this book:
B.E., D.E., S.F., F.H., D.M., K.R., T.R., and S.S.

CONTENTS

Father India

Introduction
Travels in Alternative Modernity

Do those of us who go to India in the late twentieth century resemble our more daring predecessors who traveled there in bygone eras? Probably yes and no. In the early seventeenth century an eccentric Elizabethan, Tom Coryate, *walked* to India in order, he said, to ride an elephant and to write a book. Later travelers chose more efficient locomotion to propel them into Coryate's double destination of adventure and profit in India. "Come. Come to the exotic," India sang to them as they flocked there to hunt tigers or to convert heathens or to emulate sages. Criminals and cretins in earlier centuries got packed off to India, where their families could draw the curtain across their antics and disgraces. In the twentieth century businessmen came, as colonial administrators earlier had, to enhance power or purse. More cerebral westerners wished to understand India but (so goes the Orientalist indictment) understand it in a way that justified westerners' increasing power and purse there.

On a flight to India recently, who came into my mind was none of the above, however, but someone from long ago who never even considered going there. That figure was James Boswell, and he entered my imagination, not as Samuel Johnson's great biographer, but as a young rake, eager to bite off as much of experience, of the odd strangeness of life, as was humanly possible. In the early 1760s, like all idle young scamps Boswell was touring the Continent, when he did something quite rash: he hopped off the well-mapped itinerary of the European Grand Tour and onto a small boat that would take him to the uncharted, untamed island of Corsica. I wondered which came first, Boswell's foot or his brain—the traveling itch or the traveler's imagination? For no sooner did Boswell abandon familiar, known locations than his journal also abandoned familiar, conventional thinking, and he was speculating daringly about sex, politics, and religion. These were not exactly hushed or forbidden subjects in eighteenth-century polite society, but the way Boswell in Corsica began to write about them was unprecedented. Suddenly, from his vantage point on the road, he saw (or believed he saw) that faith, society, and erotic impulses were relative, malleable, and they could all be remolded to gratify an individual's happiness.

I now see why Boswell became my mental traveling companion on the flight to India. In my mind, he was the first of a new kind of traveler, who voyaged out not for profit or preaching but rather to spill his innards all over the map—a voyage outward and inward simultaneously. I can imagine calling the westerners in twentieth-century India whose adventures unfold in this book Boswell's Children, for they had his gene for outsized impulse and restless dreaming. Their trips, too, transported them over a terrain as much intellectual as geographical—journeys undertaken in search of new thought as much as new sights. They made the oddest travelers, for they labored the voyage to India not to understand it but to understand the very country or world they were leaving behind. The psychoanalyst Carl Jung, for example, journeyed in India in the late 1930s to put in perspective the western psyche that was causing such havoc back in Europe; in 1960 Martin Luther King Jr. spent a month in India, hoping to return with a new vision for America. *Father India* is a study of travelers like them who quit more comfortable conditions to find somewhere, somehow, in India, an alternative track through modernity that would lead them back to a "Boswellian" better home.

They booked passages to Bombay and Delhi and Calcutta but secretly hoped (so secretly they sometimes failed to confess to themselves) that those passages might deposit them at ports for which no shipping agent vends tickets. They looked up the Deccan, the Punjab, and the Coromandel Coast in atlases, yet no map has areas shaded "spiritual possibilities," or "personal adjustment," or "wiser politics." With such nongeographical destinations in mind, they, like Boswell, stacked their emotional and intellectual baggage high, halfway to the ceiling. When your luggage is in danger, V. S. Naipaul said, that's your clue you have arrived in India. The contents of these travelers' luggage, however, were the most cherished assumptions of the modern western mind, and, in truth, they put them at risk in India.

I saw how their forays into India—if taken collectively—could be thought of as an experiment, one conducted by many and supervised by none, spanning the twentieth century from beginning to end. Of course *experiment* was not exactly in Lord Curzon's mind when he set out to establish an enlightened empire of empires, unlike anything the world had known. E. M. Forster hardly supposed himself conducting any sort of trial when, unable to write another novel of the private life and the tête-à-tête, he escaped a mammoth writer's block by larking off to India. Annie Besant certainly pictured no laboratory when she set sail to forge a more just basis for politics on the subcontinent. And V. S. Naipaul wanted merely to sample the antiquarian land of his ancestors, but he inadvertently placed the Enlightenment values of individuality, rationality, and progress into a living crucible there. Collectively, their experiences in India, or rather the patterns of expectation and disappointment that repeat through them, test many a European-born assumption about how the individual will fare in society. The accidental experiment, which no individual intended, proceeded thus: put the random ingredients of western cultural history in a test tube, and over them pour a different catalyst, India, and see what change in coloration or chemical combination then occurs.

Each pleasant surprise, every harsh shock that India yielded, put a question mark after the well-ordered world these people left behind. Outwardly the travelers in this book had little in common. Naipaul excavating family roots in India, Martin Luther King Jr. plucking Gandhian inspiration, and Madame Blavatsky waving her mystical wand hardly appear to be bearing down parallel tracks. Where nonparallel tracks converge, what makes such dissimilar figures siblings after all is they each wanted from India what the Hungarian-born writer Arthur Koestler declared he wanted: "to look at the predicament of the West from a different perspective, a different spiritual latitude." They expected India to be different and that very difference to suggest (in Koestler's words) an "answer to our perplexities and dead-locked problems." When Koestler deboarded the plane in Bombay in 1958, though, the city's heat and smell of backed-up sewage enveloped him as if "a wet, smelly diaper was being wrapped around my head by some abominable joker." Soon he felt India might be *too* different, and eventually he concluded, like Hermann Hesse and Jung before him, that India had no answers whatsoever for his questions. But there was a "deeper," a more receptive sort of traveler than Koestler—Forster, say, or Christopher Isherwood or Madeleine Slade—who felt India's difference just as keenly but instead of feeling defeated, used its overwhelming dissimilarity to revise their questions and categories, and this act of revision often eased or dispelled quandaries for which there was no direct answer. Their triumph or disappointment on alien terrain in India does obliquely tell us something about that terrain, but far less than it thus exposes about the "worldview" they had both left behind and brought with them.

The drama began as soon as these travelers arrived and started projecting onto India the unconscious assumptions of their religion, their society, or their own identity. Selfhood, politics, and religion, those sprawling subjects, supply our themes because selfhood or identity orders personal experience at the intimate level; politics is a social ordering of group experience; and religion structures experience at that largest, nebulous level, the "universal." Identity, politics, and religion were in fact for these travelers merely different vocabularies for getting at the same thing—the troubling uncertainty, the horrible ambiguity of their positions— which, in its severity, makes the earlier Victorian crisis of faith look by comparison like an exercise in bright confidence. The strange, unanticipated bumps that jolted them in India shook and altered what they had oppressively taken for granted about society or religion or sometimes their very selves. Theirs might be counted modern voyages of exploration, but voyages that did not redraw the atlas so much as rewrite the dictionary of contemporary experience.

Rather than making the unexpected they encountered abroad conform to preexisting understandings of behavior back home, as tourists usually do, these travelers generally used such encounters to challenge that understanding. The stylish novelist Christopher Isherwood left the familiar behind when he acquired an Indian guru but continued to lead a hedonistic life, being religious and atheistic simultaneously. Forster accepted his homosexuality not by confronting it, as the psychologists said he should, but by letting its value settle out differently while his back was turned attending to other matters in India. The biologist J. B. S. Haldane dismissed India, conventionally enough, as a scientific backwater until he discovered he could practice his profession better there than in England. Contrary to conventional wisdom, the more the Frenchwoman Mirra Richard immersed herself in an arcane Hinduism, the more she undertook progressive projects such as founding an advanced school à la Dewey and Montessori and inaugurating the most international utopian city in history. This is not what the textbooks said should happen. Mirra Richard, Haldane, Forster, and Isherwood didn't fit the models in standard sociology and psychology texts, as they strained to inhabit a different sort of modernity. Suffering initially from a hangover of the

Victorian worldview, many of these travelers used a stay in India homeopathically, to doctor the hangover into a better vision for the unimaginable century to come.

※

The historian always wants to ask: why at that particular date? Why as the twentieth century opened did the great Irish poet W. B. Yeats shake his white mane over the Upanishads, and later why did sexual misfits like Forster and Allen Ginsberg loiter in strange corners of India, and for that matter why did Naipaul, after decades of excoriating the country, suddenly declare India the model for civilization after all? What thread, if any, can connect travels disparate as King's, Besant's, Naipaul's, and Forster's across the subcontinent?

It was after the First World War that the tectonic plates of global interaction began noticeably to shift. The beginnings of the long death of colonialism meant a westerner and an Indian no longer viewed each other so distortedly, so unequally—a head craning downward, a neck straining upward. Besides, the Great War had caused a crisis in confidence in the West. Its aftermath was not Woodrow Wilson's lasting peace but dictators and camps and the likelihood of bloodier war to come. On a personal level, the preening self-confidence of an earlier era came to seem grotesque to a younger generation in such a troubled world—nearly as grotesque as their own uncertainty. Contemplating this overcast prospect, thinkers might suddenly find themselves wondering about India as they searched for some vantage point outside (in Spengler's famous phrase) "the decline of the West" from which to reenvision the future of the West. If you like symbols, consider: after Woodrow Wilson's postwar vision failed to materialize, Wilson's own daughter Margaret moved to India and settled in a religious ashram, to see whether it might hold the keys to lasting peace that the White House had so blatantly failed to provide.

Gandhi's answer to the question *why now?*, as he observed one westerner after another come to his own ashram, was reminiscent of Spengler. The contemporary West had misplaced its soul, and pilgrims like the Reverend Charles Andrews or Admiral Slade's daughter were on a mission to retrieve it. But Gandhi in his anti-modernism was almost simplistic, in a way that none of the major figures in this study was. A woman socialist attuned to class inequities (Besant), a homosexual knowing history as a persecution (Forster or Isherwood), a psychoanalyst helping patients adjust to present circumstances (Jung), or the grandson of indentured servants (Naipaul) could hardly romanticize the past as a better country. Waltzing back to the Middle Ages with Henry Adams or pining with T. S. Eliot for some fine reactionary monarchy was for them not an option.

Instead they went to India. These particular travelers did not repudiate western rationality or individualism or progress but toted them there along with their bags. They put on the colored spectacles of India not to block out the ills of the contemporary West but to see them in a different focus, to begin the healing diagnosis. During the 1930s, though in his sixties and feeling his age, Carl Jung decided an India trip was in order. With the fascist evil darkening in every direction, Jung wanted to explore how another civilization had integrated the human propensity for evil into the psyche. Similarly in the 1930s the poet Yeats, though approaching seventy, decided to study with a Hindu holy man to see whether Indian philosophy might help stabilize the European imagination. In a kindred spirit the poet Louis MacNeice, although claiming to be "allergic" to India, felt it a fortunate turn when the BBC assigned him there after World War II. "You don't want to go," MacNeice told himself as he prepared to go,

> and that is why you must go. . . . There is [an] East from which you've been too long parted. You must go back beyond Rome, Athens, Jerusalem. The earth is not the moon, one can cross to the dark side, can see how the other half lives. And even a glimpse of their lives may throw some light on your own half. . . . Come on, come on, start packing.

Martin Luther King Jr. was among the many who over the ensu-
ing decades followed in MacNeice's footsteps. Although King dutifully toured the monuments and sights, the view he wanted from
India was of a different America—from the middle of the journey
a view of what to do at the end, when he returned to the United
States. For Yeats, Jung, MacNeice, King, and many others, the
vision of a more humane modernity led not *to* but possibly *through*
India.

Gandhi had his finger on their collective pulse, after all, when
he diagnosed a pervasive discontent. On a personal level, their
excursions to India compensated for a voyage inward that had
become too restricted in Europe or America. If *intelligence*, to take
one example, increasingly has meant analytic ability, then
Hermann Hesse and Isherwood canvassed India for a less narrow,
less I.Q. test–like rationality. If *home life* defined a woman's lot in
Europe, then Mirra Richard and Madeleine Slade assumed such
active public roles in India that they might have crossed into not
another country but another species. And if western paradigms of
political economy restricted legitimate change to one model,
stages of development, then King and the Reverend Charles
Andrews found in India a communal dynamic more complex than
a simple material forward-march.

The shock of India—kindness and generosity mixed with barbaric poverty and disease; exquisitely refined individuals amid
archaic taboos; magnificent intelligences honoring religious
superstitions—defied old, neat systems of values. The title of this
book—*Father India* instead of the customary Mother India—is
meant to evoke a little of these travelers' disorientation and surprise when they discovered that tradition, and everything else,
were not what they were supposed to be. At times they felt as
though they had stepped through the looking glass, where everything was now reversed. In India Annie Besant, the Shavian arch-
rationalist, immersed herself in religion. Madeleine Slade, the
lonely woman, toiled in communal ashrams lacking in privacy.
Lord Curzon, the aloof egotist, indignantly investigated cholera

camps and cases of racial injustice. So busy were they in their altered courses they scarcely noticed that, inadvertently, they had stumbled into a reexamination of what a moral person is and what an ethical society means. Each of their cultural collisions in the Indian corridor thus composes an essay about possibilities—about the different possible ways religion, politics, and personal life can combine to enrich or oppress. Recapturing a century's worth of these Indian adventurers uncovers no shortage of things horrible happening. But alongside the horrors, now and then they reimagined the pieces of the world dovetailed into a better moral order.

What do you think of western civilization? Gandhi was once asked. He answered, "It would be a good idea." This book is about a good idea in India. *Father India* tells the story of those persons— Curzon, Besant, E. M. Forster, V. S. Naipaul, Christopher Isherwood, Mirra Richard, and oddly Gandhi too, as well as a chorus of minor characters—who attempted to comprehend or even to perfect western civilization through India, and of how their successes and failures returned to the modern West a changed understanding of itself.

PART I
Society

In Heaven as it is on earth: George and Mary Curzon became near-monarchs in India. Here, exploding fireworks light up their silhouettes in the night skies over Delhi. *The British Library, Oriental and India Office Collections.*

The Politics of the Past
Struggling to Be Reborn

If they had only been content to be brutes, plunderers, and oppressors, how much easier, how much better in the long run, it all might have gone. But when the British conquered India, they determined to justify their conquest as being, quite possibly, the best thing that had ever happened to the Indians. The empire builders boasted they were introducing into the subcontinental turmoil and social disarray a new rule of law, an orderly house of politics, for which the Indians would eventually thank them. Earlier, when the Mughals had swept over much of north India, they did not claim their raj was a great boon to the Indians; nor, as the Mughal empire disintegrated, did the native Maratha princes who often replaced them care whether their oppressions and onerous taxation were good for their new subjects. But there, right in the English parliament, the great eighteenth-century orator Edmund Burke raised his portly frame and sounded his peroration: Britain must, he declaimed, secure the "prosperity" of the Indian before seeking an ounce of gain for itself.

There is rarely a new idea in history, but possibly this wild notion, that a (nonmissionary) conqueror was conquering for the conquered's benefit, might qualify for just such an ideological first. When the British East India Company's charter came up for renewal in 1833, the historian Thomas Macaulay shook his head over how bizarre the exchange was: England importing Indian spices and goods and exporting English political notions and ideals. Macaulay called Britain's emerging Indian empire "the strangest of all political anomalies," a social experiment that "resembled no other in history." Its closest kinship may have been to the Spanish annexation of the Incan, Aztec, and local kingdoms in Latin America, but the English considered the Spanish tyrants and determined not to duplicate their fanatical despoliations. Much earlier, when the English had conquered the Welsh and

Irish, they had endeavored to incorporate them; when conquering the North American natives, they had driven them over the edge of the world and replaced them. But the British could neither incorporate nor replace the faraway Indians, and so instead they resolved, through institution building and education, to turn them into demi-Englishmen of a browner hue. Lord Curzon, the new Viceroy as the twentieth century began, called this effort at the political education of a whole people the noblest mission in the history of the world. The British rule of India, he liked to imply, involved a trust as sacred as marriage and as inviolate as parenthood, and any Englishman who violated that trust for his own gain deserved unconditional perdition.

What England gained from India is obvious, material, and calculable almost to the decimal point. But what did England offer India that justified its lordship over the subcontinent? Intellectuals such as James Mill, Henry Maine, and James Stephen wrote out the answer to this question at learned length, but at the time any Englishman, scratching his chin a bit, could have told you. England was bringing or teaching the Indians lessons in life—in how to lead a good life.

A good life—was ever there a vaguer cliché? But every cliché has a history, and the idea of a good life was once fresh, charged, electric. The eighteenth-century Enlightenment had supposedly transferred salvation and happiness from a heavenly goal to an earthly destination, to a desideratum in the here and now. As the British were laying the foundations of their empire in India, the idea of happiness in its new definition was enjoying a vogue in Europe. During the nineteenth century, it had ceased to be as ineffable as divine dispensation, as rarefied as an angel's aureole, but become instead something hard, knowable, and utilitarian. Happiness occurred matter-of-factly when three factors—a person's rational self-interest, his material betterment, and progress in the conditions and opportunities in society—converged, and this happiness was, for the first time, available to any individual determined enough to pluck it off the branch. In instructing his readers to strive for "a careful and constant pursuit of true and solid happiness," the philosopher John Locke offered no tired platitude but bold new secular advice. Following Locke, Thomas Jefferson in writing the Declaration of Independence substituted for property "happiness" as one of the inalienable rights to which every individual was entitled. In India many of the early British empire builders were disciples of another philosopher, Jeremy Bentham, and Bentham's famous calculus of "the greatest happiness for the greatest number" was the gift they believed they were delivering to India. In exchange for ruling their land, the British traded the Indians, in effect, nothing less than the secret of happiness.

It was a political secret. The English system of governance was the mechanism that would hoist India's decrepit civilization into a happy prosperity and healthier condition—the kind of health that only a legalist, enterprising, modern democracy enjoyed. In England where rational economics, Adam Smith's "Invisible Hand," had supplanted divine laws, each individual could even pursue his own good and the result still be the good of the whole. England's material accumulation and technological superiority during the nineteenth century had proven conclusively (certainly in its own rulers' minds) that their system was the finest machine for delivering happiness the world had ever known.

Europe's attractive-sounding ideas about governance were, however, alien to hierarchic, autocratic, theocratic India. When the British brought their sapling of liberal politics and laissez-faire economics to India, they were dismayed that it would not readily transplant in the hard native soil. Different ideas of a polity confronted each other, but that was not how they experienced it. They experienced it as shock over the barbarous state of Indian society—shock over suttee, the practice of immolating a widow after her husband's death; shock over mere children of five and six married to each other. Obviously, these practices did not illustrate an individual making a contract with society to secure his happiness. The individual and his or her happiness seemed irrelevant, dispensable, in India. The new British over-lords immediately set upon their business of progressive reform. They forbade suttee and passed the Widows Remarriages Act (1856); they enacted the "Age of Consent" law (1891), deeming all sexual intercourse between children under twelve, whether mar-ried or not, rape.

But there was a more fundamental reform the British Raj needed to legislate into being, if its gifts of rational governance, liberal civil rights, and individual happiness were not to wither away in the harsh climate of India. India's backwardness and its opposition to individual happiness were established in British eyes by the caste system and particularly by its offshoot, Untouchability. Arundhati Roy's novel *The God of Small Things* (1997) describes Untouchability as it appeared as late as 1969:

> Paravans [an untouchable caste] were expected to crawl backwards with a broom, sweeping away their footprints so that Brahmins or Syrian Christians would not defile them-selves by accidentally stepping into a Paravan's footprint. . . . Untouchables were not allowed to walk on public roads, not allowed to cover their upper bodies, not allowed to carry umbrellas. They had to put their hands over their mouths when they spoke, to divert polluted breath away from those whom they addressed.

If this was what Untouchability was like in 1969—two decades after Article 17 of India's Constitution had abolished it—then imagine the spectacle that appalled educated Englishmen a half century or more before. When Gandhi's friend the Reverend Charlie Andrews entered an Untouchable's cottage to ask for water, she screamed, knowing she'd be beaten or stoned for pol-luting his presence. Perhaps one in five Indians was classified, or condemned, as an Untouchable, fit only to remove carcasses or carry away excrement, and whose very presence was, like leprosy, dangerous to normal members of society.

But the British could not outlaw Untouchability, as they had widow burning or infant marriage, for it belonged to the very foundations of Indian society—the caste system. "If there was one social institution that, to the colonial mind, centrally and essentially characterized Indian society as radically different from western society, it was the institution of caste," writes the political scientist Partha Chatterjee. "All arguments . . . about the inherent incapacity of Indian society to acquire the virtues of modernity and nationhood, tended to converge upon this supposedly unique Indian institution."

The word for caste in India, *jati*, means simply, birth. During the Raj, an Indian baby was born into a caste, which meant his loyalties, his position in society, his job, and his spouse were almost entirely predetermined. The system resembled (to British observers) more a hive of bees operating by instinct than a human society governed by intelligence and justice. But if the British legislated caste away, they tampered with the communal foundations of India's complex society. So instead of abolishing the caste system, and having the whole social structure possibly tumble down about them, the British authorities compromised their ideas about political happiness and acquiesced into the contradiction. When Gandhi arrived on this scene, in 1914, he declared that the conflict was less a contest between India and England than a battle for the soul of the world between two contending ideas of what a society should properly be.

The empire builders had proudly convinced themselves that the edifice they had erected in India, built on bricks of logic and justice, would last for a fair portion of all time. But it vanished, relatively, in an instant—in a single long lifetime: there were people born when the British crown began governing India (in 1857, replacing the East India Company) who were still alive in 1947, when the British exited and left India an independent nation. Instead of bricks, they had built on sand, on blatant paradoxes and contradictions. The British brought their handsome political principles—rational governance, laissez-faire economics, secularization, individual choice, and equality of opportunity—but attempted to graft them onto social anomalies such as caste where they could hardly take. On a larger scale, they brought their nationalist, liberal democracy to India but denied that country democracy and liberalism and nationhood, in the name of administrative rationality, economic prosperity, and "happiness." Some like Thomas Macaulay noted the incongruities of British India—"the strangest of all political anomalies"—but they were few, compared to the many colonialists who preferred seeing the serene mirage of their Empire as the greatest gift the Indians had ever received.

What follows is the story of three towering persons who were among these few, who embodied in their persons that battle for the soul of India. Lord George Curzon, Mrs. Annie Besant, and Mahatma Gandhi each tried in his or her own way to integrate progressive western politics with obdurate Indian social realities like caste. Each presided over the impossible marriage and joined things rarely or never combined—equality and caste, progress and tradition, rationality and religion, individualism and community—to create a social good that India, or for that matter the world, had never quite known before.

Curzon's, Besant's, and Gandhi's paths could have easily crossed anytime from, say, 1900 to 1920. Yet, though their stories overlap chronologically, they represent three different eras of endeavor in India. As the century began, Curzon imported western politics into India in order to build a benevolent empire—the glorious, modern equivalent of Rome's achievement in antiquity. While he pictured Englishmen heading this noble polity, Annie Besant subsequently turned his empire upside down and had Indians leading the vanguard of modernity. When Gandhi in turn supplanted Mrs. Besant, he discarded even her radicalism as out-of-date or misguided and instead combined western and Indian notions to create a fundamental redefinition of what power itself was and what modernity itself could mean. The line from Curzon to Besant to Gandhi thus defines a changing conception of what politics in the modern world is and does. This change, this story, takes place in

India, but its implications have reverberated, from Martin Luther King Jr.'s America to Nelson Mandela's South Africa, the whole world round.

❉

After independence, when Nehru surveyed the roll call of British overlords in India, he declared only one worth remembering: Curzon. In 1899, on the eve of the new century, when the newly anointed Viceroy sailed for India, the cheers of the English rang in his ears as he departed and the cheers of Indians greeted him as he arrived. Curzon was deemed the great promise, the best assurance that the union of England and India would be a happy one benefiting both parties. From youth onward all Curzon's accomplishments had piled high, like so many velvet cushions, so that the viceregal crown would rest atop them. His ambition never pointed him in any other direction, nor would it have settled for any position less glorious.

The political history of the West appeared to be compressed in Curzon's magnificent personage. In his very style and manner he brought to India, all mixed within himself, at least three centuries of approach to governance. Accomplished, disdainful, autocratic (supposedly the only person who could make a speech in his pajamas and not forfeit his dignity), Curzon was an atavistic reversion to the eighteenth-century aristocrat. As such, he would by his will alone mandate India into modernity. Beneath the ermine majesty and pride, however, Curzon approached his task like a good nineteenth-century bourgeois, trusting in reason, fair play, and ceaseless effort to make the world run right. As such, the bourgeois Viceroy bravely rebuked English racial injustices, so all passengers regardless of skin color received fair treatment, even as he made the trains run on time in India. But beneath even that layer of bourgeois pragmatism, Curzon anticipated the late-twentieth-century technician-bureaucrat who, skeptical about social forces, believes precision with the organizational blueprint—a better computer program, as it were—will fix any malfunction in the system. As the technician-bureaucrat, the Viceroy labored perfecting minuscule administrative reforms, in the belief that administrative efficiency was "a synonym for the contentment of the governed." Surely such a multilayered approach to reform, combining the political know-how of the centuries, generously motivated, arduously applied, could not fail in India. But, to anticipate our story, fail is exactly what it did.

Curzon failed because, though the subcontinent was large, there was nowhere on it for his reformist vision to alight. Educated, westernized Indians, who should have been his natural allies, Curzon simply detested, for they threatened to take over his role and make his function unnecessary. For the mass of rural Indians, enmeshed in their caste system and locked in ceaseless rounds of toil, Curzon had declared sympathy, but his programs scarcely touched them. With an older, legalist, administrative conception of government, he did not believe that politics could operate at so fundamental a level as to tamper with the social structure. Curzon's vigorous administration, since it dared not fiddle with too many of the underlying realities of Indian life, lived for the horrible catastrophe, when it could jump into action.

> I think you only see the Civil Service at its very best [Curzon wrote] when it is working under the strain of some great affliction or disaster in India, such, for instance, as plague or famine.

During famine or cholera outbreaks his machine of superior benevolence could descend, deus ex machina, and administer relief, but when it ascended again, nothing basic was changed in Indian society. Being a good aristocrat, being a good bourgeois, and being a good technocrat, and being all of them all at once, could not compensate for Curzon's limited definition of politics, which restricted who might participate and what might be done. Curzon's efficient ineffectuality, his good intentions continually misfiring in India, may be attributed to the contradictions inherent even in a benevolent colonialism, which condemned him to being like a father who will do everything for a child but let him grow up. It was an already antiquated vision of politics by the time Curzon put on its spectacles—a vision that proposed policies and regulations but left the underlying body of society intact as it found it, decreeing most of the world's misery and problems politically off-limits.

On a government tour, Curzon once entered a village that had prepared a banner to welcome its admirable lord. Regrettably, though, the sign announced GOD BLESS OUR ABOMINABLE LOUT. Curzon, always in the best of humor on tour, chuckled heartily over the error. But, in fact, his rule depended on just such mistakes occurring regularly: they furnished the proof that the Indians were sincerely trying to emulate the English but could not yet pull it off. The story of how an admirable lord became an abominable lout in India is not really an occasion for laughter, however, and in Curzon's condescending chuckling one hears the tragic undertones of an old order coming to an end without understanding why it must end.

※

Annie Besant, the infamous radical, was Curzon's contemporary (actually she was born a decade earlier and died a decade later), but in her attitudes, in her orientation to current issues, she had already left behind the ancien régime he inhabited. They were both English, both members of the human race of course, which, according to some observers, was the limit of what they had in common. To know Annie Besant's stance on anything concerning India is simply to flip Curzon's position on its head. The decayed, backward Indian civilization Curzon found in such need of English restoration and repairs, Annie acclaimed as on a par with, and in many ways superior to, Europe's own. The passive, uneducated Indians whom Curzon wrote off as beyond the reach of politics, Annie proceeded to draft as active citizens and political shapers of their own fate. Consequently, while Curzon assumed responsibility for his brown Indian brothers until in some unforeseeable futurity they could be responsible for themselves, Annie shortened futurity to today: Indians, she announced, were ready for independence *now*. Lord Curzon and Annie Besant were like the North and South Poles of Anglo-Indian politics, and any specific disagreement between them only hinted at the larger, more general difference. Annie Besant had already moved into a new definition of politics, where its function was no longer formulating trade policy, overseeing the army, or even administrative efficiency, but giving birth to a better and more just society.

Curzon was one of the last Englishmen of his stature to consider cultural commerce between England and India as a one-way street, in which ideas, education, and instruction flowed in one direction only. He expected to exercise his prodigious talents on behalf of India, but without India radically affecting or altering him. Basically, he expected nothing from India, except to be its uncrowned king. By contrast, Annie Besant was the first English person of her political prominence to believe that the Anglo-Indian corridor permitted a two-way traffic. She expected India to change her as much (almost) as she changed it, and change her, India did. She went from being England's most notorious agnostic and the author of *The Gospel of Atheism* to composing works on spiritual chemistry and even anointing a new messiah. Her newfound vocation in India, however unbalanced it may appear, permitted her to see what Curzon found unthinkable: that progressive politics, to be effective in India, might need to ally itself with traditional religion. Only she could never effect that alliance herself, as she alternated between pursuing her political programs and then forgetting them and chasing after religious goals. She could, incredibly, be elected president of the Indian National Congress; she could also be president of the Theosophical Society; only she could not be, as it were, president of herself. Her vision kept breaking apart, falling off into unrelated tangents, and never combined into a basis for the new politics she wanted.

In some ways Annie Besant floated as much on the surface of Indian life as Curzon had. Her vision for India was European radical politics wearing a sari (her wearing a white sari herself made her enormously sympathetic to her Indian audiences). Her vision for the Indian independence movement ignored the Hindu traditions she professed to admire and instead merely copied the Irish Home Rule movement, with herself, if necessary, serving as a one-woman Sinn Fein. Whatever was too incongruous or singular about Indian society to fit into her European-born vision of justice and the good life, she ignored. How democracy and egalitarianism could combine with a caste system never overly troubled her because she tended to identify India with one caste, the Brahmins. In a similar triumph of imagination, she identified India with one person—herself—though here the cracks in the identification became perceptible with time. During the 1920s, as anti-English sentiment mounted, Indian youth, hitherto so ready with applause, booed her as she spoke to them. But she assumed they were merely reacting like Irish youth who booed any English orator, so she turned to her companion on the podium and whispered, "At last! Things have become normal."

❖

Both Curzon and Besant prided themselves on the vistas of possibility they glimpsed, where their more conventional colleagues saw only obstacles. But in 1914 there showed up in India a western reformer whose Euro-Indian synthesis—whose challenge to the status quo—was so original and unprecedented it made Curzon's and Besant's visions appear positively myopic. Of course M. K. Gandhi may not be considered a western reformer, even if he had spent years abroad. Yet his assassins—his one successful and many unsuccessful ones—sentenced him to death for exactly that crime, for being a foreigner in native dress and for tampering with inviolate customs. Although wrong to kill him, the assassins were perhaps not mistaken in their verdict. Gandhi pushed western reforms to the very heart of Indian society, and there mixed them with native ingredients and caused new possibilities to leaven the dough, beyond anything Curzon or Besant had imagined. (Gandhi's story is related at length in part 3 of this book, but he impinges everywhere and for the argument needs to be introduced here.)

More than any Englishman ever did, Gandhi waved a political wand of westernized change over the subcontinent. While India's communal traditions minimized individualism, Gandhi made each person's right to live by his own truth the ultimate priority. While Indian society subordinated women, Gandhi enrolled them equally in the public sphere as Lenin and Mao never did. While the upper castes considered Untouchability sacrosanct, Gandhi ranked its abolition above national independence. Hindu culture had shown indifference to struggles for justice and equality, but Gandhi defined service in such a struggle as the only means to attain *moksha*, or salvation, in a politics-dominated age. Western political idealism speaking in Indian language—how strange at first it sounded! So strange that neither Indians nor westerners at first recognized what Gandhi was doing. Emerson, Mill, and Tolstoy had expressed similar ideas before him, and more eloquently, but through his ventriloquism these "western values"— equality, individualism, feminism, social justice for all—voiced themselves in Indian society.

When Gandhi returned to India in 1914, after living in England and South Africa, he was denounced as a mouthpiece of westernization, someone trying to christianize Hinduism. But he soon learned to wrap his imported reforms in Hindu expressions; more than that, he made them live in social contexts supposedly antithetical to their very existence. He experienced an easier time moving politically onto new and open ground than Curzon or Besant had because he could dismiss things they considered requisites of a progressive society. Almost all of modern, industrialized, urban life—its machinery, its legislatures, its newspapers— he thought could go, and politics to him consisted of coming up with a better alternative. His religious view of politics, as undertaken for personal salvation, made less necessary an impersonal, parliament-engendered system of rights and duties. (In his *Hind Swaraj*, or *Indian Home Rule*, he had likened the Mother of Parliaments in England to a prostitute.) The communal Indian village he held up as a model for economics obviated the capitalist structures of production and distribution. Somewhere in Gandhi's wild propositions Marx's anticapitalism, Tolstoy's fanatical piety, Thoreau's rugged individualism, and Shaw's socialism were all lodged. But all together, they gave politics a sense and direction it had not possessed before. Indeed, for those people who could not go down the official route of modernity, here was a cutoff, an alternative, a detour.

Many plunged down that detour, desperate for another description or prescription for modern politics. From King and Cesar Chavez in America to Lech Walesa in Poland to A. T. Ariyaratne in Sri Lanka, those who felt trapped in a system that would not budge or move looked to see how Gandhi had once dislodged the set-in-stone British Empire. Had not Gandhi declared his ambition was to bring about not a change in governments but a change in hearts? And, with a change in heart, might not the body politic in which it beat then change in ways currently unimaginable? Gandhi, as Curzon and Besant had done in more modest ways before him, rewove hope into the political fabric where it had worn too thin.

❖

Tales of King, Mandela, Chavez (et al.) are still told and still fascinate, but the story of "Gandhism" itself would be more stirring, or at least would better conform to the rules of old-fashioned narrative, had not Gandhi in the end written over it FAILURE. What are we to make of his negative verdict? Gandhi, like Annie Besant and Lord Curzon, left contemporaries behind gasping at the boldness of everything they dared and changed in the name of the public good. In calling himself a failure, Gandhi had certain dismal specifics in mind—the Hindu-Muslim hostility he could not end; the Untouchables he could not integrate into society—but even here he judged his efforts by too ahistorical a criterion. He achieved accords between Muslims and Hindus that no one else then could have, until his Hindu opponents called him "Mohammed Gandhi"; in 1932, his fast-unto-the-death to end Untouchability had, for the first time, Brahmins and Untouchables sharing meals and embracing one another in the street. The unimaginable is what Curzon, Besant, and Gandhi typically imagined. With a dizzying daring that Gandhi would (and did) admire, Curzon insisted that reforms that ordinarily would have taken six months be put into effect within six hours. Like Curzon, Besant accelerated the speed at which long-intractable problems moved on the national agenda. If these three are reckoned failures, who may be called a success?

And yet in one regard they all fell short of what they intended. For all their radically different approaches, none of them could fully import the western political system for securing an individual's happiness into Indian society. Too early on the scene, Curzon never saw what Besant and Gandhi later cautioned about: namely, that "happiness," the "good life," if exported over the globe, might father a Frankensteinian version of itself. Gandhi warned that if everyone's rational self-interest required a greater material accumulation for its happiness, that formula, like locusts, would strip the globe bare. Annie Besant hoped that Hinduism might counterbalance western materialism, but ricocheting between "progress" and "spirituality," she never achieved that balance. Gandhi, however, proposed a practical model. The ancestral villages of India, with their all-but-forgotten cottage industries of spinning and weaving, made, he claimed, exploitative capitalism unnecessary. He founded different ashrams to demonstrate just how economically rational, individually satisfying, nonracist, and feminist this old village model could be. But after independence, Nehru politely informed Gandhi that a modern, advanced state had as much use for his village-nation as for a flying carpet. Nehru and others at the time never quite understood why Gandhi fretted so about modern, progressive politics. By the end of the twentieth century, many economists and environmentalists do understand. Whether individual liberties, whether even a civil society, can coexist with a sustainable economy despite rapidly diminishing resources is, so they declare, *the* problem facing the twenty-first-century world order. Annie Besant and Gandhi, presciently, looked that problem in the face much earlier.

Their work is thus not so much a failure as unfinished business. Their labors still invite curiosity, for the questions they raised are still being puzzled to their uncertain conclusion. Had Curzon's or Besant's or later Gandhi's vision attained fruition, it could constitute the entirety of this study. But as their European-born political programs floundered in India, a cry went out for greater changes in society than any politician's methods could introduce. Ordinarily a political figure does not stop to ask what the individual unit in society is or what social adhesive holds those individuals together; acting on the consensus, he skates immediately into action. But when Curzon brought his Enlightenment political order to traditional, "communal" India, it rested on the shoulders of a different kind of citizen than it had in Europe. For Curzon's vision to prosper there, it required a new individual, and for that individual to appear, something had to happen outside of politics. That "something" did occur, in miniature, when E. M. Forster arrived in India. England's finest novelist of intimacy, Forster surprised himself by so relishing the *un*-intimacy of boisterous social participation in India. Here, in an unlikely, sensitive writer, was oddly the example Curzon needed, the demonstration that western individualism and Indian communalism could mix and at least momentarily inhabit the same body.

Most modern politicians—to take one more case—have held that religion is a private affair, but they could not so easily hold that position in India, where religion glued the ethnic and linguistic fragments together in that jigsaw puzzle of a country. Aware of the importance of religion, Annie Besant required for her schizophrenically political-spiritual ideal of society the model of someone simultaneously religious and secular, such as, say, Christopher

Isherwood, to show how Hinduism could integrate with contemporary westernized existence. As Curzon and Besant (and Gandhi) expanded the scope of politics, they opened up a public sphere in which normally private souls like Forster and Isherwood had secretly defining parts to play, and in playing them, they changed the meaning of modernity.

This book begins with an ending—with George Nathaniel Curzon, who represented the last, best hope of an old order. But as his missed opportunities left the gate open for Besant and then Gandhi, and as their stories connect to Forster's and Isherwood's, the collective tale that unfolds is anything but one of conclusion. Annie Besant embarked, as in his own way Curzon did, hoping that a new beginning just might be possible, and to try it somewhere, each brought that hope to India.

CHAPTER 1

The Great Game Gone Mad

On the third Friday in May 1923, George Curzon left London for his country house in Somerset to await—curiously—a telegram from London that would demand his immediate return to the City. Not just any telegram; this telegram would make the wrongs of a lifetime right. Its sender would be Lord Stamfordham, the king's private secretary, proposing a meeting in London, and at that meeting Stamfordham would on behalf of His Majesty request Curzon to form a government in which he would become Prime Minister of England. That history would conform to this plan not only Curzon but practically no one in England doubted.

Because of illness the old Prime Minister, Bonar Law, had resigned unexpectedly. In service, in ability, and in preeminence, Curzon simply had no rival to be his successor within the Conservative Party. In his Somerset villa, as the lights illumined the great columned halls and cast a subfusc golden pallor over the exquisite furnishings and priceless paintings, Curzon reined in his impatience, waiting for the business of government to resume on Monday and the telegram to come. Becoming Prime Minister was the second great ambition of Curzon's life. When the first, to be

Viceroy of India, had been fulfilled—though perhaps this was not the weekend for that analogy—everything jinxed and cursed had ensued, as in a fairy tale where misfortune follows from the wish fulfilled.

While he awaited the telegram, Curzon may well have returned in reverie to those glory days, those soul-trying days in India two decades before. Certainly no other Englishman ever coveted the viceregal crown so fervidly, none served as Viceroy of India longer, and if any viceroy is remembered today it is Curzon. Nor, as for that, did any other match his vision, for Curzon instituted massive reforms in India that—while they would have brought the country neither democracy nor independence—might have achieved the streamlined economy, the administrative efficiency, and some of the prosperity that other Asian countries like Singapore or South Korea achieved nearly a century later. "For the rest of his life," the newspaper magnate Lord Beaverbrook observed of Curzon's tenure as Viceroy, "Curzon was influenced by his sudden journey to heaven at the age of thirty-nine and then by his return to earth seven years later, for the remainder of his mortal existence."

And yet as in a mirage, the harder he worked in India, the more his vision receded from fruition. His policies, meant both to maintain the British in India and to benefit the Indian populace, had the uncanny effect of alienating both. When Curzon went to India in 1899, everyone predicted that, as surely as day follows dawn, the new Viceroy would return to England to become its Prime Minister. When seven years later he did return, his chances for that high office were, in fact, reckoned in permanent ruin. But, confounding all expectations, Curzon emerged from purgatory, from his years in the wilderness, when he had grubbed for minor and unworthy offices. His iron will and paramount abilities were unstoppable, and by 1923 he had held nearly every major office available to an Englishman, most recently Foreign Secretary (equivalent to the American secretary of state) and leader of the House of Lords. Every major office except Prime Minister, and on Monday that would be his.

If during that May weekend Curzon needed further proof that fate had finally turned favorable, he had only to glance across the room at his wife. Grace Duggan, his second wife, resembled his first: both were American, both alluring beauties, and both rich beyond reckoning. But Curzon's first wife had adored him and made her life one long, unbroken service to his needs. Grace Duggan adored Curzon's social position, and having married him for it, she appeared hardly to require him further. When he pleaded for her to join him at Kedleston, his cherished ancestral home, she replied that, home being where the heart is, she "would rather not go at all." When Curzon mildly reproved her for not even inquiring about his health after a serious illness, she replied that no good could come of such charges and they should attempt to spend more time amiably apart. But now that her "dear Boy" was about to become Prime Minister, all that was changed, and she had dashed back from Paris to be at his side and make it clear that at his side is where she would ever remain.

Monday came round. Curzon's old-fashioned sense of grandeur had not permitted that newfangled contraption, the telephone, to be installed in his home, and as luck would have it, the telegram delivery boy was on holiday. But the local policeman surmised what the telegram portended, and he puffed and panted on his bicycle all the way out to Curzon's estate to deliver it. Not only the policeman, but all England seemed to know. The newspapers were talking of little else, and Curzon's progress to London, after receiving Stamfordham's message, was lined solidly with curious gawkers and well-wishers cheering and photo-cameras recording for posterity every stop made along the way. When Stamfordham arrived at Curzon's London house, punctual to the minute, he began formally by recounting that the king's decision had been delayed because he had not been informed in advance of Bonar Law's intentions. On behalf of the king, whose new Prime Minister he was to be, Curzon grew incensed that His Majesty had had to learn of Law's resignation from the newspapers.

Quick as Curzon's mind was, however, he was slow to take in Stamfordham's delicate message that he had been passed over, and someone else, a lesser politician Curzon considered a nonentity, junior to him in service and inferior to him in abilities, had been selected. Curzon—who had suffered pain every day of his adult life because of a spinal injury, who had traveled the world on horseback and worked twenty-hour stints in physical agony, and never breathed a word about it—broke down and hung his head and wept. Being Curzon, though, he recovered immediately and in rotund periods lectured Stamfordham about the monstrous injustice and illogic of the choice.

Days later Curzon learned that it was India that had undone him, India that had come back to haunt him. Contests and controversies from long ago in India, superseded and supposedly forgotten, had suddenly raised their heads like sleeping vipers, struck, and poisoned his chances. The chief figure, the quiet force, in this small drama was old Arthur Balfour. Balfour had been Prime Minister of England during Curzon's last three years as Viceroy. A philosopher by training and a man of infinite charm, suavity, and diplomacy, Balfour had a mind described as the most nuanced that ever applied itself to politics in England. In those years when they had clashed over Indian policy, the Prime Minister's and the Viceroy's behavior in office could scarcely have differed more. All Curzon's fury whenever his policies were not endorsed in London, his sullen behavior toward Balfour himself, his petulant threats of resignation—all these the unflappable Balfour had simply let glide by, like a discordant tune heard in the distance. But evidently Balfour forgot nothing. Perhaps Balfour considered that a man like Curzon, who made mountains out of molehills, should not be Prime Minister; perhaps he was taking retroactive revenge on Curzon's rude effrontery.

In any case Balfour had risen from his sickbed and suffered the weary train ride to London to counsel the king. He could have marshaled a dozen arguments against appointing Curzon but instead limited himself to making one small point, which sounded less like an opinion (which it was) than a fact. In the new temper of England, Balfour told the king, a Prime Minister would no longer be acceptable or effective if chosen from the House of Lords. After his interview with the king, Balfour felt well enough after all to attend a party in Norfolk. "And will dear George be chosen?" was almost the first question asked him upon his arrival. "No," Balfour replied, "dear George will not."

Oddly, before their contretemps over India, Curzon and Balfour had been friends and cronies, but their quarrel signified more than personal loss. In it the best hopes, the shining ideals of a generation, became cracked and damaged. Balfour and Curzon had shone as the most golden members of that gilded coterie called "the Souls." The Souls—so dubbed by the popular press, because they were supposedly always inspecting theirs—provide a rare modern instance of knowledge and power uniting in the same persons. Curzon's and Balfour's golden gang valued learning, ability, and wit as the English aristocracy had not since the Renaissance. They appeared to usher in a new renaissance in crusty Victorian England; and the two most prominent Souls, Balfour as Prime Minister and Curzon as Viceroy—two philosopher-princes—came to rule over a significant portion of the globe.

They began in such high hopes, with such promise, and yet in the end it had all come to little, to so very little. To return to that abortive renaissance and what was intended to be its apogee— Curzon's administration in India—is to enter a historical tangle. For if the investigation begins simply enough, with the question of why colonialism could not reform itself, it quickly proceeds— given the high intelligence of the actors and the unparalleled scope of their opportunities—into examining the puzzling nature of what politics can and cannot achieve.

"No," Balfour repeated with bland relish to the partygoers, "dear George will not be chosen."

※

But to begin at the beginning. Never did a morning dawn brighter, it seemed, nor boisterous spirits overflow more intelligently than when Curzon was launching his career in the great world. One London club to which the frolicking young bachelor belonged was the Crabbet, its name appropriated from Shakespeare's "Crabbed age and youth cannot live together," and bearing the motto *Mens insana in corpore sano* (A Deranged Mind in a Sound Body). Crabbed age, that was how Curzon and his friends thought of Prince Edward's overweight Malborough House set, always hunting game or devouring gargantuan meals of game. By contrast, youth was Curzon's friends playing games like "Clumps," a twenty questions to guess a philosophical abstraction, or "Style," where everyone composed poetry or prose in the style of a famous author. At Crabbet or Souls dinners over champagne, Curzon contributed his share of "doggerel awful" (his description) to amuse his dazzling and self-dazzled chums. One specimen went:

> Charms and a man I sing, to wit—a most superior person,
> Myself, who bears the fitting name of George Nathaniel
> Curzon.

The *"person/Curzon"* couplet has entered some unofficial English anthology of nonsense verse, and many people can still recite it, having little idea who the "superior person" was or why he should be considered so. Curzon did not pen the couplet, however; some satirical fellow undergraduates at Oxford did. Perhaps no mocking ditty ever so harmed its subject, plaguing Curzon's entire career with its insinuation that he was a creature aloof and apart. In fact, Curzon was aloof and apart; yet nothing about this Superior Person was ever quite what it first appeared.

Curzon's life can be recounted as two distinctly contrary narratives. In version number one, the red carpet he stepped onto when he disembarked as Viceroy in India extends, symbolically, from cradle to the grave. He was born privileged, in 1859, at the Derbyshire estate that his family had possessed for nearly nine hundred years. A favorite of the gods, he glided to Eton, where he effortlessly took more honors and prizes than any other boy in that school's history. Next he duplicated the feat at Oxford. While still at Oxford, the speeches he made were repeated in Parliament. After he entered Parliament at age twenty-seven, his promotions and advances occurred as regularly as if he had stepped onto an upward-ascending escalator.

But concealed behind that charmed fairy tale exists another version of his life. His father was a country parson, a younger son of a younger son, who unexpectedly inherited the estate when one claimant died and another six were declared illegitimate. His ascendancy to English grandee ill suited his father's plain temperament, as though he had donned someone else's expensive suit that was sizes too big for him. If George's childhood home had floors of *opus alexandrium* and columns of alabaster, it remained in spirit a disciplinary, cold, and uncomfortable mid-Victorian vicarage, with everything that image evokes. His childhood sounds less like an aristocrat's pampered upbringing than a term in a gulag, ruled over by a tyrannous governess who conducted trials in which little George was made to confess to imaginary crimes and then punished for them. In the study halls of Eton, Curzon learned that achievement could win him esteem and liberation from misery. He applied himself to that lesson with a vengeance, but the prizes did not fall into his lap like overripe fruit. He would hole up for days and then nonchalantly turn in, say, a 216-page essay on John Sobieski, the king of Poland.

At Eton and Oxford he received an education, such as possibly no young man will ever again obtain, in the classics and history, in Latin and Greek, in rhetoric and poise, and to these he later added through his travels an immense practical knowledge of the world. Yet this formidable weight of learning was supported on two rickety intellectual poles that made it, at certain crucial moments, collapse into uselessness. First, his stern governess had drummed into him that life is an account book, where everything is entered as either a credit or debit. Then his Eton tutors had instructed him that intellectual attainment consisted, foremost, in an accurate command of detail. Young George's mind dazzled all, but its philosophic underpinnings could hardly have been narrower. He had learned to anatomize knowledge into tiny detailed bits and to insert those bits into plus or minus columns. His had, in fact, been one of the worst educations possible for someone who later wanted to unite diverse peoples into a living, organic empire. This shortcoming was of course not apparent when Curzon left Oxford in 1885 to launch the juggernaut of his career.

Though he was the golden youth of legend, he lacked one crucial element—gold. Curzon's character was independent, his confidence strong; but dependent upon a meager allowance from his father, his pocketbook was empty. He had a fluid pen, though, and for the thirteen years between Oxford and his marriage, his journalism and then his books paid for his travels over the globe. Those books, *Russia in Central Asia* (1889), *Persia and the Persian Question* (1892), and *Problems of the Far East* (1894), established him as one of England's preeminent authorities on questions Asiatic.

In either biographical version—either as son of heaven or as self-made man—one factor in Curzon's life remains constant: India. There are people who fasten early upon some notion, usually harebrained, of their destiny. Often they ruin themselves or others by manhandling whatever happens to make it conform to that notion. One thinks, for example, of an awkward Texas boy deciding that he must be first a congressman, then senator, and finally president, and that he would pursue no other goal in no other sequence—even though the odds were a billion to one against Lyndon Johnson's vainglorious dream. In his more privileged milieu, George Curzon stood more favored in the lottery of life's chances when as a youth he determined to become the future ruler of India.

Curzon has recounted variant versions of first hearing the auguries speak. In one recollection, the old India hand Sir James Fitzjames Stephen (an uncle of Virginia Woolf's) delivered a talk at Eton. Stephen enthralled the lads, telling them, Curzon recalled, "that there was in the Asian continent an empire more populous, more amazing, and more beneficent than that of Rome; that the rulers of that great dominion were drawn from the men of our own people; that some of them might perhaps in the future be taken from the ranks of boys who were listening to his words." The individual words in that single sentence—*Asian, empire, beneficent, Rome, dominion, our own people, ranks, rulers*—supply the vocabulary of Curzon's ambitions. Ever since hearing Stephen talk, Curzon would later say, "The fascination and, if I may say so, the sacredness of India have grown upon me."

But sometimes Curzon dated his encounter with destiny later. In 1887, Curzon first visited Calcutta and beheld a mirage: there stood Kedleston, his childhood home in Derby. Kedleston is an impressive house—a whole village was relocated to leave its view unencumbered. Sir Nathaniel Curzon had built this *folie de grandeur* in 1761, and it was far grander than the Curzons' funds to maintain it. When Samuel Johnson and James Boswell visited Kedleston, Boswell effused, "One should think that the proprietor of all this *must* be happy." Johnson harrumphingly dissented, "It would do excellently well for a Town Hall." Johnson was correct, for Government House in Calcutta had been modeled on Kedleston. On that day in 1887 Curzon saw not just an architectural copy but also a portent, a sign. He vowed that "if fate were propitious," he would one day "exchange Kedleston in England for Kedleston in India."

Curzon left nothing to fate, however, propitious or otherwise. He began to make for himself the perfect résumé. Four trips to India gave him more expert knowledge than a library of books contained. So qualified, he was barely out of his twenties when he became parliamentary undersecretary of state for India—the number two man in England behind the viceregal throne.

More than a store of knowledge was required to be Viceroy of India, however. One needed a supply of that more elusive commodity, money. Especially on the splendid scale Curzon envisioned it, being Viceroy was hardly a paying proposition. In 1895 he acquired the fat purse necessary: he married the American heiress Mary Leiter, daughter of a partner of Marshall Field's Department Store. The Curzons' marriage was not simply cold calculation and a dowry, for affection united the new bride and groom. But that affection had little chance to flourish in London, where Curzon worked all hours into the night, attending to the ninety thousand telegrams and dispatches received annually at the Foreign Office.

Three years after Curzon's marriage, Lord Elgin's term as Viceroy was due to end. Curzon had made himself the most qualified man to succeed Elgin and didn't mind saying so. Indeed, he could not restrain himself. Although the Prime Minister, Lord Salisbury, detested political jockeyings for position, Curzon could not resist setting out in a nearly interminable letter to Salisbury the credentials requisite to be Viceroy, which coincided with his own. When that letter produced no result, Curzon sent another, confessing that he had sometimes entertained the notion of the possible good he might do as Viceroy. But considering the exhausting rigors of the position, he would accept only were it offered to him in the full vigor of his prime—that is, before age forty. Salisbury understood the implication: Curzon was then thirty-nine.

Fortunately for Curzon, Salisbury reckoned his junior associate's abilities at a high estimate, and Queen Victoria endorsed that estimate. After ratifying the choice of Curzon, Victoria proceeded to more general reflections on the role of Viceroy:

> The future Viceroy must really shake himself more and more free [the Queen wrote] from his red-tapist, narrow-minded Council and Entourage. He must be *more independent, must hear for himself* what the *feelings* of the Natives really are, and do what he thinks right and not be guided by the *snobbish* and vulgar, overbearing and offensive behavior of our Civil and Political Agents, if we are to go on peaceably in India.

How, one wonders, had Victoria—then in her eightieth year, and a semirecluse since her beloved Albert's death—obtained such an accurate picture of her often abrasive civil servants in India? Curzon might have judged any letter making him Viceroy a handsome specimen of correspondence, but Victoria's, in truth, voiced his own sentiments. He recognized that India sometimes served as a combination spa–mental hospital–penal colony, where England deposited its mentally and morally enfeebled sons. In Britain's Indian Civil Service (ICS) many a dullard and incompetent found a place, but they were not the worse. Vicious, sadistic officers—possibly not so many in number, but not many were needed to do untold harm—viewed the native populace as a semihuman species, whose understanding was limited to a boot in their arse. But he would change that, Curzon reassured Salisbury; the British government would do more good for the Indians than they could do for themselves.

What bars us now, a century later, from imaginatively reentering the India Curzon entered as Viceroy is, curiously, our clearheadedness. We are able to bisect the Raj into parts properly Indian and parts British, but to Curzon's contemporaries, Britain and India overlapped and undergirded each other. The English and the majority of educated Indians concurred, as the twentieth century began, that the two lands were inextricably linked, with immense good as well as evil possible in that conjunction. With trumpets sounding acclaim, Curzon sailed to India to maximize the good and eradicate the evil. And so began one of history's failed experiments—Curzon's attempt to create a benevolent colonialism, a kind of "post-Raj Raj."

※

There is a poetry of verse, of course, but there may exist a "poetics" of action, of deed, as well. If the former employs meter, simile, and rhyme, then the latter uses the character of men, the materials of the earth, and the ironies of struggle to produce an aesthetic effect. In 1898 Curzon brought to the subcontinent a sense of India as an immense but malleable terrain, an awareness of his own power, and a large view of the reforms to be accomplished. He brooded over the possibilities with the relish, the savor, of a poet revising a stanza to perfection. There was no other task on which he would rather have expended the mortal hours allotted to him. Curzon's predecessor was a nonentity, but before him the great grandee Lord Landsdowne had served as Viceroy: and nobody remembers him. Landsdowne would have preferred occupying a post other than Viceroy and inhabiting a place other than India. By contrast, if—to borrow the second Lady Curzon's banality—home is where the heart is, George Curzon arriving in India had come home. He was the only Viceroy who, instead of sighing with relief when his term in office expired, requested another term. Curzon wrote verse, both doggerel and serious, but what remains readable today are his official dispatches as Viceroy, for in them the drama of men, policies, and consequences assumes almost artistic form. India, it appears, was Curzon's poetry.

And sumptuous poetry it was, for the privileged few like him. When the new Viceroy landed in Bombay a crimson carpet overspread the docks, cannons fired volley after volley, and the crowds lined the miles, cheering as the Curzons' carriage rolled past. In London Mary Curzon had suffered all the agonies of the servant problem. In Simla, the British summer capital in India, their house hummed with seven hundred salaaming, bowing, wishfulfilling minions. When the Curzons traveled, they boarded their own private train—a tiny palace hurtling along on tracks, painted all shining gold and white, in which Mary had her own bedroom, her own boudoir, her own bathroom, her own dressing room, and additional rooms for her maids. Masterpiece Theater or Merchant-Ivory could have dramatized Curzon's viceregal reign for the sheer succession of deluxe period-piece sets—though it would require a Cecil B. De Mille to direct the thousands of extras who kept such a show running. Mary Leiter Curzon, the Chicago girl who stumbled into the highest-ranking position an American ever held in the British Empire, exclaimed: "We might as well be monarchs."

Curzon would not have been Curzon had he not relished the opulence. But it was not for the grandeur foremost that he valued India. Nayana Goradia's *Lord Curzon: The Last of the British Moghuls* (1993) admirably places Curzon's administration in its Indian context but typically assumes that the Coronation Durbar of 1903, unparalleled in lavish display, "was the supreme moment of his [Curzon's] career." In fact, Curzon believed Edward's coronation would be better celebrated by reducing the onerous salt tax that Indians paid, and when the home government in England refused such a reduction, the showy Durbar became so distasteful to him he wanted to cancel it. Goradia depicts the Viceroy's state entry in the Durbar atop a large elephant as Curzon's "playing out fantasies of being the Great White Moghul." Curzon detested riding elephants, and whenever possible avoided it (among other reasons, it wracked his injured back with pain). He believed that out-maharajahing the maharajahs was hardly the way to bind the hearts and minds of Indians to the Empire. Curzon liked his position not so much for its magnificence as for its hardships. He inspected disease-ravaged slums and cholera hospitals and relief kitchens, where titled Englishmen never trod, until Mary grew sick with worry. "I have been absolutely miserable over the accounts of your doings in hospitals," she wrote him, "and Colonel Fenn [his doctor] shares my horror and anxiety."

Curzon savored it all, down to the quirky detail. He delighted to ride into a village where the banner welcoming him, meant to celebrate A Gala Day, read A GAL A DAY. But the amusement could hardly keep pace with Curzon's ever-mounting labors. Soon the days had not enough hours, and the nights not hours enough, as Curzon virtually dispensed with sleep, working to all hours.

But what was he trying to accomplish? What *did* a viceroy do? Curiously, many accounts of Curzon's career omit what he actually did in India. Instead they plunge into the controversies that shook his administration. Possibly this is the right emphasis, for a few headline political battles would finally obliterate all Curzon's fine intentions and blot out the benefit from all his toil. But important and noxious as they were, the controversies occupied little of Curzon's actual time compared to the endless hours he devoted to the hundred tasks necessary to govern the sprawling empire.

In a public talk Curzon joked about his responsibilities: "The Viceroy is expected to preserve temples, to keep the currency steady, to satisfy third-class [train] passengers, to patronize race meetings, to make Bombay and Calcutta each think that it is the capital city of India, and to purify the police." In fact Curzon executed those tasks, only the list extended to the nth power. He had, first, to awaken a sleeping bureaucracy, to jump-start a dormant machine into motion. Curzon could be amusing, at least initially, about all the upset he caused the old "civilians" (officers of the Indian Civil Service) as he attempted to push India into the modern world. "Nothing has been done hitherto [in] under six months," he wrote an old friend. "When I suggest six weeks, the attitude is one of pained surprise; if six days, one of pathetic protest; if six hours, one of stupefied resignation."

At work in India, Curzon instituted twelve major reforms that he believed would see the country through the next twenty-five years. He improved education and stabilized the rupee. His agricultural reforms attempted to eliminate famine, develop irrigation systems, and redistribute land more equitably. He set up a Railways Board to improve transportation; he proposed measures to overhaul manufacture, and he sought protection for the sugar industry. In addition to these major reforms, Curzon set in motion minor reforms by the hundreds, if not thousands, from the establishment of an Imperial Library to the preservation of the Burmese pony. "The Burma pony," he recorded in his notes, "is a damned good little piece of stuff." Most people, regardless of how they view his ideology, would approve of the industrious particulars of Curzon's administration. (Not everyone: Gandhi thought that the improvement of the Indian railways destroyed forever the self-sustaining tranquillity of the Indian village.)

In addition to everything else, Curzon was obsessed by the antiquities of India, relentless in cataloging them, unsurpassed in preserving them. From the Lahore Mosque-in-the-Fort to the Taj Mahal, he rescued the neglected, crumbling monuments of old India and restored them to shining form. At Fahtepur Sikri—the magnificent Mughal capital that the Emperor Akbar built in the desert and abandoned a dozen years later for lack of water, and which survives because of Curzon's efforts—the guides will inform you, "Curzon. Very little time in India. Very good man." A more eloquent formulation of this appraisal goes: "After every other Viceroy has been forgotten, Curzon will be remembered," so Jawaharlal Nehru said, "because he restored all that was beautiful in India."

❀

Yet Curzon might be more accurately remembered as the Bastard Father of Indian Independence, though an independent India was the last thing he wanted. Early during his term he lectured the British civilians that unless they genuinely liked both the country and the people, their work in India would be to no avail. Curzon genuinely liked both, but all his labor on India's behalf—as in a nightmare where up is down and forward is back—tended to produce the opposite effect than he envisioned.

Upon his arrival, the crowd's cheering was not simply for Curzon, known for his Indian sympathies, but represented a qualified cheer for the British. The Indian nationalist leader Bipin Chandra Pal vouched at the time for his countrymen's loyalty "because we believe that God himself has led the British to this country, to help it in working out its salvation, and realize its heaven-appointed destiny." Seven years later, such expressions of fidelity had turned bitter in the mouths of Indian leaders. Instead of praise for the British, antigovernment rioting sounded through the streets. What had happened in between, to reduce it to a word, was Curzon.

He had the top-heavy intelligence that often led him to be right in every detail but wrong overall. Consider the time in Gwalior when he lectured several of the greatest princes of India on their profligate extravagances. Their revenues were not for their own gratification but for the good of their subjects, he reproved them, and their sphere was not the polo grounds of Europe but the administration of their own states. Curzon was not wrong in the substance of his remarks, but the dry screech of chalk on blackboard sounded in his schoolmasterish delivery of them. He was lecturing heads of state as though they were misbehaving schoolchildren. Possibly Curzon's secret wish was that Indians should remain children, his children.

Children should be educated, and Curzon was an ardent proponent of education, even if he would deny Indians permission, as it were, ever to graduate. For after graduation comes adulthood, citizenship, the governing of one's own affairs, and there Curzon drew the line. When the Prime Minister in England requested that at least one Indian be appointed to India's government counsel, Curzon replied that it simply could not be done, for not one Indian in the whole of the country was qualified.

Half a century earlier, liberal Englishmen had considered themselves merely tutors until their native students mastered the sciences of self-rule. Their task in India, Macaulay said, was to create "a class of persons Indian in color and blood, but English in tastes, in opinions, in morals, and in intellect." If Macaulay's dream of brown-skinned Englishmen sipping tea and playing cricket in the tropic heat smacked of patronizing chauvinism, it at least implied that Indians could eventually govern themselves. The English were in retreat from *that* implication by the time Curzon arrived as Viceroy.

Curzon could express a new thought—English permanency on the subcontinent—because he availed himself of a new way of thinking: Darwinism. Fifty years earlier, Englishmen had spoken of the "relative backwardness" of India that time would remedy. By Curzon's era Social Darwinism, whose reference point was biological races, talked about not the *relative* but the *absolute* deficiencies of the Indian subspecies. Curzon's rationale for empire thus linked to an ugly racial ideology that, all over the world, was claiming its victims. In the United States, new Jim Crow laws began segregating southern whites and blacks, who had hitherto lived in close quarters, out of fear of racial pollution. In Europe anti-Semitism switched from denouncing the Jewish religion to demonizing the Jew *race*, which conversion could never change, and thus paved the way for Hitler. And so George Curzon, a superior person of a Superior Race, arrived in India to shoulder the burden of the inferior subcontinental version of man.

Curzon possessed a mind logical in the extreme, but his position could hardly have been more contradictory. He would neither deny the Indians education nor grant them the political fruits of it, so what rational position could he retreat to? Curzon's untenable position was, in effect, that the English would do so much good for India that the Indians would not notice, or mind, that they were not allowed to do it for themselves.

Curzon was surprised, and surprised too late, to learn that many Indians thought otherwise. Working and building a great noble edifice in India, he was too busy to heed the carping of native malcontents, except to wave them aside as ephemeral and unrepresentative. David Dilks's two-volume *Curzon in India* (1969, 1970) supplies a step-by-step account of Curzon's effort to erect a new political structure, streamlined and modern, unlike the unwieldy apparatus of the Raj he had inherited. Unfortunately, most steps along the way alienated the very people, the Indians, his edifice was intended to benefit. One controversy (by far the most important one) will represent the hundred lesser ones that could equally show Curzon's touch at work—a touch that could be called the velvet hand in the iron glove.

The controversy began in the government apparatus he inherited, whose unwieldiness confronted Curzon daily in the shape of the overlarge, overdispersed province of Bengal, where he resided as Viceroy. Here Curzon's superior accountant's logic applied to messy human affairs had an obvious answer: split the province into two. The gods of administrative efficiency would smile upon its partition for the sensible, red-tape-cutting reform it was.

Partitioning Bengal would, incidentally, divide Indian nationalists into Hindu and Muslim areas, from which they might then oppose each other instead of joining forces to pester the British government. Curzon had a passing awareness of this advantageous side effect of partition, but efficiency was his concern, his goal.

Indeed, Curzon never took the Indian nationalist movement seriously enough to work out measures like partition simply to weaken it. But an act that he treated as aboveboard and administrative, Indians in Bengal and elsewhere interpreted as underhanded and treacherous. Through 1904 and into 1905, as the British debated the pros and cons of partition, no fewer than five hundred protest meetings were staged beginning in Bengal and spreading throughout India. In East Bengal alone a petition opposing partition collected seventy thousand signatures. Curzon observed this agitation but remained unimpressed. It was all so emotional, he was confident, all so atypical of the true India whose interests were represented—well, by him.

On October 16, 1905, Curzon prevailed, and partition passed into law. Partition divided a geographical landmass, but it also divides two eras in history. Before partition, most educated Indians believed, with reservations, in the fundamentally good intentions of the British. After October 16, they increasingly suspected the British were pursuing their own ends and acting in bad faith. Day after day, in response to partition, protesters crowded the streets in growing numbers, often erupting into violence. Fires burned at night throughout Bengal, setting cotton goods from Birmingham to flame. The *Swadeshi* (literally: self-nation) movement started to encourage manufacturing native goods, and *Swadeshi* schools began to educate the young. In Calcutta, where the violence caused by partition raged most fiercely, Curzon contented himself by observing that such behavior ill suited the residents of the capital of a great empire. Trusting his intuition, refusing to allow a commission to investigate, Curzon reported back to London that all this hue and cry represented only a tiny minority and would soon pass into complete oblivion.

Five years after Curzon left India, the partition of Bengal had to be revoked, but what it had set in motion could not be recalled. A drawer in Curzon's desk of efficient administration had opened into the inferno, and the fires that flamed up would not stop with a campaign for independence. About partition, Curzon was like a stone shooting downhill with the force of gravity, unaware of the avalanche he was starting. Forty years later the ever-mounting avalanche crashed full force, when a Muslim Bengal became East Pakistan (now Bangladesh) and Hindu Bengal became part of India, and a million people lost their lives in bloodshed, ten million became homeless refugees, and millions more suffered indescribable misery. Curzon's bold stroke of efficiency had culminated in one of the overwhelming tragedies of the twentieth century.

❖

Of the thousand bonfires in India protesting Curzon's actions, barely the faintest gleam reflected back to England. The shouts of outrage in Calcutta echoed dimly if at all in London. The Empire may have been doomed when it mistook a man who antagonized so many Indians for their champion and chastised him for being too pro-Indian in his sympathies.

Despite the ruckus over partition, Curzon continued to imagine himself the Indian's best friend. For though he barred Indians from the halls of power, he was determined that the laws of the land would apply without discrimination to everyone in the land, Indian and English alike. During the Boer War, he reproached the Cabinet for taxing Indians to pay for a war in which they were barred from fighting, and his denunciation of the whole shabby treatment of Indians in South Africa won the young Gandhi's praise. Curzon's was in fact a novel experiment in modern history where the idea *separate but equal* was not, after all, a euphemism for separate *and* unequal.

He even stepped blithely before the army—as in front of an oncoming tank—to teach his rule about justice and fairness for all.

The most famous instance of Curzon's moral intrusion involved two Ninth Lancers who had beaten their native cook so badly he died from the wounds. Colonial justice, complete with withheld evidence and bribed witnesses, hushed up the crime. But when the outraged Curzon got wind of the affair, he punished not only the guilty soldiers but their entire regiment. "I will not be a party to any of the scandalous hushing up," he exploded, "on the theory that a white man may kick or batter a black man to death with impunity because 'he is only a d— nigger.'" Possibly no other high British official in India then believed that a "colored" person's rights were the same as a white's when Curzon attempted to inaugurate a new era of color-blind justice.

The Ninth Lancers were, pity for Curzon, a famous and fashionable regiment, the darlings of the British public, fresh from victories in the Boer War. Had Curzon researched the most effective means of alienating English public opinion, no better method could he have produced than punishing the Lancers. At the Coronation Durbar in 1903, the English cheered loudest and longest when the Ninth Lancers rode past. The rebuke to the Viceroy rang in his—indeed, in everyone's—ears. Curzon claimed not to be discomfited by this show of support for the Lancers but rather to feel "a certain gloomy pride in having dared to do the right." Curzon's gloomy pride, as in the adage, went before a gloomy fall.

Heedless of opposition and controversy, for three years Curzon had wielded a power unrivaled by any Viceroy before or since. Little wonder he unconsciously grew to think himself a king by another name. By 1903, though, the political temper in England itself was entering a new era. Victoria was dead; her last great Prime Minister, Lord Salisbury, who had retained confidence in his Viceroy's judgment, had retired from office. The change in administration, from Curzon's viewpoint, could hardly have been more propitious, for his great, dear friend Arthur Balfour succeeded Salisbury. But old friend was soon old friend no more—or at least Curzon interpreted it so, when Balfour's Cabinet refused to take down verbatim his policy dictation from India. The unruffled Balfour responded to Curzon's tirades with conciliatory moderation:

> You seem to think that you are injured whenever you do not get exactly your own way! But which of us gets exactly his own way? Certainly not the Prime Minister. Certainly not any of his Cabinet colleagues. We all suffer the common lot of those who, having to work with others, are sometimes overruled by them. I doubt whether any of your predecessors have ever received so large a measure of confidence from either the Secretary of State or the Home Government. I am ready to add that probably none has ever deserved that confidence more.

Balfour's compliments could not alter the infuriating fact that he was not getting his way. Ignoramuses in England, who could not know or comprehend the situation in India, were getting their way instead. Curzon's protests grew in number, seasoned with his usual threat of resignation—a possibility more unthinkable to the Viceroy in India than to an ever more exasperated Cabinet in London.

The tragedy that followed tells us something about the nature of aristocratic politics. Government by aristocratic clique, whose members have known one another's habits and thoughts since childhood, is ideal for settling small differences in a club or during a country house weekend. But large differences of state, instead of being debated objectively, so mingle the personal and the political that both are often poisoned. The drop of poison was now ready for Curzon's cup.

✵

Though turn-of-the-century India bustled with English (and native) rogues, mountebanks, and scoundrels of every description, Curzon's tenure as Viceroy had blessedly lacked an essential villain. He was at sullen cross-purposes with the army, but the British Army in India possessed no strong figure to oppose him. It was Curzon himself, on his own perverse initiative, who imported the engineer of his own downfall.

Curzon had a stroke of inspiration: to recruit, as head of the army in India, Horatio Herbert Kitchener, the Hero of Omdurman, the avenger of General Gordon's death, and British commander in chief during the South African War. Lord Kitchener was idolized by the British public and reckoned then (though not subsequently) the finest military strategist of his time. Personally, Kitchener was a man of towering physique and towering ambition, too; if there was anything dwarfish about Kitchener, it was only his sense of honor. Curzon was warned against bringing out such an untrustworthy creature as his military commander. But in recruiting the most glorious soldier of the day as his commander, Curzon annexed a secondary glory to his own. And since the Viceroy was worried about war with the Afghanis, military pressure from Russia, and other fighting along the northern frontier, he wanted a strong, iron-willed general.

Kitchener's complex personality belongs to a character configuration that has largely ceased to exist. If someone were as crude as Kitchener today, he would hardly be deemed charming. If he had Kitchener's power to charm, he would lack his coarse nature. Kitchener came by his vicious streak honestly. His father, an English Army officer who had bought up estates cheap in a famine-ridden Ireland, crossbred eccentricity and tyranny. When the young Kitchener angered his father, his punishment consisted of being spread-eagled on the lawn, his hands and legs tied to croquet hoops, as the hot sun or winter rain mercilessly pelted him. Kitchener carried his father's sadistic temperament into the next generation. Once he had the buried body of a military opponent dug up in order to employ its skull either (so hard to decide) as an inkstand or a drinking cup. Queen Victoria had her Prime Minister request of Kitchener that he kindly bury the body again. Yet this same Kitchener, as refined as a cowboy on a bronco, could when he wanted win over whomever he wanted. The beguiled who succumbed to his spell included the Queen, the Prime Minister, and George and Mary Curzon.

Great thinkers are said to have one main idea (Marx = the economic basis of historical change; Freud = the sexual character of human energy) and Kitchener's idea was Kitchener. As the army's commander in chief, he came out not to serve India but for India to serve him. Two temperamental egotists like Kitchener and Curzon would need mature tact and restraint to deal with each other, but about both there was something of the schoolboy who if he doesn't get his way isn't going to play. A disagreement to either was not serious unless accompanied by his threat of resignation— a prospect that, to their minds, should cause the very heavens to shudder.

Curzon early on realized the major issue behind the endless quibbles Kitchener raised: he would be dictator in all matters military. As relations between the two men worsened, Curzon recognized that if Kitchener actually resigned, "However trumpery the issue on which he [Kitchener] might elect to go, public opinion in England would side with him, and say he had been driven out by me." What is puzzling is that Curzon knew the explosion was inevitable and simultaneously ignored that he knew it. Even in bringing Kitchener to India, Curzon had been like the patient who carefully notes every ingredient on a medicinal bottle, while ignoring the warning *not to be taken internally*.

Curzon turned a blind eye to Kitchener's capacity for mischief, the way he could be blind to his own failings. Indeed behind their blatant dissimilarities—gentility versus coarseness, mandarin versus barbarian, philosopher-aristocrat versus soldier-adventurer— their failings were curiously similar. Both were egotists, both were relentlessly ambitious. There was a further parallel. Kitchener was a closet homosexual, who surrounded himself with young officers, "Kitchener's boys" as they were called. Although Curzon did not suspect the sexual reason for Kitchener's all-male household, he did remark on its unsalutary effect upon the master:

Kitchener is an extraordinarily lonely man: being unmarried, he has nobody in his house except young officers greatly his inferiors in age and standing; he takes no advice from anybody, he spends his whole day in thinking over his own subjects and formulating great and daring schemes.
. . . He stands aloof and alone, a molten mass of devouring energy and burning ambitions, without anybody to control or guide it in the right direction.

In suggesting that Kitchener was the loneliest man in India, without friend or confidant, Curzon ignored the fact that he himself may have been the second loneliest, with a total of one intimate—his wife, Mary. If the above quotation deleted marital status and substituted Curzon's name, it would lose little in accuracy. Kitchener's isolation seems to move Curzon to pity and to censure; in fact it was what had attracted him to the soldier. "Curzon's instincts," David Dilks wrote, "lay with the strong man who found obstacles in his path." In his attempt to master Kitchener, there was just the slightest hint of Curzon's attempting to control externally what he could not control within himself.

A further parallel: their inner compasses pointed both men to India. Even before Curzon's approach, Kitchener had already determined to go to make his political fortune on the subcontinent. In that earlier era, men whose overlarge vanity outgrew their own country's law tended to become a law unto themselves in India. Since the old English order did not quite adhere there and the various Indian regional customs did not govern them, a space opened to imagine *l'état c'est moi*. Their personal civil war could have raged so intensely perhaps only in that period and possibly only in India—because the realities of India did nothing to mitigate it. Later figures, like Charlie Andrews and Madeleine Slade (or Forster or even Naipaul), had to figure in local customs and social conditions in any disagreement or difficulties they experienced in India. But as English demigods above the laws in India, Curzon and Kitchener waged their feud on a platform above all social constraints, in a pure empyrean where there was nothing to deflect the blows or restrain the animosity.

For such people who embody the law in their own person—take, for example, Robespierre during the French Revolution—of all activities, the most dangerous is a holiday. In the summer of 1904, between his two terms as Viceroy, Curzon returned to England to enjoy a much-earned, much-needed rest. Exactly then Kitchener struck. In Calcutta he became the beast unchained, spreading unholy terror, galloping in a phaeton wildly down the wrong side of the road, with reins, gloves, and cigar all held in one hand. His letters flew just as wildly to England. In them Kitchener resurrected his threat of resignation unless all civilian control over the army be turned over to him. Kitchener thus proposed to dispense with the regulated system that prevailed in England and in almost every country with claim to being a democracy.

Unlike Salisbury, who cared not a fig for popular sentiment, Balfour beneath his mask of affable indifference cared very much. He worried that his shaky government could not survive a public riled by its hero's resignation. Balfour's Cabinet dutifully stripped the civilian military administrator in India of nearly all powers and transferred authority to Kitchener. Had Curzon resigned then and there, over precisely that issue, he would have been a hero to every knowledgeable figure from the old commander Lord Roberts to Winston Churchill. But for all his political abilities, Curzon lacked the indispensable one of timing. He wavered, he hesitated, he was Prince Hamlet. When, after returning to India, he tried to act retroactively and resigned over some lesser issue, he was reckoned less a martyr than a fussbudget. In fact, he was probably performing his periodic, cathartic exercise of merely threatening to resign. But Balfour pretended to take Curzon's perfunctory threat at face value. The response, penned under the king's name, came in the form of a telegram: "With deep regret I have no other alternative," the royal telegram informed Curzon, "but to accept your resignation at your urgent requests."

With a single sentence, seventeen words, an era ended. Curzon had dedicated his *Problems of the Far East* (1884) "To those who believe that the British Empire is, under Providence, the greatest instrument for good that the world has ever seen." If that belief seems in retrospect vainglorious and arrogant, it compares favorably with Kitchener's chief concern about Anglo-Indian relations, which was a horrified fear that his soldiers would pollute themselves by sleeping with Indian women. Curzon was the last avatar of an old dream, a once-shimmering dream, that the best of European knowledge could guide Asian lives for their own benefit. In the government mansion in Calcutta, on that sweltering August day in 1905, as Curzon stared at the king's telegram, the dream evaporated into air.

❖

When a Viceroy returned from India, the Prime Minister and other government representatives rallied at the station to welcome him. When Curzon arrived at Charing Cross station on December 3, 1905, however, no government official waited on the platform. Even his old friends from the Souls—who seven years earlier had pledged to celebrate his return gloriously—were absent, away at a country house weekend. They interrupted the party momentarily to deliberate sending a telegram but for the life of them could not think what to say. One wit cautioned that, unless they were careful, "Glad you're back" would slip into "Glad your back's worse!" Everyone laughed and the telegram was forgotten.

When a Viceroy returned from India, he received the title of earl. The king urged that no time be lost before Curzon received this compensatory honor. But Balfour, wishing to avert attention from the recent Curzon-Kitchener fiasco, decided "the waiting game" was the game to play, and then he was swept from office in the next election. The newly elected Liberal government had little reason to strengthen the Conservatives in the House of Lords by making Curzon an earl. Curzon might have resurrected his political career via the House of Commons (the "Lord" in his title derived then from an honorary Irish peerage, which did not bar his election to the Commons). But the king thought it unseemly for a former Viceroy to demean himself on the hustings. Curzon thus not only lost India, he also lost politics: the man without a country became the man without a vocation.

His one solace was his wife, Mary. Their marriage had been a "love match," though in its early years the relentlessly driven Curzon had little leisure for that luxury, love. In India, cut loose from London's social orbit, without friends or true equals, he began to rely on Mary's support, as increasingly her charm smoothed over ruffled situations that his own imperious personality had created. (The wags of the day were on to something when, punning on Mary's maiden name, they dubbed her "the Leiter of Asia.") After a couple of years in India, it pained both husband and wife to be separated from the other's company for even a few hours. In India a marriage of affection bloomed into a romance out of a fable.

Curzon had thrived in India, feeling physically better (when not absolutely overworked) than ever in England, but the climate and the strain of duty wore on his wife. Some days Mary existed on a biscuit and a spoonful of brandy, every ounce of her will tightened to conceal her debility from her husband. In 1904 she became gravely ill, but against all expectations recovered enough to resume her round of duties. A reporter commented she looked as though returned from the dead. "Yes," she replied, "but one may not do these things twice." Concealing her premonition from her husband, she feared she might not live to witness his magnificent achievement completed in India. "One of the humble inconsequent lives," she noted in her diary, "who go into the foundations of all great works." Curzon suspected little and so was spared the anxiety she wanted him free of; perhaps he looked the other way, because the other way was where his great work lay. By late 1905, her unrelenting efforts in India had taken their toll, and, though she was still lovely, still young, only thirty-six, her strength was obviously ebbing. Her death, soon after their return to England, devastated Curzon. "Every man's hand," he said, "has long been against me, and now God's hand has turned against me too."

Postmortem

If this were a drama—Sophocles, Shakespeare, and Ibsen would be various authors amenable to its theme—Curzon would stand as the man who challenges the gods and brings the wrath of heaven down upon himself. He once asked his private secretary what had gone wrong with his viceroyalty, and the secretary had the temerity to answer him honestly: "Too much hubris." Curzon made no attempt to defend himself. "I was born so," he said, "you cannot change me." Hubris, the fatal flaw of an Aristotelian hero, sets in motion a course inevitably tragic.

But this is not a piece performed in a theater, and Curzon's fall derived less from flawed character than a flawed vision. He admitted that he was personally limited, but his vision was meant to be impersonal and limitless. "The British Empire is," he claimed (forgetting about Christianity), "the greatest instrument for good that the world has ever seen." Curzon was like some Pope of Imperialism, fallible as a human being but embodying an infallible institution that transcended human limitations.

That overblown claim should reawaken interest in Curzon, now when nostalgia for empire glistens with a high sheen. At the end of the twentieth century, "ethnic cleansing" in the Balkans, civil war in the former Soviet republics, and starvation in Africa have given, respectively, the Austro-Hungarian, the Soviet, and the French and English empires a better report card posthumously than they received at the time. The Cold War itself in fact reflected an imperial world order, reduced to two empires, and even its welcome demise is secretly lamented by some ideologues who preferred its clearly demarcated dangers to the uncertainty that has replaced them.

Lord Curzon's career furnishes a case study for empire. Human intelligence, he believed, had to order the globe's various geopolitical units, and empire performed that orderly function. A world without empires, a world only of nation-states—with no overstructure to contain national rivalries and only commercial advantage to dictate transactions—would have struck Curzon as a recipe for rapacity and conflict. Imperialism, to him, involved not simply national rivalry or favorable trade balances but a moral arrangement as well. Late in his life he employed statistics and tables and calculated investment, export, and construction to establish that, during his viceroyalty at least, England had given as good as she got in India. If the British Empire thrived, he believed, so did the international order in which it played its part.

The question is why his viceroyalty did not thrive. Why his viceroyalty was all toil, struggle, controversy, and then a mighty fall? There is of course the Aristotelian explanation: the ideal was eaten away, as if by termites, by defects in the very foundations. In his nursery Curzon had learned that all actions went in either plus or minus columns, which ill prepared him for political compromise and for dealing with plus-*and*-minus characters like Kitchener and Balfour. At Eton he had learned to master details but not that the details themselves are culturally conditioned, which ill prepared him for governing other cultures. The creed of empire found in the cultivated mandarin Curzon an eloquent, accomplished, but ultimately inadequate apostle.

Besides, his political timing was off. As a politician, Curzon was increasingly an anomaly, out of sync in his own milieu. While he endeavored to extend the great Empire to the horizon, other English politicians were retrenching to a more manageable proposition. Afghanistan, to the northwest of India, tempted Curzon like a piece of forbidden fruit. (As a young traveler he had penetrated Afghanistan's forbidden borders, impressing its chieftains with his resplendent uniform, which he'd bought in a costume shop.) Indeed, Curzon would have extended British suzerainty into even more forbidden Tibet. On Tibet's snowy peaks a Curzon-sponsored expedition planted the Union Jack, and British power achieved, literally and symbolically, its highest pinnacle. But even as Curzon's imperial vision was reaching fruition, it was forced to recede. "I should greatly deplore it if [Tibet] should fall under our influence," Balfour announced from London, repudiating Curzon's policies. "Let the Tibetans manage their own affairs . . . I desire nothing better." Ditto for the Afghanis. From the moment of Balfour's statement, the British Empire, which sung of itself commanding the waves and omnipresent in the sun, began its slow retreat until one day it would be but one country among others.

A half century after Curzon's death, in 1979, the Russians invaded Afghanistan, belatedly verifying his argument about the Great Game for influence in the Asian heartland. During the 1950s, the Chinese invaded and brutally annexed Tibet, justifying his argument that Tibet would fall to some outside sphere of influence, either Britain's, Russia's, or China's. These are not exactly faraway events, as Balfour thought, that concern only remote folks on the edge of the world. The debacle in Afghanistan contributed to the collapse of the Soviet Union; the massive forests in northern Tibet—second only to the Amazonian rain forests in preserving the earth's ozone layer—were largely denuded in a few years for Chinese profit, causing serious flooding as far away as Bangladesh. The lion shall be followed by the jackal, Curzon had prophesied: if the British imperial order retreated, national powers would supplant it that would prove even less rational and restrained and more rapacious.

As a prophet, Curzon was without honor in his own country—whether his country is considered England or India. In England, "ignorant" politicians five thousand miles away defeated the Viceroy laboring so diligently on the scene in India. Or so Curzon liked to believe; it salved his humiliated pride and stimulated his unparalleled capacity for righteous indignation. Ultimately, the enemy who defeated him was not Balfour or Kitchener or, for that matter, even Curzon himself, but rather a retiring country gentleman and shy naturalist named Darwin. Curzon planted his feet firmly on the ground, believing himself more than a match for any man, but it was an idea—or the social uses to which Darwinian ideas about the races were put—that dislodged him and swept his viceroyalty to wreckage. In India his new, enlightened imperialism was undermined by the racial theory that justified it. The British Empire would bring good governance to India because, ultimately, the Indians were congenitally as a race unable to govern themselves. Curzon despised his colleagues' increasing use of the slur *niggers* to refer to Indians, but he nonetheless found it congenial to think in racial terms himself. Under Social Darwinism, his overlordship of the lesser races was proclaimed by biological science, by nature ordained. Were one thus to list the victims of late-nineteenth-century racialist thinking, atop the list would have to go Curzon himself.

All that he planned was undone by racism and all that he built was thus dismantled. The post-Raj Raj, the new era of harmonious Anglo-Indian cooperation, was canceled out by a contradiction to which he remained blind. His desire to escort the Indian people rung by rung up the ladder of prosperity was at odds with his kicking them down to the bottom of it racially. A number of English writers—H. G. Wells, Arnold Bennett, George Bernard Shaw, Joseph Conrad—pointed out that to expect a foreign people to thank you for demeaning them was a trifle much to ask. But these were not writers Curzon read, and thanks were, he thought, his proper due. "Poor Pappy [Mary's pet name for him] gets so downcast sometimes," Curzon complained to his wife in India. "Grind, grind, grind with never a word of encouragement." He had worked so hard on their behalf, and to the end Curzon never understood why the Indians had not showered him with gratitude.

Curzon's role in history (a subject never long absent from his thoughts) was to call down the curtain on not one but two epochs. England's blithe confidence, the golden hope Curzon couriered to India that it would happily lead the Indian through the twentieth century and beyond, to the increasing satisfaction of both, was after his term put away in a drawer. Simultaneously, his viceroyalty closes the era of the politician-prince, of men like Gladstone and Disraeli and himself, who ruled within a well-demarcated sphere of politics. It was, ironically, Curzon's superbly honed political intelligence that caused him to misjudge Indian politics: he ignored its nationalist movement because, fueled as it was by religious sources, it did not fit his narrow definition of the political. After Curzon's fiasco in India, the line between the political and the nonpolitical would never be so clearly drawn again, and a different kind of western-Indian exchange began. Curzon might well have called it the Great Game Gone Mad.

※

Picking up a pen was as automatic for Curzon as talking is for most people, and his estate overflows with private papers, boxfuls and roomfuls of them. Among them is a lone sheet of stationery, whose brief jottings betray a certain poignancy. That stationery is embossed *No. 10 Downing Street*, the residency of the Prime Minister. Curzon had intended it to be his ultimate home on earth—that glorious mirage that receded the nearer he approached.

Ten Downing Street was where the British Cabinet met in full session when, late in his life, Curzon served as Foreign Secretary. Evidently at one such Cabinet meeting Curzon, bored, absented himself mentally and began scrawling on a sheet of notepaper. A sense of mortality, and of history's verdict on him, was never far from his thoughts, and he began to compose his epitaph. Scarcely had he written two lines when he reconsidered and began again. The first epitaph is in prose; the second, in poetry. In the first, the excitement of India rose before him once more, and he proposed the measure of his life's worth thus: "A faithful servant of the Empire, he explored the secrets, and loved the peoples, of the East."

No, not good enough—it lacked *gravitas* (a favorite word of Curzon's). So, with his Cabinet colleagues droning on in the background, he set himself again to the task of memorializing his history:

In diverse offices and in many lands
as explorer, writer, administrator,
and ruler of men,
he sought to serve his country,
and add honour to an ancient name.

These two versions represented the opposing claims upon Curzon's loyalty—the great work of India versus his country's and his own aggrandizement. Curzon was called the Last Roman, but at moments, indignant with righteousness, invoking the fury of heaven, he resembled an odd throwback to a Hebrew prophet. He was indeed a man who had seen the faceless face of God in that unlikeliest of places, the British imperial adventure. In Curzon's version, imperialism heaped such a jumble—the sacred and the profane, the visionary and the trivial, the idealistic and the exploitive. What was to be the final judgment? Curzon's first epitaph suggests that his life's work, his achievement, lay in India; the second, revised version, that the truer poetry inhered in English patriotism and in being Lord Curzon. For one second his pen hovered over the first epitaph, which inscribed his love for peoples of the East, and then the pen dipped down and he scratched it out.

CHAPTER 2

Old Priestess for a New Politics

On that hot August night in 1891 the world turned upside down, and subsequently nothing would ever make any sense again. Such was the impression newspapers around the world created as they reported that—that *lunacy* which had transpired at the London Hall of Sciences. Only George Bernard Shaw, never at a loss for words, found metaphors commensurate with "the calamity." It was, he said, "as if some one had blown up Niagra [*sic*] or an earthquake had swallowed a cathedral."

The "cathedral" he was referring to was Mrs. Besant, "Militant Annie." Annie Besant was the one, the only woman of her day whose oratory could sway crowds, and when she mounted the podium she became a force of nature—or, some said, an unnatural force. Even the feminist Beatrice Webb, supposedly sympathetic, was appalled that Mrs. Besant manipulated audiences with a voice that should have sounded to more homey purposes. "To *see* her made me shudder," Mrs. Webb confessed. "It is not womanly to thrust yourself before the world." Annie Besant was forty-three in 1891, and she had been thrusting herself before the world for two decades, advancing from one radical cause to another, the way (her critics charged) a drunk reels from bar to bar. But Mrs. Besant was always sober, ever sensible, invariably serious. Her career had made her, except for Victoria, possibly the most famous woman in England. As she rose to speak that night, the audience hushed in anticipation of being transported, of having its sense of indignation awakened, of being thrilled to the marrow, and, for the duration of her talk, feeling that crowded, dingy hall converted into a gilded center of righteousness and wonder. They were in for a big surprise.

Still, rumors had been afloat. Precisely to avoid any surprises, the sponsors of that evening's meeting had instructed Mrs. Besant to talk on a standard Freethought topic suitable for the National Secular Society. When the applause died down, Annie made it clear exactly how far she intended obeying instructions. "I did not break with the great Church of England and ruin my social position," she declared in ringing cadences, "that I might come to this platform and be told what to say."

The hall was overcrowded to the point of suffocation, and at that moment not a sound, not a single cough disturbed the silence as she paused. Annie reminded them that they had long known her, she'd long known them: struggle after struggle, through thick and thin, they had stood together. "You have known me in this hall for sixteen and a half years."

Cheers broke out through the room.

"You have never known me to tell a lie."

Further cheering, louder cheering ensued, punctuated with shouts of "No!" and "Never!"

"My worst public enemy has never cast a slur upon my integrity."

The racket was deafening, the shouts of approval thunderous. "Never!" "No!" "Never! never!"

And then the bombshell came. Annie revealed that she had been in communication with Madame Blavatsky. Of all people in the world—Madame Blavatsky! Madame Blavatsky was certainly notorious, but what she was—a satanist? a departed spirit in human form? a criminal fraud?—most members of that audience could not have said. For several decades people like Oscar Wilde and W. B. Yeats had visited her to find out; others had satirized her, as T. S. Eliot later did in *The Waste Land*, under the name Madame Sosostris:

Madame Sosostris, famous clairvoyante,
Had a bad cold, nevertheless
Is known to be the wisest woman in Europe,
With a wicked pack of [tarot] cards.

In *Ulysses*, James Joyce called Madame Blavatsky's *Isis Unveiled* a "Yogibogeybox" and described her disciples as "functioning on astral levels, their oversoul, mahamahatma. The faithful hermetists await the light. . . . Hesouls, shesouls, shoals of souls." As the high priestess of Theosophy, Madame Blavatsky did not increase her credibility by claiming to receive letters written on rice paper from Spirit Masters or "Mahatmas" who dwelled out-of-body in Tibet. (The exact method of franking and postal delivery was left vague.) But, as Annie Besant confided to her audience, she herself had begun receiving just such letters, in the same handwriting of the Mahatmas, on the same rice paper. Annie was speaking to the National Secular Society, and her auditors that night consisted of materialists, rationalists, agnostics, and atheists, who were stupefied by her confession. "I do not ask you to believe me," she told them, "but I tell you it is so."

The consternation went out from that hall to around the globe. Newspapers in Europe, America, and Australia denounced Mrs. Besant's "Buddhist craze" or else predicted that the famous atheist would next convert to Roman Catholicism. In London a fashion designer created that indispensable wardrobe item, a Mahatma hat, and wags took to inquiring of each other, "How's your karma today?" After a century crowded with every craze and fad imaginable, it is now nearly impossible to re-create the shock that Annie Besant caused that night. It would be as if the media learned that

Einstein had derived his formula $E = mc^2$ using a Ouija board or, closer yet, that Margaret Thatcher when prime minister had been found dancing the midnight streets with the Hare Krishnas. Annie Besant, the rationalist's rationalist, had joined that band of loons, the Theosophists. No, all was not right in the world.

❊

Still it was *Mrs. Besant* claiming to receive these impossible letters—the same Annie Besant who had never been known to fudge, fabricate, or falsify. Even without the Mahatma letters, Annie's conversion to Theosophy would have been a hard pill to swallow. All her adult life everything she had done, everything espoused, pointed in exactly the opposite direction.

By the time she was forty-three, Annie had enjoyed or suffered a career no other Englishwoman could rival. Perhaps, she surmised, her marriage to a cold, unloving Protestant minister had led her to question the Victorian axioms about God, good, and country and landed her in rebellion. Perhaps—this was her other hypothesis—her sensitivity to the sufferings of the poor had rendered her suspicious of all the social pieties. Under whichever motivation, she had reasoned herself from orthodoxy to materialism, from materialism to agnosticism, from agnosticism to atheism, and she had reaped the reward. Her husband judged such a woman an unfit wife and divorced her; the courts judged her an unfit mother and took her children from her. When she championed what is now called birth control (having observed the toll of unwanted children upon working mothers), her name was damned from pulpit to pulpit across the land. She was vilified as no good Victorian girl in the mid-nineteenth century had ever been.

Around the time she turned forty, however, the most bizarre, unpredictable twist of all transpired. Annie Besant was becoming respectable. People who had only cursed her, or refused to speak her name at all, began finding good words to say about her. Her unprecedented campaign to provide thirty-six thousand free meals and free medical care to poor schoolchildren had impressed even the socially proper. At age forty-one, she was elected to the powerful London School Board—probably the most important elective office open to a woman at the time.

But no sooner had Annie become the respectable cathedral Shaw alluded to than the earthquake of her conversion to Theosophy threatened to swallow her. Theosophy! Madame Blavatsky, for all her ethereal folderol, was earthy and humorous, and she had a favorite word: *flapdoodle*. Flapdoodle, in fact, seems a perfect description for all the wild hares, occult borrowings, and cockamamy cosmology out of which Madame Blavatsky had constructed Theosophy. In her nearly interminable books, *Isis Unveiled* (1877) and *The Secret Doctrine* (1888), Madame Blavatsky explained that before human beings set up house on Earth other races—Hyperboreans, Lemurians, and, more recently, Atlanteans— had preceded them. She revealed that hidden Masters in the Himalayas convey divine messages through human vehicles such as Christ, the Buddha, and, more recently, Madame Blavatsky herself. Anyone today attempting to penetrate the thicket of *The Secret Doctrine* may soon turn to reading railway timetables for relief. But many Victorians, stranded high and dry by an increasingly rational Protestantism, thirsted for miracles and hungered for the wondrous, and to them Madame Blavatsky served a satisfying manna, apparently baked in Tibet and India. (Other prophets, for whom even India was too tame, claimed to receive their source materials from Mars. See the early psychologist Theodore de Flournoy's *From India to the Planet Mars* [1900].) In converting to Theosophy, Annie Besant subscribed to a farrago of incredulities one part Hindu and most parts unadulterated fantasy—and this was the same Mrs. Besant whose motto had always been *The Truth*.

Bernard Shaw consoled himself with the thought that Annie had never been one to resist a fad. "She was a born actress," Shaw said, as a way of discounting her conversion to Theosophy. "She was successively a Puseyite Evangelical, an Atheist Bible-smasher, a

Darwinian secularist, a Fabian Socialist, a Strike Leader, and finally a Theosophist, exactly as Mrs. Siddons [a famous actress] was Lady Macbeth, Lady Randolph, Beatrice, Rosalind, and Volumnia." Her latest role—what actresses won't do to claim the stage—was now Theosophist priestess. Such a diagnosis scarcely conceals Shaw's hope that this little Theosophical farce would soon have its run and Mrs. Besant would be on to a better role.

Even if one allows Shaw's actress metaphor, the role didn't fit—rather like casting a ballerina as a sumo wrestler or vice versa. One newspaper reader at that time wrote in suggesting the whole report of Mrs. Besant's conversion was simply a hoax, part of a plot to discredit Secularism. The reader was wrong in his facts, less wrong in his conclusion. Annie Besant's conversion did—and, to a certain extent, still does—discredit secularism. In addition, just conceivably, there may have been an actual plot to lure the unsuspecting Mrs. Besant into the Theosophical web.

In those years when Madame Blavatsky was spreading the gospel of Theosophy in countries high and low—before her own body grew so fat it could only spread out in a big chair—she believed that she suffered rebuffs because she was a woman. Nowhere more than among the authorities in British India did she feel her public role frustrated, her seriousness ridiculed, because of her female sex. What she needed was a woman who would outshine all male competitors in public arenas like the lecture forum. The candidate for the job seemed obvious. And why not? Mrs. Besant had penned fierce denunciations of Christian hypocrisy, and Theosophy offered Hinduism as an alternative to Christian hypocrisy. And while endorsing every other reform under the sun, Annie Besant had declared herself in favor of some self-government for India. Was not all this a sign, a prelude to Mrs. Besant's joining the Theosophical band?

Madame Blavatsky was hardly aware of the obstacles in the way. In the *National Reformer*, the paper that Annie Besant and her friend Charles Bradlaugh edited, few subjects provoked their mischievous mockery more than Theosophy. Madame Blavatsky's utterances were, the *National Reformer* commented (November 2, 1884), "startlingly at variance with the possible." To "treat members of the Theosophical Society as serious persons," the *National Reformer* went on, defied possibility. "Many of them are very good, very respectable, and very mad. Some of them are less mad and less good."

Nonetheless in her own monthly, *The Theosophist*, Madame Blavatsky began to print only favorable notices about the *National Reformer* and in particular about Annie Besant's work. In one editorial she planted the bait, dangled the worm:

> For one so highly intellectual and keen as the renowned writer [Annie Besant] to dogmatize . . . after she had herself suffered so cruelly and undeservedly at the hands of blind bigotry and social prejudices in her lifelong struggle for the freedom of thought seems absurdly inconsistent.

Annie knew what it meant to be a bigot's victim; that she should now become the bigot herself was more than she was prepared to do. Henceforth she was more cautious, and more curious, in her remarks about Theosophy.

And perhaps Annie was not so far-fetched a convert, after all. Even among steadfast Christians, new ideas like Darwinism had undermined the old religious fervor, and unsatisfied spiritual longings—like so many loose electrical wires—spluttered dangerously in the air. As for the socialism she championed, Annie observed that while correct in its analysis, it seemed powerless to move the hearts of men. Another way of putting this was that she herself, while confident intellectually, was feeling emotionally dissatisfied. She who could thrill others was, it seemed, unthrilled and unmoved.

Not even Madame Blavatsky could have plotted the next fortuitous turn of events. In early 1888, she published her mammoth two-volume *The Secret Doctrine*. The editor of *The Pall Mall Gazette*, W. T. Stead, had not the foggiest idea what to do with it. He shrank

before the dank prospect of opening it; he knew his regular contributors would quail; and so he wrote Annie, hoping that she
would be quite mad enough to review it. After Madame
Blavatsky's recent challenge to her fair-mindedness, Annie felt
she could hardly refuse. Soon Stead received a merry note: "I am
immersed in Madame B! If I perish in the attempt to review her,
you must write on my tomb, 'She has gone to investigate the
Secret Doctrine at first hand.'"

Against all odds, Annie initially liked *The Secret Doctrine*, then
she began to thrill to it, finally she succumbed. She sensibly
ignored the Hyperborean and Lemurian nonsense to see beneath
it human life recharged with a high purpose. Out of the Darwinian
cold she had stumbled indoors, via *The Secret Doctrine*, into the
warmth of myth and meaning. Blavatsky's own writing played
upon those same tender emotions that fantasy-moralities like
Pilgrim's Progress had touched when she was a girl. After warning
Reformer readers away from Theosophy, she now determined to
meet the Grand Theosophist herself. Annie Besant, whose religion was rationality, whose drug of choice was work, and who did
not distinguish pleasure from morality, was about to enter the
world of romance.

Yeats called Madame Blavatsky's lodgings in London a "romantic house." The lamplight raised a dull gleam on the bronze statu-
ary, Indian rugs subdued and suffused the rooms with color, carv-
ings of Indian gods and goddesses hinted of a supernatural aura.
(The smoky effluvium the rooms floated in arose though, unmys-
tically, from Madame Blavatsky's cigarettes, puffed on one after
another.) It was a house where people met—Annie first met the
young Gandhi there—but when Yeats encountered the sensible
Annie he later remembered nothing about her except, vaguely, a
nice dress and nice manners. By contrast, he remembered and
talked about Madame Blavatsky his whole life, one moment likening her to an old Irish peasant woman, the next to a female Dr.
Johnson. Other regulars *chez* Madame were less constrained in
their comparisons. "You know," one man whispered to Annie,

"Madame Blavatsky is perhaps not a real woman at all. They say that her dead body was found many years ago upon some Italian battlefield."

In that hushed, awed atmosphere, Madame Blavatsky reigned, full of gaiety and good sense. She sat at a table covered in green baize, constantly scribbling on it with white chalk. She was decoding the structure of the universe's design, some said (actually she was recording her scores at solitaire). What did Annie, who appreciated hard analysis and social significances, make of straying into such odd otherworldliness?

In fact, she didn't have to make anything unusual of it. Madame Blavatsky gauged her visitors, knowing intuitively how to approach them. After meeting Annie, she noted that Mrs. Besant must be shielded from any exaggerated claims or nonsense about occultism. So that first evening at Madame Blavatsky's, Annie heard from the seeress's lips only brilliant, easy talk of the world and sophisticated tales of travel. "Nothing special to record," Annie noted afterward, "no word of Occultism, nothing mysterious, a woman of the world chatting with her evening visitors." But just as Annie rose to leave, Madame Blavatsky fixed her eyes upon her visitor—those eyes that fascinated even her enemies, so sparkling and crystal blue were they—and said, with a voice full of longing, "Oh my dear Mrs. Besant, if you would only come among us!" Annie felt a peculiar urge to sink then and there to her knees and kiss Madame Blavatsky's hand. But Annie summoned all her self-mastery, and she extricated herself with a polite good-bye. Yet those eyes, those words, haunted her until a suitable interval passed and she could visit the wondrous Madame Blavatsky again.

Some historians propose an explanation for Annie Besant's conversion to Theosophy: lesbianism. Madame Blavatsky's letters to Annie begin "Dearly Beloved One" and conclude "Very adoring." In memos about Theosophical Society business, Madame Blavatsky addressed Annie as "My Darling Penelope" and signed herself "Your female Ulysses." Today a lover in the pitch of passion hardly utters such endearments, but a century ago they could be blameless innocence. Certainly innocent for Annie, who found little desirable in desire and the irresistibleness of sex only too easy to resist. Though labeled an immoral woman, she may have never experienced sexual congress after her divorce. At Madame Blavatsky's, Annie found a combination more intoxicating than sex for her: the warmth of affection commingled with the cool metal of purpose. Though ridiculed in the West, the Theosophical Society occupied a place of some esteem in Anglo-India, and in picking up that Indian thread in Theosophy's shaggy weave, Annie may have intuited how it could lead to her eventually exercising a leadership impossible for women in the West. (By the time she joined the Society, Annie was already a widely read, respected writer in India.) From her side Madame Blavatsky gladly relied upon her new friend's lucidity and strength as her own vigor waned. She might expound some esoteric point, lose her thought, and then say, "Annie dear, you explain." Theosophy is metaphysical cosmology on the grand scale, but through it, Annie sailed into the tenderest human haven.

Oddly, though, what clinched Annie's conversion to Theosophy—more than Madame Blavatsky's mothering hand; more than any glimmerings of future glory in India—was Theosophy itself. One must remember (though in those years Annie herself often did not) that her whole upbringing had been religious. She still felt a religious need to believe in something, but the endless suffering she had witnessed in Victorian England ruled out comfortably believing in an all-powerful, all-loving Judeo-Christian God. The Theosophists came to her spiritual rescue. Theosophy had up its sleeve unheard-of explanations, such as karma and reincarnation, that claimed to make sense of inequality and human misery. And Madame Blavatsky claimed that a deeper understanding of science would reveal a spiritual design beneath the scientific materialism of the day. Without quite realizing it, Annie had been longing for the Consolations of Theosophy.

Her adult life had not been happy. She had toiled unremittingly, but there was always more to do; she had investigated innumerable questions, but there never was a final answer; she had championed numerous causes, but injustices remained. Words never failed her, but one word she apparently didn't know: *pleasure.* Theosophy was like a window being opened, letting in fresh air, letting in the possibility of happiness. It furnished, she said, "the means of realizing the dreams of childhood on the higher plane of intellectual womanhood." And so she signed the membership card and became a Theosophist. And so that August evening she climbed to the podium of the Hall of Sciences and let her voice ring out. "I do not ask you to believe me, but I tell you it is so."

With her conversion Annie Besant's life divides into two. Nothing in her first four decades foreshadows the last four. Part 1 of Annie's life was constructed of entirely western materials, and even her rebellion against British tradition looks like, from this distance, an intramural English sport. Part 2 would live itself out miles, oceans away, in India. Had she not become a Theosophist, her remaining career might have gone thus: sooner or later Parliament would admit women, Annie would be one of the first women elected, and for all her earlier notoriety, she would end covered with honors— and then be quickly forgotten. (Such a career, such a fate, with only the gender changed, describes her friend Charles Bradlaugh, whom nobody remembers.) Instead she went on to resettle in India, robe herself in a white sari, become president of the Indian National Congress, and adopt God as her son (as some saw the boy-messiah). Even Bernard Shaw, who relished the preposterous, could have invented nothing so preposterous as that.

But for the moment—the moment, that is, when he first learned of Annie's conversion—Shaw was less concerned with its ridiculousness than with putting a stop to it. Faced with the loss of a colleague who had become a staple of his existence, Shaw determined to bully her out of the nonsense—no, better to tease her out of it. Rushing round to Annie's office in Fleet Street, he began haranguing her with an eloquent denunciation first of Theosophy, secondly of feminine inconstancy, and thirdly, and most particularly, of Madame H. P. Blavatsky. Annie merely sat there and smiled.

"Why need you go to Tibet for a Mahatma?" Shaw needled her. "Here and now is your Mahatma. I am your Mahatma."

Annie answered that she had become a vegetarian—vegetarianism was Shaw's pet nostrum—and evidently vegetarianism had weakened her brain, so no point trying to reason with her. She was making something like a joke—by gumption, a joke! Annie, who had never been known to tell a joke, was now making a joke at his expense. Perhaps the whole thing, Shaw concluded, was hopeless after all.

⬡

A biographical note: whereas India stirred Curzon's boyhood imagination and ambition, in Annie Besant's upbringing India was like a fairy-tale book not even opened. Yet Annie went on to spend five times longer in India than Curzon did, and Theosophy plunged her deeper, more permanently, into the country than Curzon ever ventured. A little biographical background is needed to make sense of the puzzle of her career, which was scarcely imaginable for a Victorian man, much less a woman.

Annie was born in 1847 into the comfortable mid-nineteenth-century English middle class. Her father earned a livelihood in London as an underwriter, but, like a good Victorian, devoted his leisure to intellectual interests that ranged from languages to philosophy. An amateur fascination with medicine prompted him to accompany physicians on their rounds. Attending the postmortem of a tuberculosis case, he inspected the cadaver's breastbone and scraped his finger. Three months later he was dead.

With her father's death when she was five, the prescribed path of Annie's life entered its strange, altered course that would eventuate in India. Little Annie was reared by a wealthy spinster, Ellen Marryat, who "adopted" children from genteel but impecunious families and gave them an education that was a marvel of eccentric rigor. "What do you mean by that expression?" Miss Marryat would ask her new student, to teach Annie to question and to think for herself. Annie would reply, "Indeed, Auntie [as she called Miss Marryat], I know in my own head, but I can't explain." "Then indeed, Annie, you do not know in your own head or you could explain so that I might know in my own head." Young Annie forfeited an easy, affectionate family life, but she gained a superior intellectual training, one then nearly unheard of for a girl, and one without which her later career would have been inconceivable.

If Curzon's education taught him that the world was an accountant's ledger ruled with plus and minus columns, Annie was schooled to a severer vision yet. A strict evangelical, Miss Marryat taught that all roads led to perdition save one: duty, duty, and more duty. Children's tales, novels, drama, even Shakespeare, were forbidden reading at Miss Marryat's. Catching Miss Marryat's evangelical fervor, Annie ("little prig that I was," she recalled) vowed to abandon worldly frivolities like the theater and balls, though she had been to neither. No wonder Annie would later so often misjudge character, for in her formative years there were few characters around, either in person or in books, for her to learn to judge it by. Annie was trained at Miss Marryat's to think rigorously, but more or less deprived of anything to think about.

"There is a lot of foolish courage in the world," the writer Colette observed, "or else there would not be so many young girls marrying." No sooner had Annie peeked out of the sheltered surrounding of Miss Marryat's, at age sixteen, than there appeared that curious phenomenon, a prospective groom. Frank Besant had little to commend him except that he was a Church of England minister, which haloed even the stiff, gloomy young man in a reflected glory. When he unexpectedly proposed to Annie, she was simply too inexperienced to know how to say *no*. Rather like Dorothea Brooke in *Middlemarch*, Annie envisioned marriage less as a sexual relationship or emotional intimacy than as a kind of profession. She viewed her role as a clergyman's wife as a calling, a noble round of attending to the sick, feeding the poor, and cheering the afflicted. Mistaken though she might be about it, it was practically the only career open to her.

At Cheltenham, the fashionable parish of the young clergyman, there were—hard cheese for Annie—no poor to minister to. The new wife had little to do and a domineering, unsympathetic husband to tell her how to do it. Nobody in his right mind would confuse the failings of a marriage with the failure of religion. But during the five years of their wedlock Annie was hardly in her right mind, and her cold, hard husband infected the whole religion for her. A friend commented that Annie "could not be the Bride of Heaven, and therefore became the bride of Mr. Frank Besant. He was hardly an adequate substitute." To idle away her tortured leisure, she tried writing stories, in which the husband drops unaccountably out of sight and the wife enters into a heroic career of public deeds. The real Frank Besant was not to be so simply wished away; in real life only an ugly legal suit could accomplish that editorial deletion. As Annie forfeited her role as both wife and Christian, a suicidal prospect opened before her: all respectable society would shun her on Earth, and hell and perdition await her thereafter.

To lose religious faith a century ago, though, was not as dreadfully simple as in Annie's nightmare. So pervasive was the Christian worldview that if anyone did extricate himself, he stumbled out into—not empty space, not a neutral sphere—but into something very like Christianity minus the name. Like any respectable church, the atheistic Freethought movement had its own meeting hall, its own Sunday gatherings, its weekly sermons, even a Secular Hymn Book. And like any proselytizing faith, the Freethinkers sounded their message of welcome to lost souls and potential converts such as the recently divorced Mrs. Besant. Annie, after her divorce, did not lose faith so much as find a new one.

Like Paul in the Bible, she became the effective spokesperson for her new secular religion. Under the bold Freethought banner, Annie began to act out in daylight the stirring deeds she had once trembled to dream of. One injustice after another—war, flogging, capital punishment—became her latest cause célèbre. One activity alone—producing a pamphlet instructing working-class mothers how to prevent unwanted pregnancies—branded her a moral leper. When during this period she managed to earn a degree in science, Birkbeck College refused to list her publicly among its graduates. The only woman in Great Britain with first-class honors in botany, she was refused a pass to the Botanical Garden in Regent's Park. (The curator explained that his daughters sometimes walked there.) In 1879 the courts deemed such an atheistic, immoral woman an unfit mother and removed her daughter from her custody, and that, finally, nearly crushed Annie. "It is a pity there isn't a God," she snarled. "It would do one so much good to hate Him."

Still she carried forward—championing national education, public libraries, and children's health care, but she felt herself championless. She defended workers' strikes and women's unions but felt herself undefended and lonely. Shaw commented that Annie Besant rocketed from feminism to Fabianism with the ease of an actress assuming and discarding a part. But Shaw had got it wrong. Each new cause represented not a new role but a new religion, and if Shaw did not recognize this, Annie did. "If 'morality touched by emotion' be religion," she acknowledged, "then truly I was the most religious of Atheists." The trouble with her imitation religions, though, was exactly that—imitation. In her heyday as an atheist, she rousingly chanted her heroes' names at rallies— Bruno! Priestley! Voltaire! Paine!—failing to see what a thin pantheon they composed. If she succored herself on Voltaire and Thomas Paine—and not Plato and Augustine and Shakespeare— no wonder she was feeling "spiritually undernourished." By 1890 Annie had exhausted all her substitute religions and inwardly was preparing herself for something else. Silently she formulated the syllables of a new experience before she surprised herself by uttering: Theosophy; India.

❈

The precise origins of most historical movements can be dated but hazily. By contrast, we know exactly when the New Age began: on

November 16, 1893—at 10:24 A.M. For the benefit of posterity, astrologers carefully noted to the exact minute when, in the tiny village of Tuticorin, Annie Besant first set foot in India. The West, particularly England, had long poured its best and most celebrated into India: famous administrators like Warren Hastings and Curzon, famous soldiers like Kitchener, enterprising merchants and naturalists and explorers had filed through the land. But never before had one so famous brought to India what Annie carried there: sympathy, respect for Indian culture and faiths. Surely it heralded a new era. Two years before, the pandemonium that Annie had caused at the London Hall of Sciences contributed to the general belief that the East was on the eve of directly influencing the West. Annie's arrival in Tuticorin signaled the reverse: that the West was about to set foot in India on a new favorable, positive footing. At 10:24 in the morning, the sixteenth of November, in the year 1893—a new world, without the old demarcations and limitations, without East and West, began its birth throes. The twentieth century might know no more auspicious moment.

Already Ceylon lay behind her, conquered, in a swoon. Through Sri Lanka Annie had progressed under a rain of flowers tossed by schoolchildren, endlessly serenading in her honor. Pale stuff compared to what awaited her in India. She lodged one night in a palace whose furniture was made of pure crystal, upholstered in satin; the next night, in a flea-infested hut. One day she dined off banana leaves; the next, off plates of solid gold. A yellow palanquin transported her, hoisted high in the air, to indicate here was one esteemed above others. In Bangalore no auditorium was large enough to accommodate the crowds, so she lectured outdoors, stationed between two sacred bulls. Indian women in purdah attended their first public lecture to marvel that one of their own sex should so speak. Few private citizens (before the age of rock stars) ever received such adulation and applause. Enough to unbalance one less sensible and sober—nor perhaps was Annie entirely immune.

Oddly, Annie Besant had done everything in her power to avoid or at least postpone going to India. After converting to Theosophy, she had headed in the opposite direction. Her successful American lecture tour caused one jealous observer to note, "She can make plenty of money in America; in India she can't make a cent." But finally in 1893 Annie ceased her dawdling, knowing India was unavoidable. It was simply the next step. A century ago India, for a Theosophist, was the required college, as it were, furnishing credentials—the equivalent of a Ph.D. in occult studies. In the three years since her conversion, Annie had been living India vicariously and voicing its wisdom puppetlike. Once there, she might learn to manipulate the strings and become the mastermind herself.

Ultimately, though, Annie Besant traveled to India for—if one had to reduce it to a word—confusion. In England, after her conversion, she was the high priestess of a fringe group of spiritualists and was cut off from the social reform that had been her life's blood. A scarlet *A* could have adorned her blouse, not for adulteress but for abbess: she was Theosophy's occult abbess, and that stigma might have harmed her more ultimately than the press's and pulpit's denunciations ever had. A priestess is a priestess is a priestess, but in India she might be something else as well. There, as the spokeswoman for Theosophy, she would be—who knew what, for the border between politics and religion would not be so closed there. Moralistic, somewhat prudish, Annie Besant certainly furnished no prototype for the later '60s hippies in India, but she early hunted the same redeeming confusion of the categories they later did.

Besides, her appearance in India was practically a command performance. Superhuman pen pals, disembodied Mahatmas in the Himalayas, had been writing her on rice paper, summoning her. It will perhaps not surprise the reader to learn those Mahatma letters were forgeries, and it should not have surprised Annie either, because they were written in such awful American slang. (An American Theosophist, William Q. Judge, forged them to snare Annie's support in an intraorganizational feud. The Mahatmas thus dispensed such Tibetan mysticism as "Stick with

Judge.") Once they got her to India, however, the Mahatmas ceased to matter: wherever Annie went, her purpose blossomed before her. She was in India, as she had been in England—and, if possible, would be on Mars—to tweak the bulbous nose of British authority, to champion the underdog, and to furnish the leadership in right's struggle against wrong. If anything protected Annie from the chimeras and chicanery that had all but swallowed up Madame Blavatsky in India, it was her political commitment. She ventured to India for visions, but her eyes inevitably focused on social conditions. She had come for Theosophical Truth, but daily facts compelled her attention.

After arriving in India she traded the respectable black clothing she had worn in England for a white sari. She insisted this wardrobe change be taken as a sign she was in mourning for the wrongs that England had inflicted upon India. The sympathetic appeal of a celebrated Englishwoman in a sari was not lost upon local audiences. Soon various Indians were secretly approaching her to lead their national movement.

Mrs. Besant was a private citizen in India, but from a British official's point of view, she was a public nuisance. The British were an infinitesimal fraction on the overpopulated subcontinent, and their rule depended on the Indian majority's subscribing to the hypothesis that they could not rule themselves. And now this Mrs. Besant had arrived to inform Indian youth that the English model was suspect. "An English lady 'spiritualist' is wooing Bengal audiences to her last new faith by assuring them that 'if the youths of India would act up to the traditions of their past,'" *The Times* back in London reported, "they would not remain long under a foreign yoke." The British authorities put pressure on the Theosophical Society. The Theosophical Society put pressure on its newly arrived spokeswoman. If her ambitions were political, she should have remained in England on the London School Board, where her influence was paramount. Under official pressure from within the Theosophical Society, Annie took a vow never to meddle in matters political.

If a tiger swore off meat, eyebrows might be raised. When Annie vowed to shun politics in India, doubts were equally in order. The surprise is not that she broke those vows but that she kept them *apparently* as long as she did. The two decades from 1893 to 1913 were her nonpolitical years in India, yet scratch their surface and there, raw and red, is political meat barely camouflaged.

In old age, looking back over her long career in India, Annie Besant declared that it all had unfolded according to plan. Her early years awoke a dormant religious pride among Indians, which made them receptive, during her middle period, to her educational reforms, and with those educational reforms fostered in her last decades the new political climate. This hindsight seems a little too tidy. Yet Annie's "religious phase"—an accident mandated by the Theosophist quarantine on politics—does in retrospect look like a shrewd political maneuver. For most reformers begin simply too late in the game. They change a law, tamper with an institution, fix a grievance, while the basic social structure remains intact and cynics comment, *Plus ça change.* . . . Annie situated politics in a broader context than Lord Curzon could ever have imagined.

Within a mere two years of her arrival, Annie had translated the Bhagavad Gita into English. Surely a harmless, apolitical activity. Yet an English version of the Gita, given to him by a Theosophist in London, turned the young Gandhi's thinking back toward India. (Years later, on his political travels through India, Gandhi carried Annie Besant's translation with him, saying read it, it can never be improved.) The Bhagavad Gita, in Annie's translation, suddenly sounded a contemporary message. "Union with the divine life," she wrote in her introduction, "may be achieved and maintained in the midst of worldly affairs." Were worldly affairs and religious enthusiasm conjoined in India, however, the lid of Pandora's box would come flying open and likely smack the British in the face. Annie had misconstrued the Hindu injunction to free oneself from the sufferings of reincarnated existence and read it as an imperative to end the suffering of the unfortunate around you.

The Gita in her hands issued a call for social action and even implied an endorsement of democracy! Such misunderstandings of Annie's proved over time more influential than the impeccable analyses of a thousand disinterested scholars.

A few years after Annie's Bhagavad Gita appeared, the nationalist leader Bal Gangadhar Tilak was imprisoned because, like her, he tied political demands to a religious movement. But the British government could hardly lock up an English gentlewoman merely for rendering a religious document into English. Nor could they imprison her for her next endeavor, which boded worse to come, of founding the Hindu Central College in Benares to educate Indian youth in their own traditions. The authorities were flummoxed, at a loss about how to handle "naughty Annie" (as the governor of Bombay called her). "The weakest thing in the world is to repress a little," the Viceroy's secretary lamented, aware that the damned House of Commons in London would not tolerate the extensive repression necessary to stifle, once and for all, the unrest that Annie and her cohorts were igniting. For two decades Annie and the British authorities coexisted in an uneasy, genteel stalemate.

In 1913 the sheep's clothing fell away, and Annie announced her open involvement in Indian politics. "At last I became convinced that nothing but a change in the Government was of any use," she explained, "and no education work for the uplift of the people was possible as things were; and that drove me . . . to take up definitely political work." That year she joined the Indian National Congress, and the next year she purchased a Madras newspaper, one with no circulation, it's true, but with a license to publish. She rechristened it *New India* and converted it into an organ for undermining the British Raj. The Great War had begun in Europe, and many Indians were proud to support England in her hour of need, while even the firebrands declared a political truce during the war. Not Annie, who supplied *New India* with a motto for the war years—"England's Need Is India's Opportunity." And she had a name for that opportunity: Home Rule.

Here was a novel element in Indian politics, actually, two novel elements. Even Indian radicals conceded it would take years before they could rule themselves. Annie proposed a different chronology: India was ready now. Second, her activism in England had taught her the importance of organizing at the local level. She initiated a grassroots campaign without precedent in Indian politics. Previously, Indian activists had cloistered themselves in elegant debating societies, where resolutions were so suavely, so impeccably drawn up that no one troubled to act on them. Before Annie Besant, one Indian politician recalled, nobody proposed "the vision of going to villages, of speaking to the people at large, of making them realize what they could do, and what it was their duty to do." Annie brought politics to the wretched of the earth, and in doing so she made the ground tremble.

The British authorities in turn made a new category for Annie: she was classified after 1914 as "an all-India problem." She desired to be nothing less. In 1916 in Lucknow she endeavored to make that classification official by running for the presidency of the Indian National Congress. When she lost, she knew what she must do. Martyrdom. As an Englishwoman she would make a far-fetched president of the Indian National Congress; as a martyr, though, she would be a plausible candidate. When an English policeman was killed in Calcutta, Annie Besant's *New India* described the assassins practically as heroes. The authorities feared she had god-knows-what-else up her sleeve—strikes? boycotts? encouragement to arms?—so that there might be no undoing the damage. The British government reluctantly decided it had no choice but to intern the harridan.

Internment, in a pleasant cottage at the lovely hill station of Ootacamund, should have amounted to a well-earned holiday for a seventy-year-old woman whose nonstop labors exhausted coworkers half her age. But not if that septuagenarian was Annie Besant. Deprived of her drug—work—she sank listless, fell ill, and appeared to be dying. Rallies protesting her internment were mounted all over India. She was interned on June 15, 1917, and already by the end of June, twelve protest meetings had rocked Bombay; twenty-eight, Madras. The internment of Annie Besant "in my humble opinion," Gandhi observed, with considerable understatement, was "a blunder."

A bad blunder. The prospect of her dying in confinement, the mounting protests, and the appointment of a more sympathetic viceroy all conspired to secure her release, on September 16, from Ootacamund. Wherever she went crowds gathered, flowers were strewn at her feet, admiring hands lifted her into the air. As the year 1917 ended, the impossible happened, and one who was too pale, too old, and too feminine became president of the Indian National Congress. Annie prepared her acceptance address, which would make clear that she and India were now one cause, one person. More plausibly than Victoria, Annie Besant might have thought herself the Empress of India.

※

But what about Theosophy? Theosophy had brought Annie to India, but once there, she let her attention drift far afield. As for the Theosophical Society, it was in fact thriving in India, its name spreading, its membership growing. That success came, some charged, because Annie Besant had sealed a pact with the devil— or with a man who closely resembled him.

C. W. Leadbeater (1847–1934) was too charming, too full of mischief, to be wholly the demonic blackguard rumor painted him. He was another western eccentric who popped up in India seemingly out of nowhere. As the sons of an aristocratic engineer working in South America, he and his brother had passed their youth in a series of hairbreadth adventures, and tired of this constant danger, Leadbeater had retreated to Oxford, where he took orders in the Church of England. That, at least, was his version whenever anyone sought biographical data about him. In fact his father was an English bookkeeper, and Leadbeater had no brothers, nor had he ever set foot in Latin America. Nor Oxford. Only by the skin of his teeth, through remote family connections, had he secured an underpaid, overworked curacy in an English back-water town. Leadbeater was a liar and a charlatan—by nine-teenth-century standards. Nowadays, when personality is considered a "social construct" and one's identity is "invented," he could be a role model. Madame Blavatsky thought him a regular donkey and pretended to confuse his name, reversing his initials to *W. C.*, the English shorthand for toilet. But a Church of England clergyman converting was too good a catch for Theosophy to pass up, so in 1884 she included him in her entourage to India. To initiate him into the mysteries, she had him circle the ship deck carrying a full chamber pot. Unfortunately for the future of Theosophy, Annie Besant was less a judge of character than Madame Blavatsky.

Indeed, Annie had a problem, and C. W. Leadbeater materialized as the answer to it. Annie lacked an essential ingredient to fulfill her role as Theosophy's high priestess. As heir to Madame Blavatsky's throne, she had to inhabit realms that do not even exist without intuition and fantasy, which unfortunately had been left out of her makeup. In her Theosophical writings she always appeared to be repeating something she hadn't experienced herself. "Her pages bristle with Sanskrit jargon," one critic complained, "but no living or creative ideas move among them."

Enter Leadbeater. The phantasmagoria from the nooks and crannies of centuries' worth of occult lore was lodged in his mind. With mighty clairvoyant gaze he explored the other planets, examined the records of Atlantis, espied archangels and had little chats with them. Annie began to rely on Leadbeater for the "living or creative ideas" she herself lacked. With this man "on the threshold of divinity" (as she described him), Annie could thus coauthor works like *Occult Chemistry*, in which, with the inner eye, they decoded the structure of the atom. Theosophy in this way divided into a double monarchy: Annie directing its politics and Leadbeater the mystical end. And when Leadbeater began dictating weird dogma for the Society—though she had always opposed dogma—Annie accepted it, unable to produce any alternative out of herself.

But if Annie had a problem, Leadbeater had one, too. Euphemistically speaking, he was interested in education—that is, he liked young boys. He always traveled in the company of a couple of likely lads, had them sleep in his bed, and taught them the gentle art of masturbation. Annie was warned in time to avert the scandal but chose to ignore all discreet hints and admonitory whispers. Finally in 1906 incontrovertible evidence was produced—a merry letter of Leadbeater's to a young boy, which ran: "If it [ejaculation] comes without help 'he' needs rubbing more often," the letter advised. "Tell me fully. Glad sensation is so pleasant. Thousand kisses darling."

Oscar Wilde's trial, not long before, had initiated an era of homosexual hush-up and cover-up. From the "sexual underground" Leadbeater now sounded a new voice—insouciant, unembarrassed, unabashed. At the Theosophical Society "court" hearing on his conduct, he merely explained he had been a Greek in a former lifetime, and anyway, he could read the boys' auras and knew what they needed. Leadbeater was expelled from the Society, but he was soon back in Annie's good graces. She seemed even to condone his conduct. "His only defense," she argued, "was that he gave a coterie of premature blasé young men some advice." Never had Annie allowed a hint of sexual scandal to touch her, yet now she permitted it to swallow the Theosophical Society whole. Why so foolish? Perhaps because she remained loyal to friends and championed the underdog, no matter what. Besides, the scandal concerned sex, a subject that did not interest her, and her mind did not fully picture what the charges against Leadbeater involved. And then, this too, she needed him. How can you run a spiritual, visionary society without spirit and vision, which it was Leadbeater's job to furnish. Annie had good reasons for her advocacy of Leadbeater, only they reasoned the Theosophical Society nearly to ruin. Protests about the "Leadbeater affair" resounded, and resignations from the Society doubled, tripled, and quadrupled. The Society never fully recovered from its stigma as an abode of immorality.

Still worse was to come, when God arrived on the scene. Annie had never repudiated Madame Blavatsky's idea of the Mahatmas or masters, but she relegated them to a ghostly chorus who, when called upon, invariably rubber-stamped what she'd decided to do anyway. The Mahatmas appealed more actively to Leadbeater's imagination. With his grandiose visions, any company less exalted was practically slumming. Leadbeater set himself a mission unparalleled—to discover the next Mahatma while he was still a boy. Such a discovery would have, for Leadbeater, the not undesirable side effect of making him something like the young god's godfather. The possibility of a new avatar eddied through Theosophical circles in whispers and wonders. Few anticipated the danger: for what would happen if the new avatar were later to prove human, all too human?

Early in this century, Theosophy seemed on the eve of making a leap of quantum proportions. Annie Besant was not alone in suspecting it would be the next addition to the world's great religions. Which other faith was as suitable for the new twentieth century? Theosophy was one of the first societies to invite Europeans and Asians in on an equal footing; likewise, it was one of the first to balance an older religious cosmology with modern social activism. This satisfying combination caused Theosophy membership to soar everywhere. For people as divergent as Yeats and the young Gandhi, for members of the English Parliament as well as for Indian maharajahs, Theosophy opened the doorway to a better future. Had someone predicted then which would become the faster growing religion—Mormonism, say, founded by an unlikely angel named Moroni and endorsing polygamy and theocracy, or Theosophy, with its creed of social and individual betterment— surely all bets lay with Theosophy.

The only thing the new religion lacked, to Leadbeater's thinking, was a messiah. He scouted and auditioned budding candidates for the juvenile lead role of "World Teacher." The child of an American Theosophical couple was nearly chosen but finally nixed because an Indian lad was felt to have more mystique. Leadbeater's senses appeared to desert him, though, when in 1909 he selected a dirty, skeleton-thin Telegu boy, one constantly beaten in school for his stupidity. The boy looked unpromising, but Leadbeater promised, and Annie dutifully became the boy's legal guardian. Against all odds, the runt did grow up to become exactly what he was supposed to—a "world teacher." He wrote books translated into numerous languages, attracted followers by the thousands, and displayed an independence and courage beyond anything Leadbeater had dreamed (or approved) of. The boy's name was Jiddu Krishnamurti. After Krishnamurti's adolescence and apprenticeship under Leadbeater's and her tutelage, Annie was ready to announce in 1925 that he was *He*. "The Divine Spirit has descended once more on a man," she proclaimed. "The World Teacher is here."

In old age, Krishnamurti was asked what his life would have been like had the Theosophists not "discovered" him. His answer was simple: he would have died of tuberculosis. Yet what he experienced instead was its own brand of misfortune. With the best intentions in the world, Annie had sent Krishnamurti to England in 1911 to be educated. Evidently if the godhead was to get anywhere, he had to become an English gentleman to do so. Annie, who lived on public platforms, saw nothing cruel in forcing this half-grown boy to stand beside her on the stage. Crowds that had never seen an Indian before gawked at the dark skinny boy in his anachronistic Norfolk jacket, with his long black hair parted Christlike down the middle. "As I go about the street the people nudge each other," young Krishnamurti lamented:

> The other day one chap said to the other, "There goes that chap printed in the paper, the Messiah!" Then they burst out laughing. I should have laughed too, if I hadn't been there or involved in any way. . . . I shall have it all my life. Heavens, what have I done to deserve all this.

By the time he was mature enough to be declared the avatar, he was too mature to go along with it. In 1925, when Annie designated him the Teacher, all he wanted to teach was that there were no such "Teachers," including himself. In talks he cracked jokes about the avatar nonsense and claimed he could never finish a Theosophy book, such dull reading it made. Poor Annie! She would have given her godson Krishnamurti anything, except what he wanted—which was for her to stop giving, to stop proclaiming. "I must get out of all this rot," he thought to himself. And not merely thought, he said it aloud on public platforms, to the consternation of Theosophists. Doubtless it had been improbable from the start: a novel in which an atheistic old English lady anoints a sickly Hindu boy as the new messiah would meet sheer disbelief. Leadbeater wrote Annie what was no longer deniable or hideable: "The Coming has gone wrong."

Very wrong. Having a pervert for the church pillar (Leadbeater) and a messiah who announces there's no messiah (Krishnamurti) sent Theosophy into a tailspin from which it never recovered. The Theosophical Society declined into a fringe group (as Mormonism became the world's fastest-growing religion). Saddened and dazed by Krishnamurti's apostasy, Annie was hardly in a mood to review her career for what she might have done differently. She knew only that a decade before the world had lain in her hands: as president of the Indian National Congress, she had meant to lead India into Home Rule, and as president of the Theosophy Society, to lead humankind into a new spiritual home. Krishnamurti's defection was doubly bitter, because India was also rejecting her contribution politically. Where—how—had it all gone so very, very wrong?

❇

Annie's concentration on Theosophy in her old age grew in proportion to the decline of her political influence. Her nurturing attentiveness to Krishnamurti increased as Indian politicians refused her guiding hand. Cruelly, her triumphant moment in politics dated the beginning of her decline. That memorable day, December 26, 1917, she rose before a crowd of nine thousand in

Calcutta and in the tongues of angels and in the tongues of men addressed the Indian National Congress. Annie habitually swayed crowds as easily as lesser mortals say "How d'ya do." But for her presidential acceptance speech she spared no effort. She ransacked books; she spent hours writing; she crossed out ideas; she tried different expressions; she composed and recomposed. Her speech represented to Annie the holy vows wherein she and India plighted their troth to each other.

"I cannot promise to please you always but I can promise to strive my best to serve the Nation, as I judge of service," her voice rang out, as she vowed to lead heedless of popular approval. For once, the crowd failed to respond. For two whole hours her voice continued to ring out. It appeared to try the audience's patience. She had interwoven heroic imagery from the Christian Bible that had always stirred her but that could not stir her audience in the same way. And, in truth, she had glorified her own position. "I cannot promise to agree with . . . you always; the duty of a leader is to lead." She was, slightly, like Lord Curzon lecturing the princes—the authority who knows his (in this case, her) Indian audience's good better than they do. At the end of two hours a polite applause sounded, but her listeners remained cold, skeptical, and unmoved. How different that perfunctory clapping was from the sustained thunder of applause that had greeted Annie's arrival on the subcontinent nearly a quarter century before, when she was considered the first famous English visitor who would be intimately receptive to India. Her presidential address, with its miscalculated Christian imagery, now made her seem but another English person who found the Indian order too alien and who had come to impose her leadership upon it. Some in that audience surmised they would have to wait for another generation (just as readers of this book have to await the next chapter for E. M. Forster) for a westerner willing simply to register India along his quiet emotional capillaries.

Now that she was president, her statements frequently took the form of fiat. To the British she might sound like a ventriloquist, as though India were speaking through her, but Indians detected in her pronouncements the commanding diction of the memsahib. Her affront to authority, her radical moral rhetoric, had not changed since she mounted soapbox and platform in England. But in England she had denounced injustices that often pricked or wounded her personally. In India her voice box was not so connected, as it were, to the mechanics of the sound system: Annie spoke in India for people, causes, and ideas that for all her efforts at empathy were ultimately not her own. Like Curzon, whom she despised, she had come to imagine herself the legitimate spokesperson for a country that, many observers felt, neither could legitimately represent at all.

In 1919 the British police brutally squashed protests in Delhi— protests quite similar to ones Annie had earlier organized. Only the Delhi protests were organized by a rival of hers in the Home Rule Movement. Surprising everyone, Annie concurred in their suppression and appeared to have joined the British side. In her newspaper she editorialized that when "a riot becomes unmanageable, brickbats must inevitably be answered by bullets." Though she realized her mistake and apologized profusely, the phrase "bullets for brickbats" would not die, invariably repeated to discredit her. Instead of the garlands they had showered her with three years before, the crowds now greeted her with boos and jeers.

As we saw with Curzon and Kitchener, westerners who left behind the laws of their own country tended to become laws unto themselves in India. Tilak, the nationalist leader, complained that Mrs. Besant acted as though "she it was who alone awakened the sense of political freedom in India." "I cannot bear for a moment the supremacy which she claims for her opinions," Tilak went on. "[The Indian National] Congress recognizes no Mahatma to rule over it except the Mahatma of majority."

Tilak was referring to the Theosophists' cockamamy Mahatmas, of course, but Annie now had a more human Mahatma to worry about: Gandhi. They had first met at Madame Blavatsky's so many innocent years before. Some historians claim it was Annie who first bestowed upon Gandhi the title Mahatma (literally: "great soul"). Gandhi certainly praised Annie for "the inspiration I drew from her in my boyhood and then again in my experiences of political activity." Such flowery tributes could not conceal the fact that since his return to India in 1915, they had been locked in a fierce rivalry. Their personality differences were magnified into two different visions for India. Annie, ignoring the Muslim population, considered India a Hindu country, whereas Gandhi eventually gave his life to a nationalism that embraced both religions equally. While Annie tended to identify India with the Brahmin caste, Gandhi was determined to end caste distinctions. And while Annie hoped to educate the people up to the political requirements of an elite, Gandhi tried to level elitist standards in the name of equality. Gandhi widened Annie Besant's middle-class definition of citizenship to include all Indians, which may be why India has proved, despite turmoil and corruption, Asia's most resilient democracy. In the 1920s, Gandhi was like a signpost pointing to the future, whereas Annie was an arrow that, if dusted off, showed the way to the past.

And that was, so one might think, exactly how it should be. In 1927 Annie would be eighty years old, and it was time for her to belong to the past, time for her to rest. But *rest* was the word missing from her vocabulary, and her last decade of political activity would be, if anything, more frenzied than her first. Desperate to take the initiative—it no longer seemed to matter which initiative—she proposed that Britain give India commonwealth status, with the franchise for Indians based on literacy. Her proposed parliamentary bill to effect this could appeal only to a tiny coterie, excluding as it did the vast majority of Indians. Gandhi and Motilal Nehru would not support the bill, the Muslim leader Jinnah refused even to read it, and the English Parliament simply shelved it. It was becoming only too evident that Annie represented no ethnic group, no geographic region, no historical tradition within the country. Of course, until recently land and locals and leaders did not need to come wrapped in the same ethno-national homogeneity. The Marquis de Lafayette was, after all, a hero of the American Revolution. Unlike Lafayette, however, Annie wasn't enrolling in an already existing army but initiating policy on her own. And add to this the fact that she was coupling a nationalist movement (which many like Nehru based on secularism or socialism) with an international religion (which rejected those *isms*), and the result doomed her as the years went by to becoming increasingly out of sync.

Ancient, driven, inexorable, Annie in her seventies and eighties resembled a cursed creature in a fable, never permitted to cease moving. Her wheels were turning furiously yet she remained in the same spot. Her politics shifted by the moment, one instant siding with the extremists, the next with the moderates, then with the British, to whichever position promised her influence. Increasingly her criterion for whether a course of action was correct was whether or not she had advocated it. She became a kind of Lord Curzon of revolution, her position invariably the right one, anybody else's hardly worth considering. Indeed, subtract the uniforms of splendor, the protocol, and the acres of servants, and Curzon's and Annie Besant's Indian days bear eerie resemblance. Both of them held court, answered questions in large halls, granted private audiences, and went on tour. Once the youthful rebel against every authoritarian institution, Annie now behaved in old age as if she had finally found an acceptable authority: herself. Still vigorous in 1930, she appeared an authority that might outlive empires.

An Attempt at Evaluation

One astrologer who forecast Annie's date of death, only to see her defiantly live on long past the due date, rationalized his miscalculation. "For her the ordinary rules by which longevity is determined seem not to apply." But on September 20, 1933, at four o'clock in the afternoon, the exemption to the rule ceased. In her last conversation she rambled incoherently about the "little fairies," and why, she asked, did so many pretty animals die so young?

The Theosophical Society continues to exist, but the historical context that once gave it importance is gone. Historical contexts are usually elusive, but Annie's was symbolized in a corner of Madame Blavatsky's parlor. There on a pedestal perched a statue of a baboon, and under the baboon's arm some practical joker—surely Blavatsky herself—had wedged a copy of Darwin's *Origin of Species*. Madame Blavatsky's stunt playfully parodied Theosophy's quite serious attempt to form a union of science and religion. "We were discontented with old ideas and half afraid of new," Annie generalized about her generation, stranded nervously between religion and science, "greedy for the material results of . . . Science but looking askance at her agnosticism." Theosophy's blend of religion and if not hard science, experimental approach, made it for many divided people the heady solution to a problem otherwise intractable. That Annie Besant, who became president of the Theosophical Society, was also among the first women in England to obtain a degree in science was hardly a coincidence.

Annie intuited that in the new secular era religion would be, as Amitav Ghosh recently put it, "reinvented as its own antithesis." Most people today understand religion in one of either two ways, but neither existed much before the modern period. In the antireligious person's, say, Freud's, view, religion is superstition, to be eradicated by educational advance and scientific progress. From the believer's perspective, whether C. S. Lewis's or the Ayatollah Khomeini's, religion is the bulwark shielding an individual from the contemporary dehumanizations of life. Both views, "secularism" and "fundamentalism," compartmentalize religion in its own sphere or as its own field of activity, instead of seeing it as one aspect of everything. The Theosophists' claim upon the historian's attention comes from their attempt to fashion what Mirra Richard called a "third position"—a religious approach that is neither and both secularism and fundamentalism.

India called to them because there they might be free from the iron classifications that categorized everything as either faith *or* science, religion *or* radicalism. Annie and the Theosophists made their entrance in India as though entering a laboratory, to experimentally combine for the good of mankind things never mixed before: East and West, science and occultism, spirituality and modern politics. As a spiritualist who demanded that schools and legislatures dance to her tune, Annie was a proto-fundamentalist; as a champion of religious dissidents, she was a good soldier in the secularist camp. Besant and Leadbeater created in works like *Occult Chemistry* an unclassifiable third way through contemporary intellectual understanding. Ultimately, what shape and coloring their glorious experiment would take they, like good spiritual scientists, could not know in advance, but only after it was successful.

But that *after*, that success, never came. That glorious day when Theosophy inscribed itself as the new world religion among the world's faiths never dawned. In its obituary of Annie Besant the London *Times* explained the cause of her failure. All bright prospects dimmed when the admirable Mrs. Besant fell under the pernicious influence of C. W. Leadbeater. Others lamenting the lost promise harked back to Krishnamurti, the World Teacher who wouldn't teach. But the obituaries and the postmortems perhaps dated the ingestion of the fatal poison too late. Theosophy was like the athlete who takes a potent drug that shoots him powerfully out of the starting gate but causes him to droop and faint before reaching the finish line.

At the very start Madame Blavatsky belied Theosophy's claim to be a scientific, experimental investigation of religion with her hoax about half-human–half-deities in the Himalayas. She betrayed Theosophy's genuine interest in Eastern religion by inventing her own religion-equivalent of Tibetan Mahatmas. In India she did encounter remarkable gurus and teachers (Swami Sankaracharya of Mysore, Dayananda Sarasvati, Sarat Chandra Das) with whom she could have engaged in that East-West dialogue of which the Theosophists sweetly dreamed, but. . . . But she was impatient, short of cash, and craving attention, and more efficient were her gaseous Mahatmas, who could endorse her actions via magical communiqués and perform on cue. Invoking them, she wowed and won audiences and fame for herself—"the wisest woman in Europe, with a wicked pack of cards." But when finally the tricks got exposed and the curtain pulled back, there, rather as in *The Wizard of Oz*, sat not wizards or Mahatmas but only an old woman manipulating the knobs.

It was a critical historical moment when Annie Besant appeared on the scene, and the balance could have gone either way. She was a rationalist, a scientist, a realistic politician, but a latent Victorian impulse toward the mythological worked in Annie no less strongly than it did in, say, the poet Yeats. When she called India "the Holy Land . . . whose polity was built by King Initiates, whose religion was molded by Divine Men," she was speaking Yeats's mytho-poetic language. But to set down her poetic vision Annie used, instead of writing paper, national policies and international societies. When, out of loyalty to Madame Blavatsky but also from a deep craving within herself, she endorsed the existence of the Mahatmas, Theosophy's great historical moment silently passed. Her motto (and chosen epitaph) was *She Tried to Follow Truth*, but at a crucial moment she received rice paper letters from disembodied spiritual masters and followed them instead. Annie Besant's long drama in India still remained to be played out—the scandal of Leadbeater, the disappointment of Krishnamurti, the competition with Gandhi— but in this case the denouement, the ending, preceded the middle.

People still join the Theosophical Society, but the promise it shone with in Annie's heyday—1,500 lodges, membership growing in nearly every country, the possibility of becoming the next world religion—is extinct. At the very dawn of that heyday, Madame Blavatsky scraped together the money to purchase some land outside Madras at Adyar for Theosophy's world headquarters. Much of the above story of Blavatsky and Besant and Leadbeater and Krishnamurti transpired there. Incredibly, some very old Theosophists can still remember long, long ago hearing Annie

Besant speak beneath Adyar's great banyan tree. Ancient though she was, she spoke without microphone and after one hour exactly sounded her peroration, the electricity of which went through them and, seemingly, would keep on sounding till it reached the ends of India. Today at Adyar the beautiful gardens are going back to seed and the groomed fields to weed (and the only murmur beneath that vast banyan tree is an occasional snake rustling by). The pervasive melancholy resembles some Conradian setting of noble hopes and pristine dreams gone to rot in the tropics. Madras with its congestion and traffic and millions of people has grown up around Adyar, and India today perhaps affords no greater contrast than rustic, quiet Adyar and rushing, noisy Madras, existing side by side and separated by only a few steps. But the Theosophists could never cross those steps over into the contemporary world.

Beyond Adyar, though, Annie's influence, her life's work, may enjoy an afterlife after all, in other groups and under different names. Indeed, her critics not only concede, they make this point: wherever there is a kook—a crystal gazer, a channeler, a past-life interpreter—there is Annie Besant's monument. It seems enough to give her old pal Bernard Shaw a posthumous good chuckle, that the sober, practical Mrs. Besant might indirectly have mothered the flaky, spacey "New Age." But Annie's work in cross-cultural spirituality extends beyond the so-called New Age movement: her receptivity to other possibilities, her curiosity about other cultures, her championing of "backward" faiths, fostered the climate in which different religions could become not only the cause of hatred and war, but also the source of international cooperation and mutual enrichment. Indeed, the world's most respected religious figure today, the present Dalai Lama, preaches the same core of teachings that underlay all Annie's efforts: the hope that tolerant religion, humane politics, and scientific knowledge can combine and reinforce one another, and must, if the worst devastations are to be avoided. Theosophy may have been merely the first act of a drama, the second act of which, with a change of characters, we are witnessing today, and the third may be yet to come.

Her dreams thus came true, but the dreamer is forgotten. Her hopes for an India that would be independent, for race relations that would be more equal, and for a religion oriented not to sin but to earthly welfare have all come to pass. But, outside India, the memory of her who worked to realize these hopes has passed away. Writing fifty years after her death, the English author Rosemary Dinnage said the time had come to rescue Annie Besant from oblivion: Annie was a human exemplar, Dinnage argued, a woman with larger-than-life virtues. She may at times have been complacently self-serving, turning a blind eye to whatever did not further her purpose. But her failings were, in good Victorian fashion, indistinguishable from her virtues. If she was self-righteous, she fought for causes that were, by almost any standard of social justice or antiracism, "right." If her epitaph, *She Tried to Follow Truth*, should read *She Followed Half-Truth*, that very shutting out of complicating factors allowed her to accomplish prodigiously. If her Mahatmas (like the God of many a smug Englishman) invariably validated what she had already envisioned, she at least envisioned a humanity living in equality and nobility of purpose. She spent herself so unselfishly that, by the end, she had not a penny to her name: each year, on January 1, she withdrew her bank balance and donated it to worthy Indian causes. Any scorecard of Annie Besant's triumphs and failings is enormously complicated by their being writ overlarge, on a scale of giant intention and action such as the world may never see again. She was courageous in battle, magnanimous in victory, and in the defeats of her last years uncomplaining, nor whining for vindication.

Lord Curzon had surveyed all posterity and attempted to dictate how it should remember him ever after. Although Annie Besant had struggled like a cornered animal before relinquishing an ounce of power, in more reflective moods she declared that the greatest monument to her would be, in fact, oblivion. Her labors were successful if they helped inaugurate a free India and a new spirituality that would no longer require even the memory of her. Nearing death, Annie simply looked around her rooms at Adyar, recalled all that had transpired there, and only requested they remain more or less unchanged, once she was no longer there bustling through them.

PART II
Self

Identity dons a different costume: E. M. Forster
in Indian dress. *King's College Library*

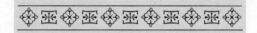

Identity in the Present Tense

Desperate souls, flee to India. Two such souls who bundled up their crises and wrote DESTINATION INDIA across them were E. M. Forster and V. S. Naipaul. Although nearly a half century separates their respective journeys, a similar situation motivated each one to drop his routines and to take off to India. Both men, as they packed their bags, were suffering from something suspiciously resembling an old-fashioned "identity crisis." Outwardly everything appeared rosy, life mastered, success won: before their initial trips to India, made when they were around thirty, Forster and Naipaul had each written four acclaimed novels that had established them as the promising novelists of their respective generations. But inwardly they tread on quicksand, in which their sense of themselves, even their means of livelihood, seemed to be sinking, and the danger was that their great promise might go forever unfulfilled.

Naipaul's four novels were comedies set in his native Trinidad, but living in England, he had exhausted the "Caribbean-ness" in himself and could not (or at least never did) write a Caribbean novel again. Forster's four novels concern the personal private life, but the secret of his own privacy, his homosexuality, was a literary taboo, and he could not (or at least never did) publish a novel of domestic intimacies again. Aside from writing, Naipaul was no longer a Trinidadian, but he hadn't become an Englishman either, and as a man without a culture, he worried that his whole existence reduced to having a name and owning a typewriter. Apart from writing, Forster shared his house and companionship with a domineering mother, whose robust health suggested that stifling arrangement might well last forever. Forster and Naipaul both invested their initial trip to India with impossibly large significance: if the journey failed and they returned to England no different from when they left, they feared coming home to the abyss. They unconsciously sought in India, though they would scarcely have worded it this way, something like self-transformation.

And what is that elusive thing, the *self*, anyway? Neither Forster nor Naipaul pondered such a vapory, ontological question as he rushed about arranging all the last-minute practical details before departing for India. Quite possibly, they should have. Forster was going ostensibly to meet a good Indian friend, while Naipaul hoped to verify whether his father's pretty tales of India had a grain of truth to them. But inadvertently, by importing their "identity crises" into a country where identity—the self, a person—was so differently defined and constructed, they stepped onto a wild roller-coaster ride into the very nature of being.

So contrary are India's and the West's versions of the self, India's preeminent psychoanalyst Sudhir Kakar has written, that patients in India come to him suffering from what in the West would be considered psychological health. Kakar recalls, for example, a young engineer who arrived at the initial session accompanied by his father and his sister, both worried about his problem with autonomy. The engineer was not experiencing a deficient sense of self, it turned out, but too secure a one. The father explained, "He is very stubborn in pursuing what he wants without taking our wishes into account. He thinks he knows what is best for himself. . . . He thinks his own life and career more important than the concerns of the rest of the family." A western psychotherapist would congratulate the young engineer—"Good! High time!"—but his Indian family bemoaned his unnatural independence and wondered what could be done. Forster, Naipaul, and other individuals troubled by their sense of self unwittingly slipped into a cultural cauldron that brewed individuality and autonomy according to a different recipe.

If Forster or Naipaul ever heard the Hindu injunction "Know thy Self" (*atmanam vidhi*), it would have sounded in their ears like the Socratic command "Know thyself." The echo is deceptive; the meanings could hardly differ more. A westerner's identity lies geographically within the contours of his physical body, and by probing there using psychological methods of examination and introspection taught since Socrates, he will uncover who he is. In India, by contrast, an individual's identity is not circumscribed by his skin's boundaries but bleeds over into the community—a community composed not only of family and neighbors but also of animals and ancestral spirits and deities as well. Identity in the contemporary West, as psychologist Kenneth Kenniston writes, presupposes a "limitless respect for the individual, [and] faith that understanding is better than illusion." Indian identity stresses that surrender to greater powers is better than individual effort and that a person becomes his true self as he enters into the living stream, naturally and un–self-consciously, of the community life and its traditions.

What a tangle, Freud thought, what an overgrown jungle was the Indian understanding of the personality. In 1930 the Nobel Prize–winning author Romain Rolland solicited Freud's opinion of the Indian approach to the self to use in his biography of the Hindu saint Sri Ramakrishna. Freud's polite, perfunctory reply could hardly conceal how uninterested he was in the whole question. "I shall now try with your guidance [he wrote Rolland] to penetrate into the Indian jungle from which until now an uncertain blending of Hellenic love of proportion, Jewish sobriety and Philistine timidity have kept me away." A jungle!—that's what so many westerners complained of as they tried to penetrate the Hindu worldview, where the human individual, social castes, and the greater gods live all on top of one another. Hermann Hesse traveling to India in 1911 remained aloof, "afraid of being overwhelmed—engulfed [by India]," Rolland reported. "Hesse tells me: 'Yes, that's so. In India there's a tiger hidden in the jungle.'"

The young Americans for whom Hesse's novels *Journey to the East* and *Siddhartha* became cult classics a half century later never suspected that their author had loathed India. But Hesse was not being hypocritical when he painted a beautiful India of the spirit, as though he had not actually gone, seen, and abhorred the country. Hesse acknowledged in advance that his trip was undertaken "out of sheer inner need"—an inner necessity projected onto outward geography—and as such, he allowed his imagination selective free play and ignored the rest. Travelers after World War I such as Forster and Naipaul, however, no longer felt so free to take poetic license with the hard realities. (Indeed, after World War II, Naipaul felt so uncomfortable tampering with the facts that, except for one short story, he never made fiction out of India.) Postwar travelers were not the romantic individualist, unbeholden to the conventions, that Hesse had fancied himself. For all his modesty, Forster was seen as the representative of the English virtues of pluck, decency, and civility; despite his Caribbean and Indian background, Naipaul became the eloquent spokesman for European rational and progressive values. Freud had called India a jungle, and Hesse warned there might be the tiger in that jungle. And into that so-called jungle Forster and Naipaul ventured as the unofficial ambassadors of European civilization, on a safari in search of self.

Sigmund Freud, the greatest investigator of the self in the twentieth century, waved India away: he was simply not interested in anything India had to say about personality, identity, or the psyche. The competition, however, thought otherwise. Freud's rival, Carl G. Jung (1875–1961), was very interested, and he even hazarded that Indian notions of the self might counterbalance certain tendencies in western psychology gone askew.

In 1938, His Majesty's government in England invited Jung to attend the twenty-fifth anniversary celebrations of the University of Calcutta. Freud would never have accepted such an invitation—what would have been the point? For Freud the human psyche, like human anatomy, was basically everywhere identical. Jung, more curious about other possibilities, accepted the invitation with alacrity. In India, so he told himself, sophisticated representatives of a highly differentiated civilization could articulate for him their psychology in their own terms. Europe, he believed, desperately needed to hear such articulations, and never more so than then. By 1938, Jung had intuited the inferno to come—war, barbaric persecutions, and unprecedented destruction—at the very heart of European civilization. "The so-called Christian West," he wrote, "far from creating a new world, is moving with great strides toward the possibility of destroying the world we have." Jung thus imagined his journey to India somewhat in the form of a quest: he would be the knight securing the grail—the grail in this case being psychological formulations to counter the mentality of destruction.

Jung's journey to India might have concealed a more basic motive, though, a mission or "grail" different from the one he consciously posited for it. Although he was a success both personally and professionally, Jung's school of psychology was dismissed and derided in Europe, while Freud's reigned everywhere triumphant. Nowhere was the battle between Freud and Jung more clearly joined than in how they understood the self or what constitutes an individual's autonomy. For Freud, a person's identity is nothing more than his (or her) conscious ego, perched hazardously above impersonal, unconscious raging forces largely sexual in character. Jung countered that one's unconscious consisted of far more than sexual libido, that it contained more individual elements, too: the unconscious had an "Indian" capaciousness to intermingle the personal with dark and shadowy forces, with archetypes both bestial and divine. Jung's hope was that more healthy individual identities—truer selves that integrated conscious personality with unconsciousness—would create a less divided and conflicted society than the one threatening to destroy Europe. But within psychoanalytic circles Freud's formulations of the self were accepted as science or fact, while Jung's were dismissed as fanciful speculations, even mysticism. He might have taken heart that one of India's leading philosophers, Sri Aurobindo, in criticizing Freud's theories, expressed a view of the self similar to Jung's own. Very well, then let the country of "Know thy Self" prove that Jung's ideas were other than mysticism: in 1938, at age sixty-three, Jung boldly plunged into India the way his younger, more conventional colleagues donned their white jackets and entered the laboratory.

Was there ever a more urbane visitor to India? Sophistication practically dripped from Jung's anecdotes of his days and byways through India. Upon returning, Jung regaled the Indologist Heinrich Zimmer with how at the Temple of Konorak his guide had pointed out the famous phallic-shaped lingams. "Do you know what these stones mean?" his guide whispered. "I will tell you a great secret." Let him not say penis symbols, Jung thought, as he hoped instead for some less obvious, more startling revelation from the East. "These stones are man's private parts," his guide softly mumbled, put there to remind husbands of their marital duties. Jung noticed the guide nodding self-importantly as if to imply, You in your European ignorance would never have thought it so! Zimmer could barely stop laughing to exclaim, "At last I have heard something real about India for a change!" Jung did not need to spell it out that his guide was like a little Freud, who proffers a sexual explanation, while behind it rises the whole temple-complex of civilization richer than a single sexual interpretation can do justice to.

But if Jung was the sophisticated traveler, he also appeared to be one who had forgotten why he had come to India. His purpose was to study the psyche there, to discover how notions of the self can either exacerbate or ameliorate the larger evils of the society. But, once on the spot, he merely sported about as any intelligent tourist, noting social curiosities, styles of clothing, outward behavior. Rather than investigate the psychology of religion (he interviewed no guru or wise man, not even those Zimmer insisted he absolutely must), he rushed everywhere. He hurried about receiving honorary doctorates from British, Islamic, and Hindu universities, one day in Calcutta, then in Allahabad, and next on to Benares, a nonstop engine of public activity. His ceaseless busyness, his frantic ricocheting here and there, portended something suspicious. And when all the hubbub proved "a little too much of a good thing" and Jung landed in the hospital exhausted with dysentery, he seemed curiously relieved. The hospital provided him a sanctuary, "a blessed island in the wild sea of new impressions." With his psychological bias, and now in a good humor because of the hospital, Jung offered a metaphorical diagnosis: "I got dysentery because I could not digest India."

What exactly about India could Jung not digest (besides the amoebas)? Had something frightened him, as it had Hesse? In his sketchy travelogue *From India* (1913), Hesse confessed the only event that affected him deeply in India was a dream he had there, and the same might be said of Jung. Though he had traversed half the world to get there, and at every turn fascinating new expressions of the human psyche greeted him, all of that apparently mattered less to Jung than an enigmatic, unforgettable dream he had one night in the hospital.

In the dream Jung saw himself touring a medieval castle located on an island. Not any ordinary castle, it is the very castle of the Holy Grail. A German professor is lecturing on the Grail, comparing English and French legends, displaying a brilliant erudition. But in the dream the German professor bothers Jung because he pontificates as though in a classroom, oblivious to the fact that the actual Grail is nearby. The island divides in two parts, separated by a narrow strait, and there, on the other shore, the Grail lies beckoning. The dream makes clear that Jung is the one person who can secure it, but as he strips himself naked to swim the strait, he wakes up from the dream.

In Switzerland, before setting off for India, Jung had been studying about medieval grails and quests and interpreting them psychologically. Upon waking, Jung gave the dream a far-fetched interpretation: it was a reprimand, he decided, reminding him his real work lay back in Europe. He cut short his trip and booked early passage home. Jung forgot his own quest in India, his search for other approaches to identity and different definitions of the self. Suddenly indifferent, Jung hastened back to Europe to become a "professor" (and, symbolically, who could the German professor in the dream be but Jung himself?)—to write and lecture on Hindu and Buddhist psychology with *academic* brilliance. His retreat into the disinterested scholar's stance in Switzerland continued that earlier retreat into the hospital where Jung had taken refuge from India.

Apparently Jung felt confronted in India. The spiritual and the primitive, the individual and the communal, all existing side by side in India corresponded to a division within himself and affected him viscerally. So much in his thinking should have made him espouse, as the young engineer's family's did, the ideal of a communally defined person. If human unconsciousness truly is collective in a positive way, as Jung insisted, then one's identity demands a collective expression and a communal approach to selfhood, outside the European individualist mode. Indian philosophy excited Jung precisely because it corroborated all his ideas about identity and the collective unconscious, which were dismissed as eccentric in Europe (e.g., *Atman* = the Jungian view of self; *citta* = the psyche; *samskaras* = archetypes; *mandala* = symbolic wholeness; etc.). But collective identity was one thing when Jung wrote about it in his comfortable book-lined study in Switzerland, and frighteningly something else when, amid India's press and throng and in its caste system, it jostled him on the overcrowded streets ceaselessly.

And in fact Jung's model, his ideal, was not the communal but the individual. Jung envisioned as the high peak of human-ness that individuated person—born in ancient Greece, reared in the Renaissance, and matured in the Enlightenment—grown so distinct he almost constituted a *genus*, a species of bloom solely in himself. If one were to seek such an apotheosis of individualism who breathed accomplishment, humor, and originality with his every breath, one could hardly locate a more charming specimen than Jung himself. But once in India, in the confusion of masses and classes and with his senses continually bombarded, Jung felt threatened in his individualistic ideal. Jung was not unreceptive to India; to the contrary: he was hyper-receptive to the conflicting stimuli, to the sheer mass of people, to the debilitating climate, to everything that would endanger his carefully built-up sense of self. When Jung woke from his dream in the Indian hospital, he told himself, "Your state is perilous; you are . . . in imminent danger of destroying all that centuries have built up." So instead of leaving the hospital resolved to make up for lost time, he booked early passage home. "I did not see one European in India who really lived there," Jung said in his defense. "They were all living in Europe, that is, in a sort of bottle filled with European air. One would surely go under without the insulating glass wall."

A conflict in his own values turned Jung into a professor of paradoxes, the dean of ambivalence, when the subject was India. He approved of so many of the communal and spiritual possibilities in Indian life but worried that any westerner risked his fragile autonomy, if he experimented with such overwhelming headiness. Not only the political systems vary, Jung cautioned; the inner history of the self in Europe long ago diverged from India's. What is a tasty morsel to the Indian psyche may prove (to return to dysentery as metaphor) indigestible in a westerner's psychological tract. Besides, a European will consider only that part of an Indian spiritual practice that appeals to him personally and not what else it may mean within an Indian community. Jung's reasoning, whatever merit it may have, unfortunately gave him the coy stance of the flirt who teases but then draws back, "No no, mustn't." Jung hugely appreciated the philosophy of yoga, but thinking of Madame Blavatsky and Annie Besant in particular, he warned that a westerner "will infallibly make a wrong use of yoga"

> because his psychic disposition is quite different from that of the Oriental. I say to whomsoever I can: "Study yoga— you will learn an infinite amount from it—but do not try to apply it, for Europeans are not so constituted that we apply these methods correctly, just like that."

As for yoga, so for gurus. So for mandalas and so for meditation. Over all the jewels of eastern wisdom Jung placed his DO NOT TOUCH sign. As for a trip itself to India, which he heartily recommended, he also carefully prepared a prospective traveler not to expect to enjoy it:

> I think, if you can afford it, a trip to India is on the whole most edifying and, from a psychological point of view, most advisable, although it may give you considerable headaches.

Jung's tempting paradoxes, his NO TRESPASSING notices posted before the spiritual Orient, in the end, needless to say, lured in the very people they were intended to keep out.

Stripped naked in the dream, Jung had stood poised to swim the divide and win the Grail, but something in his very being revolted, and he woke startled. Had he succeeded in what the dream symbolized—had finally a western knight won the grail of appropriating the Indian psyche—Jung would have gained what had eluded Curzon, Besant, and Gandhi all. Each of them had attempted to impose on India the Enlightenment moral order, which allows the individual to define and pursue his happiness on his own terms. But for a new social order to emerge in India the Enlightenment individual was too flimsy, too self-centered a customer, to replace the system of caste that had hitherto undergirded society. Curzon's, Besant's, and Gandhi's various Indo-European syntheses required a more communal individual; they needed to unite western individualist traditions with more collective traditions of identity, if their ideally casteless society was not to degenerate into mere anomie. In short, they required a Jung whose grail of a differently conceived selfhood actually lay somewhere in India and not in medieval manuscripts lying back on his desk in Switzerland. But if the great Jung, a *maître* of comparative psychology, had turned back at the gate, how likely was it that a couple of mere word mongers like Forster and Naipaul would persist and prevail where he had faltered?

✠

But Naipaul and Forster were not merely writers. They were highly evolved representatives of European civilization who inadvertently put its values and insights to the test at every corner they rounded in India. Even more important, each bore a different notion of the self to India. For not only philosophers have ideas about the nature of identity; ordinary people do, even if they never formulate them in so many words. On a popular level float two contradictory assumptions about selfhood, about what makes an individual what he or she is. Some people consider that people are defined by what they do. Other people believe people, regardless of their actions, are defined by what they intrinsically are. Forster and Naipaul each carried one of these two assumptions about identity to India; indeed, each wrapped himself in it, his garment of protection against the perils of travel and the hardships of the road.

For Naipaul, a man was what he did. Naipaul may not have been a Trinidadian, nor exactly an Indian, nor exactly an Englishman, but so what? He was what he did, which was write books. An author seems a tenuous peg to tether one's identity to, especially in the beginning, but Naipaul was a good writer, and his sense of well-being grew more secure over the years, with the publication of each new volume. When Naipaul went to India he was thus less curious about the Indians' psyche than about what they *did*. To his scandalized dismay, he discovered they made a bloody mess of it. Four or five men often joined to do the simplest task, and then bungled it, when one Indian as efficient as Naipaul was at writing could have dispatched the job in half the time. And on top of everything else, god forbid, Indians meditated or did yoga or otherwise sailed their sense of self-identity into an empyrean of pure idealism, as though the execrable, bungled mess below it were not the final truth of the matter. Naipaul in India resembled, curiously, Jung. Curious, because as a psychologist Jung would presumably focus on what people *are*, behind the mask of social doing. But because collective identity interested him, Jung could study it only through what they collectively did. And so India's inefficiency and squalor, as clues to the collective self, bothered him more than they did many tourists. Paramahansa Yogananda's *Autobiography of a Yogi* (1946) provoked Jung's sarcasm because its cream puff idealism contained not a single practical "antidote to disastrous population explosion and traffic jams and the threat of starvation, [a book] so rich in vitamins that albumen, carbohydrates, and such like banalities become superogatory. . . . Happy India!" Jung's harmless strain of sarcasm turned rabid, however, in Naipaul. Naipaul accused Hinduism of having caused the Indian self to turn inward, stagnant, and become defeated, yet despite its defeatism, it still dared to proclaim the loftiest sentiments—a rose planted atop a dung heap. Happy India, indeed.

The philosopher Goldsworthy Lowes Dickinson likewise recoiled before India's squalid mess on a trip in 1912, but his traveling companion, E. M. Forster, oddly did not. Forster kept an open mind concerning how much India's poverty would disturb him, and when it did not overly do so he felt relieved. He wanted to enjoy Indians and not to consider them (as Dickinson, Jung, and Naipaul all did) a "problem" to be investigated. Forster had taken from the Cambridge philosopher G. E. Moore the notion that states of mind are infinitely more interesting than kinds of actions. Unlike Curzon, Besant, and Naipaul, who wanted to explore what actions were possible on the subcontinent, Forster wanted to experience which pleasures were possible there.

What if India was a muddle? In truth Forster knew he was, beneath the surface, quite a muddle himself. He was a homosexual living in a heterosexual milieu; he was an Englishman who found other public-school Englishmen officious and cold; he prized intimate relationships above all but could not achieve such an intimacy for himself. There was no way he could say yes to a part of himself without saying no to another part. India's so-called intellectual muddle—its ambiguities, obscurities, inconsistencies—

were as welcoming to him as rain in a parched season. India's contradictions provided a way of saying yes and no simultaneously to things within himself that would not admit to a straightforward, unconditioned response. Adult maturity, Forster once said, begins not with the knowledge of good and evil but of good-*and*-evil. India, where he experienced good-and-evil, stimulating-and-boring, intimate-and-alien all jumbled together, worked its tonic effect upon him. When he wrote friends back in England, "I am in the middle of a very queer [i.e., peculiar] life" here, he was not griping but expressing blessed relief. By his courtesy, his unobtrusiveness, his wanting to be liked, and his willingness to be bored, Forster penetrated into a realm of experience in India that more action-oriented, goal-directed Europeans then did not even suspect existed.

Of course many travelers besides Forster felt, once in India, an improvement close to or at the center of their being. In particular the western Gandhians, such as Charlie Andrews or Madeleine Slade, acquired in India a newfound confidence. But in their cases the explanation seems rather obvious: to participate in a just cause, to engage in meaningful action, invariably improves a person's sense of self. One of Gandhi's biographers argued, however, that such an explanation reverses cause and effect. Gandhi saw people like Slade and Andrews as they secretly wished to be perceived, and this subtle change in identity they felt in his presence allowed them to do feats and endure hardships they had hardly believed themselves capable of. Would India likewise "see" our desperate writer-heroes differently or flush out of hiding a latent aspect of themselves, like one of their novels' characters suddenly revealing an unexpected face? If the coloration of Forster's or Naipaul's identity deepened, as it had for the Gandhians, then the larger world around them would automatically assume a richer hue, which in turn might inspire them to new work. On the other hand, if India proved too much, or too little, and they returned unchanged to their particular writer's blocks and dead ends in England . . . then what? Forster was only visiting a young Indian on whom he had a mild crush, and Naipaul merely searching for his grandfather's ancestral village in Uttar Pradesh. The stakes were considerably higher than either could have guessed, though, as the trunks snapped shut and each set nervously forth.

CHAPTER 3

Rites Europeans Seldom Shared

On March 4, 1921, when E. M. Forster sailed for India he was not vacationing but entering a maharajah's employment. A maharajah! At the very word, one's imagination takes wing. His senses would bask in the sensuous opulence of a princely court, his mind reel at its byzantine intricacy of ceremony. But India was then pockmarked by native principalities, some no larger than a town in the American Midwest and about as flat and dusty. Forster was curiously indifferent whether his destination would land him in luxuriance or parched shabbiness. What his exact position under the maharajah would be remained likewise vague, and he seemed not to mind that either. Ten years before on an Indian holiday Forster had met an eccentric princeling who now offered him employment. He gladly seized it without knowing what *it* was. Like a physician prescribing a cure in a dry climate, Forster prescribed this trip for himself at a troubled moment in his own life but also in Western history. The patient would quietly tiptoe out of England, where his novel was stuck and his emotional relations stalled, and cure himself, as it were, by doses of a different civilization. E. M. Forster, the novelist of interiority, of familiar intimacies, had determined to leap into whatever was unfamiliar, uncatalogued, outsized. He jauntily waved adieu to his friends, joking that he was off to be "Prime Minister or something."

⬧

India offers a thousand, thousand panoramas of beauty or fascination. The tiny maharajahdom of Dewas Senior was, however, the thousand-thousand-and-first. Of tourist attractions, Dewas had none; sights of historical interest, none; scenes of great natural beauty, the same. From Rajput palaces to Mughal mosques, India boasts many of the famous glories of world architecture. In Dewas, all the buildings were dingy, and their decoration meager, set in a parched and treeless landscape. The opening of *A Passage to India* deflates the golden Easts and rosy dawns that had stage-lit earlier English fiction about India. "The streets are mean, the temples ineffective, and there is no painting and scarcely any carving in the bazaar . . . so abased, so monotonous is everything that meets the eye." One need not speculate where Forster, who spent the majority of his time in India in Dewas, drew his inspiration.

But what did a little scenic ugliness matter when Forster was the person told of in tales of genies: the man who got his wish. He had wished for England to drop away, to fall behind the western horizon, and for India to wrap around him like a curtain. He had journeyed five thousand miles not for tiger hunting or pig sticking or the club with its gin and tonic, but to spend time with Indians. Upon arriving in Dewas, Forster surveyed the human terrain and nearly sighed with satisfaction, "No European within twenty miles."

And no sooner had he arrived than the fun began. The prankish holiday of *Holi* was going full tilt. On April 1, Forster found himself smoking cigarettes that exploded and sitting on sofas that jolted his buttocks with tiny electric shocks. His first evening, he was fitted out in Indian clothes, for in dealing with the British, he was *officially* an Indian. He had imagined serving as some sort of diplomatic aide, but instead—this was more a shock than the electric sofas—he was put in charge of the palace garden, the tennis courts, the guest house, the garages, the generators, etc. Since his mechanical abilities were minimal, the job description was, he felt sure, a recipe for a comedy of errors. But his real duty, his unofficial role, was to spend time with the maharajah, and here, in the area of human relationships, he was more hopeful of the outcome.

Forster had determined in advance to like Dewas. But, unfortunately, an artist carries his senses, his taste, with him, and Forster may have carried his too far—past every aesthetic shape and beyond any pleasing forms. Despite his resolve to like Dewas, whenever he left it on some outing, he confessed to feeling "like those first ten minutes after a toothache had stopped." The trouble was that the absence of beauty in Dewas conspired with other absences. Forster had brought with him his novel-in-progress set in India, which he intended to resume working on there. But whenever he unpacked the manuscript, its pages seemed to "wilt and go dead," scorched by the reality of India before him. Plop, back the novel would go into his suitcase. He had also brought his habit of sociability with him, his desire to make close, intimate friends, but though Forster knew some Urdu, the language in Dewas was Marathi, which confined him to superficial encounters. Writing, friendship, and aesthetics had been his mainstays in England, and suddenly those mainstays were gone. A psychiatrist might have said Forster's state in India was perilous, and the peril, put in psychiatric terms, was that he had lost the means to sublimate. The cathected objects of his sublimation were gone, and what was poor Forster to do?

The answer to that question was raging in his body. In Dewas, at the late age of forty-two, the sexual urge began bothering him, upsetting him as it never had in his twenties or thirties. Forster had realized fairly early that he was a homosexual, but fairly late what homosexuals actually do. Indeed, he was thirty years old and had written three mature novels before he obtained reliable information on how babies are conceived. Sex, sex. In England he sublimated its promptings, and he assumed he would do the same in

Dewas. This, of course, was not how he put it to himself. He thought, especially since he had overheard the maharajah disparage homosexuality, that the least he could do was cause "no trouble."

But trouble was in the air—in the hot, idle, unsublimated air of Dewas. Particularly during the languorous siesta hours, Forster felt he was hardly more than irritable flesh stretched over an erotic itch. Masturbation brought no relief whatsoever. To grow sickly with desire, to become wan or ill with it, was that to be his fate? One day he saw a dead cow over which the vultures were hovering, and he thought, "That's how it will end." Once his thoughts had turned toward sex, everywhere he glanced, there it was. Before his eyes Dewas mutated into a carnival of the carnal. When he rode in his carriage through the sticky heat, the Islamic postilion ogled strangely, trying to catch his attention. In the palace a young Hindu worker lashed the floor loudly with a leather strap, and Forster, startled, looked up. But as the boy lashed the floor with ever softer strokes, Forster's looking up would indicate he was interested, and he couldn't stop himself from looking up. (Their interest in the English sahib was not erotic, surely, but mercenary.) Crude jokes at homosexuals' expense leavened the court humor. A theatrical performance featured a eunuch—an obese man in a sari who flirted grotesquely with the male members of the audience. Forster had gone to India but had strayed, inadvertently, into the torpid country of lust.

Forster began studying the palace workmen and servants with a calculating, appraising eye. Whenever he looked at the coolie who'd devised that strap-the-floor stunt, the coolie was looking back. When the coolie brought over a chair, he was all smiles, and Forster accepted it smiling. Whenever the boy rounded a corner in the palace, Forster noticed his shadow stationary in place, as though waiting, testing whether Forster would follow.

What to do? His every movement in the palace had a chorus of bystanders, onlookers, eavesdroppers. At last Forster decided that his *tattie*—a grass screen that, when wet, served as early air-conditioning—required watering, and he dropped the hint that the young coolie should water it. When the boy arrived, Forster took his wrist to show him how to throw on the water. As the boy smiled, Forster whispered, "Meet me at seven-thirty on the road near the Guest House." Ah, relief. Promise of release. Which promise lasted about ten whole minutes, until Forster overheard the boy talking outside his window.

"The *burra* sahib has given me orders to come at night."

"At night?" the coolie's friend asked in surprise.

"Yes, and he will give me money."

Forster panicked. Suppose the maharajah got wind of the assignation? (Since the palace was full of spies and since everything that happened was reported, and what didn't happen was invented and reported, such fears were not amiss.) Indeed, no sooner had Forster panicked than he noticed out the window a senior clerk jumping into a bullock cart, obviously hastening to report the scandal to the maharajah. The maharajah brought me out to be his friend, Forster reproached himself, "one of the few he can trust, and this is what I do."

That night the maharajah's aloofness confirmed Forster's fears. At one point the maharajah exclaimed that all catamites should be banished from the court: "What is the good of such people? . . . I cannot get away from them." Even the other courtiers, Forster sensed, were mocking him behind his back. He passed the next four days in an agony of recrimination and indecision, until finally he resolved to confess. What choice did he have? Screwing up his courage, he asked the maharajah for a private interview. "As I think you know," he stammered, "I am in great trouble."

"Tell me, Morgan," the maharajah answered. "I have noticed you were worried."

Forster made his confession that he had attempted carnal intercourse with one of the coolies.

The maharajah asked, "With a coolie-girl?"

"No, with a man," Forster answered. "You know about it, and if you agree I think I ought to resign."

"But Morgan, I know nothing about it. This is the first I have heard of it."

The maharajah had to be prevaricating, pretending ignorance. But for every one of his innuendoes that had caused Forster such embarrassment, the maharajah offered a harmless explanation. Forster need not have confessed at all! He wished—he wished—to die on the spot. But the maharajah continued questioning Forster with interest and kindness: "Why a man and not a woman? Is not a woman more natural?"

"Not in my case. I have no feeling for women."

"Oh but that alters everything. You are not to blame."

"I don't know what 'natural' is."

"You are quite right, Morgan—I ought never to have used the word. No, don't worry—don't worry," the maharajah reassured him. "Yes, yes, it's true I don't encourage those people, but it's entirely different in your case and you must not masturbate—that's awful."

Forster was so relieved that when he tried to apologize he broke down and cried. Touched, the maharajah nearly broke down, too. "Oh devil!" he exclaimed. "Don't do that, Morgan—the only way with a thing like that is to take it laughing."

The maharajah began hatching schemes, plots for securing Forster a bed companion. Hardly the typical outcome—one confesses miserably, horribly, and then, instead of being sentenced to the stocks, gets the king for his personal procurer. Forster insisted that he no longer wanted a bed companion, that henceforth abstinence would be his better course. The maharajah would not hear such silly talk: God had made Forster the way he was, Forster was a guest and friend in his country, and remorse and chastity were entirely out of place.

Only connect, Forster had written in his novel *Howards End.* Five thousand miles from Howards End, in the dullish backwash of Dewas, that imperative for human sympathy across barriers was accomplished. Two people, neither of any consequence by history book standards, had connected: in that shining moment empathy had triumphed over obstacles. And—considering the maharajah's new mission on his behalf—for Forster connection was perhaps just beginning. Perhaps, perhaps, he would soon embark on an adventure beyond anything he had fantasized before leaving England.

⚹

Forster's boisterous spirits before his March departure to India had barely disguised that here was a man in some misery. Being in Dewas at least allowed him to forget, for a while, that last period of his life back home. What had happened to that decade begun in such bright promise? By 1910 Forster, only thirty-one, had written four novels that have become minor fixtures of English literature (*Where Angels Fear to Tread*, 1905; *The Longest Journey*, 1907; *A Room with a View*, 1908; and *Howards End*, 1910). Hardly out of his twenties, he had already been promoted to an adjective, "Forsterian," to suggest an approach that was humane, skeptical, antiestablishment, and moral without moralizing. And in *Howards End* he had penned, it seemed, a phrase destined for immortality. "Only connect" stirred a generation, at least its more cultured members, by suggesting that two individuals in empathy will redeem the deadening mass of time. But that catchphrase, the new adjective, the four novels, all that was a decade and more ago! The teens of the new century had passed with no new Foster novel— and, he feared, so would every subsequent decade. He was a young man and already posthumous. In 1912, fighting despair, he had gone to India as a tourist, and India had proved the very tonic. But no "Indian novel" had afterward issued from his recalcitrant pen. Now in 1921, the cure—if the immersion into India was to prove such—would have to be more radical, more systemic.

If, before embarking, Forster felt finished as a novelist, he also felt somewhat finished as a human being—a dried-up, useless prune. Before his earlier trip to India in 1912, he had been living in his mother's house, and ten years later he was still living there. One day he cracked a vase in the house, and though a grown man, he lacked the courage to tell his mother. He lunched with an aunt, and when she asked his opinion of a particularly nasty cheese, he did not dare admit he had tasted and disliked it. "Can I do anything?" he wondered. Living with his mother was bad, but, worse, he felt he was coming to resemble her. One evening at Virginia and Leonard Woolf's, his conversation focused not on literature, or ideas, but on the garden seat he'd painted that afternoon. He worried and worried, was it wise to have left it outside all night? The Woolfs' verdict: "a perfect old woman." And when Virginia Woolf considered that Forster had gone to India in 1912 and come back from India and the expected new novel had not materialized, she could only pity him. "To come back to Weybridge [where Forster lived with his mother], to come back to an ugly house a mile from the station, to an old, fussy, exacting mother, to come back . . . without a novel, and with no power to write one—this is dismal," she confided in her journal. "The middle age of buggers is not to be contemplated without horror."

But Virginia Woolf knew, ultimately, that to concentrate on the fussy, old-womanish side of Forster was to miss his achievement. Life had handed Forster some fairly unenviable stage directions— a nondescript, mousy appearance; a too careful, cautious temperament; a possessive mother; a homosexual predisposition in a homophobic age—but Forster had stared directly into the horror until, as in a folk tale, it revealed an acceptable face. Even claustrophobic home life with his mother he bore in such a way it became, he admitted, "a sort of rich subsoil where I have been able to rest and grow." Ultimately, Virginia Woolf recognized that Forster had made his bad lot in life luminous. Encountering Forster one day in the company of her flamboyant brother-in-law, Clive Bell, she was struck by the contrast. Next to Clive Bell's loud posturing, Forster's understated, exactly right tone was, she thought, like clear light on a spring day. "Clive showed as gaslight beside Morgan's normal day," she reflected. "His [Forster's] day not sunny or tempestuous but a day of pure light, capable of showing up the rouge and powder, the dust and wrinkles, the cracks and contortions of my poor parakeet [Clive Bell]."

Forster's personality belongs to a curious chapter in the history of character formation. In common with his friends—Virginia Woolf, the biographer Lytton Strachey, the economist John Maynard Keynes, the philosopher Bertrand Russell—Forster transformed the highest good from the public to the private realm, and they were more interested in states of mind than kinds of actions. Collectively, the behavior of the so-called Bloomsbury circle constituted an informal experiment in human relationships, which they endeavored to make more honest, conscious, subtle, precise, and enjoyable—more fully adult. They developed their individuality to the point of eccentricity (a Bloomsburyite's personality was sometimes his finest artistic achievement). As long as one was both truthful and artistic, wittily honest and honestly witty, everything was permitted, even sexually. Bloomsbury continued for Forster what Cambridge University had begun, when personal friendships and mental accomplishment, "which are elsewhere contrasted . . . fused into one. People and books reinforced one another, intelligence joined hands with affection." After Cambridge, after Bloomsbury, by the time he departed for India, Forster's achievement consisted not only of four novels but of that fact commented upon by Virginia Woolf—that in his personal life he never hit a false note.

And yet. . . . There Forster was, on the eve of his departure, fully achieved as a human being and fully discontent. He could express himself perfectly but could not express a new novel. Twentieth-century India has not lacked for misfit visitors who went there instead of to a psychiatrist's office. Forster thought psychiatric treatment might promise a solution to his problems, but only if he no longer wanted to be a writer. (Among his contemporaries, the psychoanalyst's couch was not merely a possibility; it was practically an obligation.) His particular malaise, he suspected, contained within it the malaise of his era, and if something creative could be done with his blockages, some contribution to general good might come of it. Secular, rational, cultured, humane, Forster dimly sensed that he represented the individual who had come to the historical limits of individualism. This is what colors his trip to India with a certain interest, for Forster was transporting there not only himself but also a culmination of European culture that seemed to him somehow insufficient.

The most sympathetic English male character (Cyril Fielding) in *A Passage to India* assays a brief self-analysis, in terms surely leased from Forster's own:

> After forty years' experience, he had learnt to manage his life and make the best of it on advanced European lines, had developed his personality, explored his limitations, controlled his passions—and he had done it all without becoming either pedantic or worldly. A creditable achievement.

Forster's Cambridge chums, all his Bloomsbury friends, might have made a similar boast (except for the controlling-the-passions part). They had explored their limitations and developed their personalities: they had polished their identity to a luster, they had perfected "on advanced European lines" the self—in other words, they had made the best of life. But Fielding (or Forster) proceeds to doubt whether, after all, "he was really and truly successful as a human being. . . . A credible achievement, but as the moment passed, he felt he ought to have been working at something else the whole time." When Forster sailed for India a second time (he was two years older than Fielding's forty then), with his achievement, and with his stalled novel packed in his baggage, he was quietly exploring what else he ought to be working on.

In practical terms, if Forster was no longer writing novels, he had to—what? Friends were scaring up openings at the Foreign Office. A post in the Inter-Allied Commission in Germany was particularly tempting because it came with a handsome salary, and Forster guessed he had some ability as an administrator. It also meant acknowledging that one was no longer a writer. The psychoanalyst's couch? the Foreign Office? the Inter-Allied Commission? Amid such deliberations, Forster seized upon a wild card. He fired off a letter to the maharajah of Dewas Senior, whom he'd met and liked during his first Indian travels, inquiring whether there might be some position available at his court. An affirmative reply would, presumably, plunge the cautious Forster into weeks of shilly-shallying, weighing pros and cons, hedging and wavering, before he could contemplate undertaking such a bold step.

Hardly. The day he received the invitation from Dewas, Forster cabled the maharajah back, announcing he would be leaving immediately.

⁂

The maharajah, in his new role as Forster's procurer, studied the possibilities. The barber! Brilliant! The court barber afforded a perfect solution. He came to the palace regularly, his expenses were already budgeted for; no suspicions would be raised. Thus, a few days after Forster's confession, there stood before him in his rooms a young man—pretty, cheerful, and overdressed. After his scare with the coolie, Forster simply let the barber, whose name was Kanaya, shave him without making any overture. *However,* the next day as Kanaya bent down to shave him, Forster kissed him. Lack of resistance on the barber's part promised all might go smoothly as—well, shaved skin. But then Forster nearly jumped out of his skin. A crash, an explosion, startled him as a bucket of water came splashing against his door. His servant had returned from lunch early and was sluicing the *tattie.* The servant was evidently suspicious, for he began cutting short his lunches, and since Kanaya was unpunctual, Forster was on pins and needles every time the barber arrived. It was a scene out of a farce where a man obtains a willing sexual playmate but, foiled every time, can never obtain the privacy to enjoy the object of his lust. Indeed, privacy seemed the one unobtainable wish in Dewas. Everything was public; interruptions were constant; servants entered rooms at will. Forster and Kanaya attempted meeting in the guest house garden, but slipping into the garden, Kanaya was mistaken for a thief and fled. The gardener boasted that single-handedly he had fought off a whole band of fearsome robbers.

Hearing the gardener's tale, the maharajah placed at Forster's disposal a dusty, neglected suite in the palace. The maharajah sent Kanaya a gratuity of twenty-five rupees, far better than Forster paying him directly. And he advised Forster never to take the passive position, for if that got out, his reputation would be beyond salvaging.

Soon the maharajah was complimenting Forster on his improved appearance. Encouraged by his solicitude, Forster alluded to his next rendezvous with the barber, but the maharajah interrupted. "I don't want to hear, because when the hour comes I shall think of you, and that I don't want." The rendezvous were working their effect, and as the maharajah observed, Forster was feeling much improved physically.

Physically. But physical intimacy for Forster meant emotional intimacy next. In Egypt, working for the Red Cross during World War I, Forster had picked up a young bus conductor. Lacking any common denominator of nationality, class, religion, age, or education, they nonetheless formed a lifelong friendship that survived distance and absence. (Forster's Egyptian liaison would have confirmed the maharajah's prejudices, since he blamed all perversions on the Muhammadans.) As Forster had with the bus conductor in Alexandria, he now hoped to cross a great gulf with the barber Kanaya. Whenever he tried, though, he failed: each time rebuffed, washed back into solitude. Kanaya was unfailingly smiling, cheerful, friendly, and—blank. Once, in desperation, Forster treated Kanaya sadistically and then regretted having behaved the Oriental despot with his slave. The trouble was, Kanaya insisted on behaving like a slave, which suggested to Forster how evilly deeper the trenches of difference and separation had been dug here than even in Egypt.

Forster's failure with Kanaya, however, taught him something surprising and useful: the sexual act was, in fact, an act. If good, it could be inconsequential, too—not radiant, not necessarily transforming anything. Forster had written a then-unpublishable novel, *Maurice* (published posthumously in 1971), where homosexual love goes far toward redeeming the two male characters. Sex with Kanaya redeemed nothing; it didn't even relieve much—beyond some pent-up frustration and moments of boredom. Possibly every teenager now knows this, not dopily to confuse the sexual act with emotional love. But Forster, living simultaneously at the end of a long romantic tradition and in a sexually repressed milieu, had dared believed that the missing erotic element in his connections, a sexual partner—if only located—would complete his sense of himself. Evidently not. For him, who had been late in finding out what sex was, and then only to find it choked in shame and guilt, those noon interludes with Kanaya yielded a hard but valuable lesson: sex was itself and not something else. Such knowledge, those sexual passages that led nowhere, perplexed him. What do you do when you cannot "only connect"?

As the deed and its meaning parted ways, Forster seemed to float amid erotic confusion, in a sexualized atmosphere that spread everywhere and nowhere. This certainly wasn't England, though, this intercultural vortex that was tugging his assumptions about sex inside out. One afternoon the maharajah, Forster, and some visiting Europeans were playing the English game "characters." In characters, each player assigns a number, high or low, to the other players' personality traits. It puzzled the maharajah when the Europeans appeared to prize highly the trait of "passion." "Is not passion bad?" he asked in surprise. Forster enjoyed *that* revelation, that all passions and not simply "his kind" were to be deplored.

But if in that strange fog of sexual customs not one's own the maharajah was confused, so was Forster. He could not even determine whether the woman the maharajah cohabited with was his wife, his official concubine, or his mistress. In England, such arrangements would have been perfectly clear—and perfectly damning; just as Forster's sexual preference, if made public knowledge, would have meant social damnation. Surely Forster could have had someone demystify the erotic vagaries of India for him, except he enjoyed them too much. He relished the maharajah's perplexity when a visiting English lady, learning that a certain official kept a mistress, demanded, "Do the others do it, too?" Puzzled by her indignation at this age-old arrangement, the maharajah assumed there must be some newer method in England. "Oh no," he bluffed, "the others are more up-to-date."

Such humorous twists soon had Forster likening the maharajah's court to a Gilbert and Sullivan operetta. Another Englishman who had passed through Dewas called it "the oddest corner of the world outside *Alice in Wonderland*." Indeed, in Dewas it was as though some cross-cultural Mad Hatter had absconded with Forster's beliefs, shuffled and reshuffled them, and dealt them back to him differently. Before Dewas, Forster had cherished the rapport between two individuals as the high point of human existence, and to him sexual intimacy both symbolized and intensified that rapport. After Dewas, Forster often implied sexuality was a rickety basis for connection between two people. "There is always trouble when two people do not think of sex at the same moment, always mutual resentment and surprise," goes one observation in *A Passage to India*. Disillusioned that sex was never what it promised to be, Forster sought out the maharajah for advice on how to rise above it. For though the maharajah obviously adored his "wife," he rarely visited her alone, and so Forster assumed he must know ways to dominate lust.

"Oh one can't teach these things," the maharajah answered, laughing. "When you are dissatisfied with your present state of existence you will enter another—that's all."

Forster never entered another. Even in extreme old age he remembered with gratitude the hours of sexual pleasure—hardly that numerous by today's rate of inflation—and how they had sweetened his cup of experience. Not "another state" certainly, but possibly Forster did enter into a perspective unknown to most Englishmen. At some point during his time in Dewas his rosy view not only of romantic love but also of romantic individualism fell away; the rose-tinted lenses fell to the ground and shattered.

Years before, at Cambridge, and then in his four novels, Forster had worked out a remarkable vision: exceptional individuals, cultivating their consideration, sensitivity, and pluck, will prove capable of bursting through social constraints, into an unprecedented empathy with one another. Somewhere in the heat of Dewas that youthful vision faded. Forster began to see a point to social arrangements that by all the standards of Cambridge and Bloomsbury he should have rejected. What, for example, could be more of a slap in the face to his lovely idea of "only connect" than an arranged marriage, which disregards what the two persons marrying want and feel. In *A Passage to India* Dr. Aziz, who had suffered such a marriage, expresses the typical modern repugnance to this primitive form of wedlock. "Touched by Western feeling, he disliked union with a woman whom he had never seen; moreover, when he did see her, she disappointed him, and he begat its first child in mere animality." But in an unexpected reversal, Forster goes on to endorse such marriages:

> Gradually he [Aziz] lost the feeling that his relatives had chosen wrongly for him. Sensuous enjoyment—well even if he had had it, it would have dulled in a year, and he had gained something instead, which seemed to increase the longer they lived together. [When she died] he realized what he had lost, and that no woman could ever take her place; a friend would come nearer to her than another woman.

Forster, of course, was barred from ever marrying passionately. But as the sensuous enjoyment of his afternoons with Kanaya dulled, and with them dulled his youthful idealization of romantic friendship, he saw how other patterns of human community might sustain him, as they did Aziz in the novel. Perhaps Indian social practices like arranged marriages, perhaps even Hinduism, erected as satisfying a habitation for the human psyche. Just conceivably, Forster thought, that habitation might prove as hospitable to his particular needs as English mores had. With that mutation of his perception Forster's passage to India had begun.

❊

When in old age Forster edited his letters from India into a volume, *The Hill of Devi* (1953), his chief editorial task was deletion. He cut out all the gushing—"Aren't Indians quaint!" and "How I wish you were here!"—written to please relatives back home. In reality, he didn't think Indians quaint, and he wanted to be alone with them. "I like being with Indians," Forster said. "It isn't broad mindedness but an ideosyncracy [*sic*]."

An idiosyncrasy, indeed. For this was the era when British civilians stationed in India ten years, twenty years, thirty years, would boast that they had never shaken hands with a native. One English lady whom Forster knew of recounted the story of how a servant had indeed once touched her. He did so after she had ignored his screams and to prevent her from stepping on a krait, a deadly venomous snake. She would have died otherwise; still she had the servant dismissed. Forster was an oddity in the way he bypassed such colonial attitudes and arrived at a point—"no European within twenty miles"—where racial and national differences ceased to be as poisonous as that krait.

It was liking a single Indian that had propelled him to India in the first place, in 1912. That Indian, Syed Ross Masood, had earlier come to England to prepare his entrance examinations for Oxford. Forster had signed on to be his Latin tutor, although remarkably little tutoring got done. When Forster tried, the high-spirited Masood would bodily pick him up and tickle him. Like Forster, Masood made a cult of friendship, but whereas for Forster friendship was intimate poetry, for Masood it was grand opera. Once when Forster bid Masood good-bye, Masood chastised him for his tempered English farewell. "But after all," Forster replied sensibly, "we'll be seeing each other in three days." "But we're *friends*!" Masood wailed. Masood's demonstrativeness woke Forster from his suburban slumber, he said, to the possibility of other customs, other civilizations. After Masood returned to India, he encouraged Forster to visit him there, baiting the hook with an unusual worm: "My great wish is to get *you* to write a book on India." Forster knew nothing about India, but Masood was undaunted about Forster's qualifications: "You are about the only Englishman in whom I have come across true sentiment & that [is] real sentiment even from the oriental point of view."

Masood's friendship supplied Forster a reason to go to India but no guarantee he would like it once there. Forster's companion on that trip in 1912, the philosopher Goldsworthy Lowes Dickinson, detested India. Dickinson was an endearing bungler, hopeless when it came to anything practical, but traveling to India he inhaled deeply and swelled himself up into a public figure. He approached India as a problem to be investigated; he planned to visit schools, factories, jails, and objectively analyze Indian civilization. His analysis, afterward, was that India had been awful, just awful. Its social arrangements were a muddle; its daily life, squalid; its philosophy, contradictory; its arts, all out of proportion. Unlike Dickinson, Forster did not go to investigate. He wanted, if possible, simply to enjoy himself. He wasn't interested in India so much as in Indians. "My soul is in the East long before my body reaches it," Forster wrote Masood before departing in 1912. "I don't *understand* the East or expect to understand it, but I've learnt to love it for several years now."

The writer Nirad Chaudhuri opined that never a European lived in India without coming to think less well of Indians. He was not thinking of Forster. Forster observed the same inefficiency that so rattled Dickinson—all the faucets, fans, commodes that didn't run. But that broken-down inventory was of imported, European manufacture, Forster noted, and thus no clue to Indian civilization. And while the philosopher Dickinson bemoaned the ambiguities and contradictions of India, the novelist Forster thought them a not unnatural, touching part of human experience. This receptivity to India was then so unusual as to require explanation. How did Forster escape Dickinson's glass barrier of Europeanized attitude and live among Indians and like them better for doing so? The answer will likely be found, if found at all, in *A Passage to India*.

A Passage could be used as a guidebook, only not to India (any India through which Forster could have served as guide has long vanished) but rather to thinking your way round unfamiliar terrain. Beyond its literary achievement, the novel is like a manual in code of the mental operations necessary for navigating an alien environment. And, indirectly, it tells us something about Forster's own passage to India—how he sidestepped the bog of simplistic reaction that sank many a European traveler in India.

The novel begins in "Chandrapore"—the last city, it seems, a European would choose to visit:

> The very wood seems made of mud, the inhabitants of mud moving. So abased, so monotonous is everything that meets the eye, that when the Ganges comes down it might be expected to wash the excrescence back into the soil. Houses do fall, people are drowned and left rotting, but the general outline of the town persists, swelling here, shrinking there, like some low but indestructible form of life.

The British looked down their superior noses at India, but Forster begins by rubbing those noses in even more squalor than colonials typically complained of. Suddenly changing perspective, though, the novel views Chandrapore from above, from where one can see the town's hidden gardens. "It is no city, but a forest sparsely scattered with huts. It is a tropical pleasaunce washed by a noble river." Forster then shifts scenes again, to indoors, where a party of Indians are amusing and teasing one another. Forster's easy, light prose obscures the rapidity of the changes: click, here is desolation; click, here garden; click, here civilized banter and courteous manners. Later novels have taught contemporary readers to expect such abrupt disjunctures. But Forster's multiple perspectives were not a novelist's trick; a shifting perspective, like an angle of vision rotating on ball bearings, was actually the way his mind experienced India. In a few paragraphs, Chandrapore has turned from a pitiable dump to a crust on nature to a microcosm of civilization.

As in the beginning, so throughout the novel. The novel advances a situation but then retreats from it; it sees something but then sees the contrary; it appears to endorse a position but then to endorse the opposite; the political and the private confuse each other; prospects alter, definite outlines recede. The critic F. R. Leavis in *The Great Tradition* took Forster to task for his philosophical weakness—for failing to make his message clearer and his argument more telling. The conclusion of *A Passage* might seem to justify Leavis's criticism, for the book ends in sound and confusion signifying only god knows what.

Specifically, the book ends in a bustling, crowded, tumultuous Hindu festival. To evoke this festival in the final pages Forster had, yeomanlike, to devote pages to new objective backdrop-description, at the very moment when in a traditional novel everything culminates in drama, in a final statement, in the world made sensible and right. Forster feebly justified this new jumbled mound of material at the novel's end: "It was architecturally necessary. I needed a lump, or a Hindu temple if you like. . . . [But] the lump sticks out a little too much." Why did he need a jumble, "a lump"? Probably because that was what India was then, to the majority of Europeans stopping or living there. Parts of India were exquisite, parts an enchantment, but all together it presented an incomprehensible lump, an indigestible lump. Jung claimed he came down with dysentery because he could not digest India. If Forster could digest the lump—that is, if he could take India at its most thronged, noisy, and perplexing, and make even that appealing or meaningful—his novel would be a triumph of understanding, even if every character in it ends diminished or defeated.

But would his own responses become lumpish, when facing the lump? At one time Forster had feared so. At the Gokul Ashtami festival in Dewas (the model for the thronged, noisy festival in *A Passage*) Forster knew he was participating in "rites in which a

European can seldom have shared," and that he should be grate-ful—if only he could be. During the festival, as Forster trailed bare-foot in Indian dress through the dusty streets, and sat cross-legged for hours, and napped using a cow's flank for a pillow, and his eyes glazed over viewing endless ritual detail, it was as though some-thing like a lump had knocked him on the head and left him dazed. His empathy failed him. The jarring noises of the festival never ceased, three or four bands played at once, horns brayed, cymbals clashed, drums rattled, battering, day after day, night after night. "It is the noise, the noise, the noise," he complained, "which sucks one into a whirlpool, from which there is no re-emerging." *The festival flowed on, wild and sincere*, the novel relates. In actual life the festival crashed down, an avalanche of noise and sensations, on Forster's poor senses, leveling his ability to think. Is this how India will end for me, he fretted, not with a bang but with too much banging?

If Forster had been intent on drawing philosophical conclu-sions, as Goldie Dickinson was, or as Leavis wished him to, he might have equated the festival with Indian civilization. He was not interested in making "Great Tradition" arguments, though, so much as subverting them or showing how they might be seen from yet another side. He thus merely put down the noise and chaos to questionable taste and looked beyond matters of taste for realities about the festival he might appreciate after all. His habit in *A Passage* of circling a subject from 360 degrees he applied in real life to the Gokul Ashtami festival. And as he looked and he looked, his perspective subtly shifted from distaste into approval. He spied something wonderful in the festival's transformation of the participants. Despite the noise that pounded at his temple, he attempted to concentrate on that one thing undeniably beautiful—the expression on their faces, a touchstone of unasked-for beauty. "The assembly was in a tender, happy state unknown to an English crowd, it seethed like a beneficent potion. . . . A most beautiful and radiant expression came into their faces," he writes in the novel.

Having found something to like about the festival, having gotten his perceptions in a fluid mode, he found them flowing positively, until he perceived the whole festival as unquestionably good. It abounded with jokes in poor taste—such as smearing pats of butter on your neighbor's forehead—but if Forster disliked the bad taste, he greatly liked religion's being able to joke. Christianity had too little humor, he thought. "The canonical gospels do not record that Christ laughed or played," he wrote elsewhere. "Can a man be perfect if he never laughs or plays?" The festival's raillery and frivolity bridged an important gap, Forster believed, by including more and excluding less of the participants' normal feelings. "All laughed exultantly at discovering that the divine sense of humor coincided with their own . . . God can play practical jokes upon Himself, draw chairs away from beneath His own posterior, set His own turbans on fire, and steal His own petticoats when He bathes. By sacrificing good taste, their worship achieved what Christianity had shirked: the inclusion of merriment." *A Passage to India* ends by finding for the alien, even for bad taste, a purpose. Forster's flexible mental habit of letting each thought generate its opposing perspective had paid off. In his final novel's final scene he performs the ultimate artistic feat of annexing even *the lump*, of bringing the seemingly incomprehensible into the sphere of human meaning.

As Forster's limits of tolerance expanded to appreciate that infinitely noisy, endlessly jarring Hindu festival, his receptivity somehow more easily accepted the ill-proportioned or irksome within himself. In the scenes of the Gokul Ashtami festival Forster shows how one can profitably advance even through situations that defy intellectual comprehension. The episode perhaps reflects his lessening compulsion in India to analyze or intellectualize his own identity. (His decreased need to investigate himself, his accepting instead pell-mell whatever came, may be partly why, after *A Passage to India*, he wrote no more novels.) India became for Forster the outward form of a more capacious imagination, where desires did not have to be tortuously intellectualized but belonged (as everything else did) to an encyclopedic bestiary, to a wider and odder plenitude than he had previously imagined existed. *A Passage to India* itself seems to argue that what an individual does with his own psychological complexity will determine what India's complexity means to him. "The personal is the political"—by expressing an early version of that thought and by locating it in of all places British India, Forster wrote as hopeless, and as hopeful, a novel as was ever set on the subcontinent.

The novel was published in 1924, and it changed the trajectory of Forster's reputation. Before it appeared, all his novels were out of print, and he seemed gently headed toward oblivion; after its success, the others went into edition after edition, and *A Passage* established him as one of the century's major novelists. Yet the novel was even more influential outside literature, so Nirad Chaudhuri argued, than within it. As history, *A Passage* has been endlessly faulted—for its inaccurate depiction of the English, of the Indians, and of the relationships between them—and yet the novel changed history. Forster commented in a magazine article about his countrymen in India that "never in history did ill breeding contribute so much to the dissolution of an Empire." After *A Passage to India*, however, it became truly ill-bred among most cultured English to champion a continuation of that Empire. Some British officers who read the novel on the long voyage to India threw it overboard in disgust. But, symbolically, it rose to the surface again, and Forster rose with it, washed by his Indian novel into "immortality."

⌗

The one problem solved for Forster was sex. Thanks to the barber, and those secret hours in forgotten palace rooms, Forster was enjoying sex at more frequent intervals than ever before. Gradually, though, he sensed a catastrophe in the making. Homosexual jokes and homophobic titillation, though *not* homosexual acts, pervaded court life. Forster gathered that he and Kanaya were becoming a butt of the courtiers' jokes. Once more he turned to the maharajah, and the maharajah responded cannily, as though sex counseling were a sideline of his. He advised Forster to deny nothing, conjure no alibis, but instead cheerfully agree with every smarmy innuendo. When a courtier began teasing him about the barber's visits, Forster taunted back, Are you jealous? To refute by agreeing had been Oscar Wilde's stratagem when he successfully deflected scandals in London. But Wilde was a creature of society with a theatrical flair, and here was Forster, previously shy and reserved, now acting a similar public part in the great society of little Dewas.

Forster's joining in the teasing effectively dispatched the budding rumors. When Forster left Dewas for a short holiday, he sensibly cautioned Kanaya to avoid any contact with the court. Hardly were the words out of his mouth, and Forster gone, than Kanaya made a beeline for the palace. He boasted to whoever would listen that he was under Forster Sahib's protection. "Sahib's fond of boys," he reported, and everyone listened. Forster returned from his holiday to have to brave out in daylight his fantasy nightmare. But he had changed in Dewas, and now he didn't want to hide in a mouse hole. He invited a courtier he respected on an outing, and the whole time Forster talked of neutral, indifferent topics to show that, the gossip notwithstanding, nothing fundamental between them had changed. Forster the timid had become Forster the bold.

But trouble never lay dormant for long. During the Gokul Ashtami festival, the barber had a bright inspiration. One evening when the maharajah returned to the palace, he noticed Kanaya sleeping in a corner of his room. Not even princes expected privacy in Dewas, and since this was the festival, he thought little of it. After the maharajah lay down to sleep, though, he felt Kanaya massaging his feet, which was the customary prelude to requesting a boon. Kanaya hesitated and then blurted out, "Can I have employment at the palace?"

"But you have it already," the maharajah replied. "You are Forster Sahib's barber."

"I want employment with you. I want more employment."

Silence; no answer. Kanaya steeled his courage to clarify his petition. He whispered, "Sahib goes to bed with me."

"How dare you!" the maharajah exploded. And with that explosion, Kanaya fled the room and did not stop fleeing till he located Forster, fell on the carpet, kissed his feet, and begged for mercy. Forster was furious at Kanaya's idiocy—for attempting to "establish himself as Catamite to the Crown." Forster was even more furious at himself, for all the bother he was causing the maharajah. He determined to dispense with barbers and his barber's special services. No, not wise—the maharajah advised Forster against dismissing Kanaya. To do so would arouse suspicions. So Forster permitted Kanaya to resume shaving him, and gradually that was not all that resumed. And to his surprise Forster discovered that the pleasure of the body can continue regardless of what the head dictates, and that life continues, regardless of what happens.

With Oscar Wilde's trial fresh in memory, English homosexuals of Forster's generation lived in dread of scandal. But the chances of a scandal ever ruining gentlemen of Forster's temperament and caution were in fact negligible. They might have instead feared something equally debilitating: that nothing would ever jostle the placid, dulling equanimity of their subdued emotional lives. In England private, prudent men like Forster lived out their lives free of public storms, and so never learned, as did Forster in Dewas, whether or not they had the mettle to face a public outcry. To his surprise, Forster discovered that he had the courage for public controversy; he preferred not cowering but defending himself. When some British officials visited Dewas, they slighted him in a minor matter of protocol. In England Forster would have dismissed the slight as beneath his dignity, but now, having practiced standing firm, he inflated the incident into a controversy, with both his and the state's honor at issue. The novelist of tender privacies was learning to conjoin personal and public.

In fact, Forster's whole outlook was undergoing a metamorphosis in Dewas. In the beginning, he had joined in the court humor and laughed at the homosexual jokes. One example of such humor, already mentioned, was the theatrical farce in which, when the wife goes away, the husband immediately sends for a eunuch. The eunuch barges in, a mustached man in a filmy pink sari, who camps it up and flirts outrageously with the audience. Here was a hint at least of the homosexual husband (and the homosexual fantasy of the male as wife). Initially Forster found such "naughtiness" funny, but the more he stood up for himself the less funny he found it. "There is much verbal and histrionic indecency which amused me at first," he wrote from Dewas, "not now, because I see that it takes the place of so much that I value."

In his unpublished novel *Maurice*, Forster had romanticized two men building for themselves in their little corner a world apart. But in Dewas, in his unsatisfactory corner apart with Kanaya, Forster rethought his ideal of having a romance in private but annihilating it in public. "Two men can defy the world," *Maurice* had proclaimed, but why was that better than two men taking part in the world? The neatly compartmentalized baggage of ideas Forster had brought with him to India was getting all messed and mixed up. In the Gokul Ashtami festival the low comedy of vaudeville and the high seriousness of religion were jumbled together. Similarly in Dewas, where men friends walked together hand in hand, public life ceased to be quite the alien, de-eroticized sphere that Forster had once opposed to the better private life, which appeared not to exist in Dewas anyway.

❊

Although Dewas was a small, provincial backwash, Forster determined not to have a small or provincial experience of it. He used it as a microcosm, placing it as it were under a magnifying glass, to reveal something large both about India and about himself. Doing so, he could spend half a year there, when none of his friends of fine plumage could have likely tolerated it for a month. For here were not Bloomsbury, not Cambridge, nothing literary, nothing aesthetic, and Forster's friends would have equated a passage to Dewas to banishment in the desert. In their circle, people cultivated the nuance and registered subtlest inflections, but on the hot central plain of India, subtlety and nuance seemed to evaporate in the air. The exquisite ability to discriminate elegantly, which in England counted for all, counted for so little here. In traveling to the sacred ruins of Ujjain, Forster felt those interminable barren plains absorbing him, blurring, erasing all the distinctions he had ever known. He inquired of the driver what kind of trees they were passing, and the driver answered, "Trees." He asked him the name of a bird overhead, and the driver said, "Bird." "Why differentiate?" he asked himself.

When his foppish young friend Joe Ackerley later went out to India to serve as another provincial maharajah's secretary, Forster tried to show him how to profit from time spent in such a place. His chief counsel consisted of: "As for being bored, don't mind it—more than the unpleasantness I mean: don't think you are wasting your time. You will never get hold of anything in India unless you experience boredom." But why had Forster accepted being bored there? Boredom shows that the Forsterian contract to "only connect" is no longer working. In India, whether people connected or not ceased to matter to Forster in quite the way it had before. In *A Passage to India* Mrs. Moore voiced an un-Bloomsburian idea about human relationships: "She felt increasingly (vision or nightmare?) that, though people are important, the relations between them are not."

Forster had stumbled, in effect, into a different lexicon of human experience. The lack of privacy, the publicity of private life—the fact that personal identity seemed a communal, not an individual, matter—has often frayed the nerves of westerners in Asia. Even when the doors were made to shut in Dewas, Forster noted, they did not, owing to the warping. Even when the servants could knock before entering, they did not, deeming it impolite. No privacy: so the maharajah, hardly startled at all, discovered the barber sleeping in his room. No privacy: so Forster had no chance, or if the chance, never the peace, to work on his novel in Dewas. Yet, curiously, Forster found this state of affairs appealing, everyone tromping through the doors (or lack thereof) of everyone else's life. The intimate rendezvous—two people breaking from the madding crowd and meeting in friendship—was not the alpha and omega here. In Dewas everybody lived a-jumble, the more the merrier, and Forster, strange to say, liked being part of the jumble. "It is indescribable and unimaginable," Forster wrote of the absence of privacy and reserve that so dazed other Europeans, "really a wonderful experience, for it is the fag end of a vanished civilization." He liked being *part of*.

King's College, Cambridge, would not have entirely concurred. As an undergraduate at King's, Forster had imbibed a system of values that prized privacy highly. Under its protective awning, unformed youth composed themselves into individuals, and such refined individuals vacated their privacy, ideally, only for special friendships that burned with a gemlike flame. After India, Forster wondered whether he had left "King's values" behind.

> King's stands for personal relationships, and these still seem to me the most real things on the surface of the earth, but I have acquired a feeling that people must go away from each other (spiritually) every now and then, and improve themselves if the relationship is to develop or even endure.

Only disconnect? Life in India had revealed to Forster a more complex social dynamics, a denser human texture, than the most exquisite tête-à-tête can weave.

Readers of *A Passage to India* were not slow to note that its author was hardly the E. M. Forster they had known. The London *Daily News* reviewer observed:

> He [Forster] has quite lost the touch of preciousness, of exaggerated care for nature and the relationships of human beings, that faintly irritate some readers of his earlier books. He used once to write at times too much as a graduate (even occasionally as an undergraduate) of King's College, Cambridge (perhaps the most civilized place in the world).

From New Mexico, D. H. Lawrence wrote him expressing amazement that Forster, of all people, had written a novel hinged "on a very unsatisfactory friendship between two men," and that Forster had implied "human relationships don't matter." Lawrence's comment was, "*Carito!*"

King's College values were not wrong, only insufficient. The weight of the universe could not be set upon two pairs of frail human shoulders hunched together in solicitude. "The 'King's' view oversimplified people," Forster wrote, "that I think was its defect. We are more complicated, also richer, than it knew, and affection grows more difficult than it used to be." When Forster began *A Passage*, he intended it as a little bridge of sympathy between East and West. But the carnage of the war and after the war the British massacre at Amritsar told Forster that his precious idealism, his delicate bridge between here and there, would have to go. Novels about individual salvation, about individuals crossing sympathetic bridges, Forster suspected, would in the approaching era of mass society and mass violence become passé.

In India, Forster had gained in boldness of perspective. His compass and maps of the whole had broadened sufficiently so that he no longer needed to sail from one tiny island of human empathy to another. After India, he could utter what would have been previously unthinkable. "Most Indians, like most English people, are shits," he wrote in 1922, "and I am not interested whether they sympathize with one another or not." *Only connect* had been replaced by something like "only participate"; the sympathetic tête-à-tête had yielded to, not politics exactly, but to "something wider than politics." Try and try as he did to come up with a name, Forster could not think what to call this "search of the human race for a more lasting home."

✴

In New Mexico, as he expressed with exclamation marks his response to *A Passage to India*, D. H. Lawrence proclaimed what overrode sympathy in human relations: "one's primary relation to the X." Lawrence added, "I don't know what to call it, but not God or the universe"—though Forster hardly needed warning about accepting God as the ultimate *X* or key.

Forster belonged to one of the first milieus that was entirely secular. God's being reported missing in action caused him and his friends little angst. When, as a boy, he learned about the Incarnation—that God had descended to Earth not to end war or poverty but to redeem mortals from sin—Forster, not having much sense of sin, decided he could do quietly without.

In his passage to India, though, he was catapulted from Bloomsbury, in which religion was nowhere, into a region where it was everywhere. In Dewas the maharajah in the middle of a conversation would bob his knees and tap his forehead and start praying. Afterward he would resume chatting as though nothing had happened. Forster would gaze at the maharajah; he wanted to sympathize, he wanted to understand, but. . . . But if appreciating religion was the criterion, Forster worried his trip to India was a washout. During the Gokul Ashtami festival when Forster tried to grasp the maddeningly profuse rituals and doctrines of Hinduism, they slipped from under his grip, all "mess and profusion and confusion . . . where nothing ever stopped or need ever have begun." Religion was handed to him on a silver platter, but Forster, whose appetite was not fastidious, for once refused to partake.

And he minded because the fullness of life in India might thereby elude him. Well, all he could do was acknowledge his limitation and admit that it might conceivably be just that—his limitation. He treated his failure of understanding as a tunnel that might lead somewhere darkly in spite of himself. Forster was atypical not in his confusion about Hinduism, but in his willingness to let it stand anyway (on proviso) for a body of answers or satisfactions too ineffable to name. Hinduism might at least symbolize the possibility of a "more lasting home," even if it was not home for him.

Indeed the puzzling question is why Forster, atheist that he was, felt so much at home in a religion-drenched country. But that is only the beginning of questions. One cannot help wondering why, at the height of his success in 1910, he abandoned writing novels. Why, a decade and a half later, was his one return to the novel set in India? And how in *A Passage to India* did he achieve such a leap forward—his masterpiece? What was it about a civilization soaked in god that gave him a broader canvas on which to work?

Two popular explanations for Forster's abbreviated novelist's career exist, one quite high-toned, the other coming later and in whispers. Critics of the '30s and '40s argued that the refined Forster required a civilized society to write about, and after World War I, the world became too uncivil for his pen. Later, after the censor was booted out, a new, better explanation was proposed: homosexuality. Forster was bored writing about suburban romances that didn't interest him and banned from composing (or at least publishing) the illicit romances that did. Perhaps the two explanations are not so entirely different.

One of Forster's tests for culture, whether a person's or a country's, was how it responded to homosexuality. When the scandal over the barber threatened Forster's reputation in Dewas, it was the religious maharajah who dealt practically with it. He "accidentally" let slip Forster's age—forty-two years old—by which venerable age, it was assumed in Dewas, men had done with sex and put it behind them. The saintly maharajah became for Forster an even greater saint for cleverly scotching the rumor. The maharajah had not condoned catamites, but when he saw that his attitude exiled Forster, he surmounted his prejudices and procured a bedmate to make Forster feel at home in Dewas. Such graciousness and inclusiveness were not extraneous but at the very heart of what Forster meant by civilization. Curiously India, more sexually repressive than England, passed the test of civilization, or Dewas did, or at least the maharajah passed.

Forster could not have defined Lawrence's *X*, which lumped the individual and the larger world, sexuality and deity all together, any better than Lawrence. But at one particular moment in Dewas he experienced it: during the Gokul Ashtami festival, as the noisy chanting resounded everywhere, he and Kanaya met in the secret palace suite. As the festival approached its climax, Forster—not to make a play on words—also approached his. For that moment the partition of centuries that had kept sacred and profane experience separated was effaced. After this climax as he lay beside the strange, passive Kanaya, listening to the communal chanting like the monotonous hum of eternity sounding just beyond the room, Forster considered the possibility that perhaps most erotic objects are, in themselves, unworthy. Yet, since they made him "love" and involved him more intricately with others, he judged them worthy after all. The puerile jokes of the Gokul Ashtami festival had been right: the joke was that religion was not hidden from view, in an asexual remove in faraway heaven. So, likewise, love did not delineate some sky-high experience, dwarfing all others, dependent on meeting the ideal partner; it was more a certain accelerated readiness in everyday matters, extended as appropriate to whoever came. Man's lasting home was in a place not so different from here, populated with a saintly maharajah and a lack-of-affect bed companion, amid holy festivities that also gave you a headache. Gokul Ashtami, incidentally, celebrates the coming of Krishna, the world made whole by Love.

In Lawrence's view, Forster was an overfussy little mouse, but it was he who crossed the earth, and there, half a world away, came closer to entering something like a new sexual-religious "dispensation." Forster was rather astonished that it was *he* who had stumbled into something larger—the gods and humans, sex and public life, himself and his incongruous surroundings, all so at odds, so crowded together, ultimately so connected. *A Passage to India*, indirectly, and his *Hill of Devi*, directly, are the record of his gratitude to India, where he had stumbled into Lawrence's *the X* made specific.

※

Forster made one more trip to India, in 1945. India was on the eve of becoming an independent nation; Forster was on the eve of becoming an old man. Whereas once continents and weeks had separated here and there, the airplane practically slammed the old man into the new country. An All-India PEN Conference had invited Forster to participate, expenses paid and accommodations arranged, and he blessed his reputation for netting him such a bonus. In an aside to a friend: "If this is fame, I can bear it."

The airplane did the work of sudden death, flashing the scenes of his lifetime before him in speedy succession. There below was Italy, which in his novels had made bold souls out of timid Englishmen; there was Greece, birthplace of Pan in his stories; there was Egypt, where he had first glimpsed the East. And then quickly he was in India again. "I had not realized how much of my heart had gone into this place"—thus the shock of it washed over him once more. No longer was he a private person, though, left to his own devices. Forster was whisked from place to place, delivering speeches, lecturing to clubs, giving radio interviews, which invariably ended with the question, "How has India changed?" ("The disappearance of purdah," he answered; or, "a higher level of general conversation"—he became quite fluent with answers.) Months later, on the plane home, scribbling in his notebook, he gave his overall performance a fairly poor grade. He had been a humorous, conciliatory old dear, whose apparent generosity gave away very little and, always busy, he had idled away the time instead of recording honest-to-God truths. "O lovely world," he concluded, "teach others to expound you as I have not been able to do!"

In A Passage to India, after the good Mrs. Moore dies, local Indian mythology begins to deify her. Alas, something similar nearly befell Forster during his last stay in India. From day to day, when not officially occupied, all he did in reality was sightsee and visit old friends. When one acquaintance, having given up literature for religion, was too embarrassed to meet Forster again, Forster wrote him:

> You have, you say, abandoned literature for metaphysical inquiry. I have abandoned literature for nothing at all. So please let us meet.

But—now that he was reputed to be a wise man (rather like Mrs. Moore)—his ordinary acts were sometimes mistaken for the signs of an enlightened being. Gandhi's associate the novelist Raja Rao said, "To speak of Forster is, in a way, to speak of a saint. Not a saint of God, certainly, but an anthropocentric apostle." Others in India were calling him saintly, too. Inadvertently Forster might have contributed to his own apotheosis, since he liked to steal away from official functions and to spend time alone in mosques. And in mosques, out of empathy, Forster would go down on his knees, his atheist's knees, like a believer. Emerging from a mosque, so his companions delighted to report, his face was radiant, simply radiant.

A saint! Forster, had he been more aware of it, would have despised such preposterousness; or better, satirized it. No, *saint* was the wrong word, the wrong idea, entirely. He preferred—whenever his wish was granted—to be inconspicuous, part of the scenery, to fit in India the way he once had, unobtrusively. Best would be to be there with no more fuss than an object in nature. As for which object, his imagination produced the image of a sponge. Twenty years and more had passed since he was last in India, and everything had changed—the maharajah dead, the country modernizing, he himself now old and famous. But a sponge, though dried out, deformed, regains its earlier shape when dipped into its original element: "I feel like a sponge," Forster said, describing what it was like to be back in India, "which has been dropped back into an ocean whose existence it had forgotten."

Sponge, ocean? It was a Hindu metaphor for the individual's fate, after all.

CHAPTER 4

Head of Darkness

Finally! Ready to clear out of that miserable hole. His bags were all packed and the gear stowed in the jeep, when—damn it!— another delay. An unknown boy rushed up, having just bathed, hair still wet, tucking his shirt into his trousers as he ran. Politely the boy asked, could he catch a ride with them to the next town?

"Shall we take him on?" the guide asked

"What shall I do?" Naipaul thought. "No," he decided. "Let the idler walk." Naipaul realized how mean-spirited his answer sounded, but he had the excuse of the past few days, the whole wretched mini-eternity of those awful days.

Those days had dragged him over an Earth as flat as in medieval cartography. Everywhere he looked had stretched out flat, flat and dreary, and wherever the dust thickened there was another pitiful village, but always the wrong village. He seemed to be not crossing space, but stumbling into another dimension of time. The man "without a past, without ancestors," as V. S. Naipaul called himself, had blundered—a fool's mission, an insane hajj—into searching for his ancestral past. Though a grown man, he had never set foot in India before; nor had his parents. What was he *doing* here?

Among the innumerable tiny villages dotting eastern Uttar Pradesh, Naipaul was searching for the hamlet that his grandfather had walked out of the better part of a century before. Now in 1961, when his jeep pulled into that mythic village, nondescript huts in the dirt, Naipaul felt sick. It was folly; he had blundered into not a village but a mistake.

"What should I do now?" Whispered to his guide, that question sounded Naipaul's refrain over the next days, as though whatever he knew about human behavior, about good manners, no longer applied. Few writers in our time have gained firsthand a greater knowledge of the world, but Naipaul suddenly seemed not to know what any situation required. The poised, cool courtesy that he had spent his adulthood perfecting deserted him, and he surprised even himself by a rudeness that would have done credit to a British sergeant of a century before.

As his jeep rounded into that village, Naipaul plunged into—though he hardly enjoyed thinking of it this way—an unintended family reunion. Everybody in the village was simultaneously a total stranger and a great aunt-in-law or a second cousin thrice removed. He had not anticipated beforehand how he should act, even less how *they* would. When they learned who he was, down they went prostrate before him. The wife of the clan head, clad all in white, seized his feet—his feet!—and held on to them for dear life, weeping the whole time.

"What do I do now?" Naipaul whispered to his guide.

She offered Naipaul hospitality, begged him to take some food. An internal warning light went off as he remembered the advice: "Once it's cooked, you can risk it. But never touch the water." He was in the middle of nowhere, who knew how anything was cooked—if cooked at all—here. Naipaul explained he had unfortunately not been well and the doctors had put him on the strictest of diets.

"Water," the woman said. "At least have water."

Helpfully, the guide pointed to a field of peas and suggested Naipaul would be safe asking for some and thus requiting courtesy. He had traveled halfway around the world, swum against the current of generations, back to the ur-legends of his childhood, and now he had penetrated the dark mythological land itself . . . in order to eat a pea? He ate a pod and promptly departed from the village.

The clan head, named Ramachandra, had been away from the village that day. But the next day Ramachandra walked, then took a train, then walked some more to reach the town where Naipaul was staying. He carried a sack of rice, as *prasad* or an offering, harvested from the plot of earth that had once been Naipaul's grandfather's.

"What do I do now?" Naipaul asked his guide under his breath. "I don't want thirty pounds of rice."

"He doesn't want you to take it all," his guide explained. "Just take a few grains."

Despite Ramachandra's having traveled a day to meet him, Naipaul's only thought was, Get that old man out of my hotel room. Once rid of the nuisance, Naipaul felt some relief, except for an irritating scratching sound on the barred window. It was Ramachandra on the other side, attempting a smile. "His effort at a smile did not make his expression warmer," Naipaul observed uncharitably. "Spittle, white and viscous, gathered at the corners of his mouth." Naipaul pulled the curtain across the window, making the scratchy noise no more than the sound of crickets. In effect, Naipaul was drawing the curtain on his search for a personal history, a usable past.

It was the very next morning that the boy, freshly washed, came rushing up, begging a ride as Naipaul was preparing to leave. The harshness with which he rebuffed the child was too conclusive. And so it ended, Naipaul thought to himself, his connection to India—in "a gratuitous act of cruelty, self-reproach and flight."

⬧

Only it did not end. Like a powerful magnet, India kept drawing him back, time and again. Every visit didn't result in a book, but this first one did (*An Area of Darkness*, 1962), and a fourth visit did (*India: A Wounded Civilization*, 1977), and a visit in the late '80s left another fat volume (*India: A Million Mutinies Now*, 1990). In between the books he wrote articles about India, some of the earlier ones collected in *The Overcrowded Barracoon* (1971). V. S. Naipaul's million-plus words make a mini-encyclopedia of a nation's failures and follies—if not a new circle to add to Dante's hell. In 1927 Katherine Mayo's savage *Mother India* rendered her name infamous throughout India, but Naipaul now replaced Mayo as *primus opprobrium* among Indian readers. On that first trip, though, Naipaul acknowledged that whatever might be wrong with India, something was wronger elsewhere. "I had come to them reluctantly. I had expected little, and I had been afraid," he admitted. "The ugliness was all mine."

But if reluctant, why go at all? In attempting to fathom his impulse, Naipaul used a peculiar word—*duty*. "Duty alone had brought me." Duty to what, to whom? To the Indian community in Trinidad he was estranged from? To the Indians in India he felt no attraction to? To the ancestral gods he did not believe in? None of these kept jerking him back, with invisible puppet wires, into a country he patently disliked. *Duty* is a customary translation of the Sanskrit word *dharma*—Naipaul would have known it from his childhood—and the word carries undertones of destiny. If it was Naipaul's dharma to visit his forefathers' land, how could he deny or escape it? He might well envy those figures in the Bible, though, who wrestled only with angels; he had to struggle with a whole messy, alien, violent subcontinent until it bestowed upon him its blessing. Or—as his jeep sped away and the dust settled his ancestral village into oblivion once more—possibly its curse?

※

A world away from India, perched above the South American landmass, sits the small Caribbean island of Trinidad. Winter tourists disembarking, dazzled by its brilliant blue skies, utter clichés about paradise. But when Naipaul, leaving Trinidad for the first time, arrived in a London huddled under gray cloud banks, he found his own sort of paradise. At last, so the clouds made him feel, he had a roof above him. He had come indoors, out of the sunny nothingness. Naipaul was eighteen years old. Already six years before—with a determination few schoolboys his age could match—he had scribbled in his Latin primer a vow that he would leave Trinidad within five years. Arriving in London in 1950, he was one year behind schedule.

Living in England, Naipaul became one of the unclassifiables. Is he an Indian, descended as he is from full-blooded Indians who migrated as indentured servants to Trinidad? Or *West* Indian, since all his formative years were passed in the Caribbean? Or, again, should he be considered British, by the fact that he has lived in England longest? If Naipaul has to be any of these—*has to be*—then Elizabeth Hardwick, when she interviewed him in 1979, was probably correct in labeling Naipaul British. Not only does he betray a sensibility and write a measured prose akin to other English writers', but Naipaul is an eloquent spokesman for values usually thought of as English and European.

In actuality Naipaul seems *neither* English *nor* Indian *nor* Trinidadian. The constituencies in his makeup cancel one another out or add up to some new thing for which there is yet no ready name. By the time he was twenty-two and starting to write in London, Naipaul had so parted company with every label or group identity that he knew for sure, he claimed, only where his desk at work was, where his flat after work was, and what name to call himself. Writers in exile usually identify with a national literature or culture or, at the very least, a community of dissidents back home. Naipaul lacked even these; his was the most solitary uprooting. The particular page he was writing, he said, was his only lifeline to the world. Others have biographies by addition, by new stages and developments adding onto the old, but Naipaul can make his life seem biography by subtraction.

Biographical data: Vidiadhar Surajprasad Naipaul was born in 1932, in a tiny town, Chaguanas, in Trinidad. The town was named for an (American) Indian tribe, but its (Hindi-speaking) Indian residents turned it into a Hindu caste name, Chauhan. A century ago hundreds of thousands of Indian migrants like Naipaul's grandparents got swept up in a wave that deposited them everywhere from Mauritius and Fiji to the Caribbean. Chaguanas/Chauhan was its own miniature India, with Hindu areas and Muslim areas, replete with religious and caste rivalries. Yet by the time Naipaul was growing up, this little India in Trinidad was crumbling, decaying, represented by broken objects that took up space but served no practical function. "India" in Naipaul's youth meant an old string bed, grimy, tattered, unusable, never repaired because no one in Trinidad had that caste skill. "India" was the wooden printing blocks heaped up in a corner, likewise never used because printed cotton was cheap and, anyway, the secret of the Indian dyes had been forgotten.

And what about Indian religion? What of the noble Hinduism that had lured Madame Blavatsky and Annie Besant and so many others to India? For Naipaul, it represented only more meaningless clutter. He was never taught Hindi. The elders seemed to expect the youngsters to understand it by instinct. Nor did anyone explain the prayers; no one instructed him about the rituals. The religious ceremonies struck the young boy as all alike: each was boring, each lasted nearly forever, and the food came only at the end. "So it happened," Naipaul said, "that though growing up in an orthodox Hindu family, I remained almost totally ignorant of Hinduism." When he later traveled to India, his indifference to religion, he realized, kept much of Indian life closed to his understanding.

He read about Gandhi's and Nehru's India in books, and it made sense and was part of history. But the India of his ancestors, never described to him, lay beyond history—remote, dark, an abyss where everything certain disintegrated in mists and vapors. Comfortably precise dates and ascertainable events did not belong to his grandparents' India, which was a black hole of the unexplained and unknowable. Joyce's Stephen Dedalus declared history was a nightmare from which he was trying to awaken. If Naipaul was to awaken from his particular nightmare, however, he could awaken only into history.

Better than awakening in time-forgotten Trinidad, as he did every morning during the 1930s and '40s. The semi-impoverished rural life in Chaguanas, and later his family's make-do existence in Port-of-Spain, hardly shape the background out of which writers typically emerge. But a single thin thread led out of this land under a dull, sleepy spell. Young Naipaul secured a scholarship to the finest elementary school on the island, and then he duplicated that triumph by winning a place at Trinidad's leading academy, Queen's Royal College, in Port-of-Spain. After Queen's, the miracle happened, and he won a fellowship to Oxford. Such luck befalling a poor Indian boy in Trinidad was like winning the lottery, only not by chance but by working nonstop like a graduate student preparing his exams, from age six on.

Naipaul retained no nostalgia for the place where he scored his youthful triumphs. When later a journalist asked what his upbringing had taught him, Naipaul answered everything about human behavior that one would prefer not to know. The journalist suggested surely he had learned some of the better things, too. "No, that had to be acquired later. It was one of the things I journeyed to England for." As for his education, which had netted him a scholarship to Oxford, Naipaul dismissed it as beneath contempt. The English writers he read in Port-of-Spain, Evelyn Waugh and D. H. Lawrence and Aldous Huxley (not, one would think, an unimpressive list for a teenager in the 1940s), proved to him that life was elsewhere, unconnected with anything that had happened or could happen in Trinidad. When he left the island at age eighteen, he felt only relief in leaving behind that "dot on the map of the world," that "place with no history."

In England, Naipaul continued his earlier pattern of outward success and inward discontent. After Oxford, he worked briefly for the BBC Caribbean program. It was to be his only job besides writer, and even it consisted of writing. In his free time, he approached the typewriter to test whether any combination of keys could render into language the blank hole his upbringing had bequeathed him. So uncertain were his initial forays, he wouldn't jinx the ever-mounting pages by numbering them. For his first four novels (*The Mystic Masseur*, 1957; *The Suffrage of Elvira*, 1958; *Miguel Street*, 1959; and *A House for Mr. Biswas*, 1961), he didn't feel secure enough to put his name upon the manuscripts. Someone else had to write it on them for him. Yet despite uncertainty, despite doubts whether a Trinidadian Indian had anything to say, the novels came and, with them, recognition. At an age before most novelists have even published, he was numbered among the up-and-coming writers in England, and like fruit from the trees, the literary prizes fell into his hand.

Yet, in some deep inner recess, his success seemed not to register. What he wrote and who read it were too unconnected. The mirror of recognition his English admirers held up to him was too gilded, too ornate, reflecting not him but them. He accepted success more reluctantly than most men accept failure. "I wish we could give him more than prizes," wrote a columnist in the London *Times*, meaning anything to cheer Naipaul up.

But of discomfort, of ill ease, Naipaul had a backlog stockpiled since before he was born. His family had uprooted itself from India, and just as his parents' generation was sending tender roots down in Trinidad, Naipaul had pulled them up once more. Some part of his psyche meant to be buried was apparently cast up, left dangling in air, exposed and hyperconscious. He needed to validate his existence minute by minute and so commented vehemently on all passing trivia most people ignore. In those comments, references to himself flip-flopped from a first-person "I" to a second-person "you" or a third-person "one." He never felt at home, and when he changed lodgings, he asked others, "Do *you* like it?" Besides a novelist, he became a travel writer, and it would be strange if he hadn't. Nirad Chaudhuri's remark, "To be *deraciné* is to be on the road forever," could have served as Naipaul's motto as he crossed and recrossed the globe, until *at home* and *on the road* blurred together.

For the biographical record, Naipaul did marry, an English-woman in 1955, but that marriage left no tracks, either in progeny or in his fiction. Meticulous sleuths may uncover one reference to his marriage in Naipaul's writing. The sentence that reads in the English edition of *An Area of Darkness*, "And at this point my companion slumped forward on her chair," was changed in the American edition—lest suspicions be raised—to read, "At this point my wife slumped forward on her chair." Naipaul remarked of the title character in *Mr. Stone and the Knights Companion*, "A man reaches a certain age, he wants to get married, he gets married; what more is there to say?"

Though he never acknowledged his wife in print, Naipaul showered affection on his father. In *A House for Mr. Biswas*, Mr. Biswas (modeled on Naipaul's father) and his oldest son reciprocate a fondness that is as rare in Naipaul's fiction as it is trite in other novels. The elder Naipaul might almost pass for an early, failed trial version of the later, successful son. In his brief glory days as a journalist, his father rebelled against the Indian community in Trinidad, penning articles such as "Trinidad Indians Are Not Sincere." The breakaway his father was attempting, Naipaul intuited, would require more than one generation.

Naipaul *père*, the provincial rebel, had read writers no more daring than O. Henry, but his imagination became inflamed. He decided—why not?—he would write literature, too! To forget about Trinidad, Naipaul's father fantasized romantic tales of an India he'd never seen, where village life passed in gracious rituals, amid huts and fields aesthetically laid out. In those stories, under the mango tree in the yard, by mellow fires in the evening, Old India lazed in a spell of beauty.

The real and the ideal—journalism and romance—thus divided, schizophrenically, in the elder Naipaul's mind. On the one side was gritty, grubby Trinidad; on the other, mythical, marvelous India. The effort to keep the sides in balance unhinged the father's sense of reality. As for those unreal stories, he never printed them, except in his son's mind, where they lodged "like a fantasy of home."

Inhabiting the two worlds simultaneously, his father lost his equilibrium. Many years later, Naipaul asked his mother, "What form did my father's madness take?"

"He looked in the mirror one day and couldn't see himself," his mother answered. "And he began to scream."

So one could become an invisible man. Would one day Naipaul look in the mirror and scream, too? The same recipe for disaster was there. Father's and son's identities were both alienated from the larger community; both staked salvation on becoming a writer, even as they wondered what they had to write about. Without ever discussing his breakdown, the father transmitted his fear and his dread to his son. That was his gift to me, Naipaul said. "That fear became mine as well. It was linked with the idea of the vocation: the fear could be combated only by the exercise of the vocation." Other young writers are beguiled by fame and money. In 1954, twenty-two years old, new to London, working as a freelancer for the BBC, Naipaul experienced a different motive when he adjusted his chair before the typewriter: the abyss, extinction if he failed.

Naipaul fell into the swelling flood of this century's displaced who had nowhere called home to limp forward or back to. And yet in his mind, elusive whispers, rumors, echoes from his childhood, murmured of a land where one might belong. On the periphery of his thoughts, in a corner of his being, beckoned "a fantasy of home." Naipaul was savvy enough by now to know that actual, postindependent India hardly corresponded to his father's mythic country, yet how could he refrain from going to see. In the late '50s he wrote his first four books in a diligent frenzy, in a half dozen years, and then, in 1961, there he was. . . .

※

In an essay "Salute to the Orient!" E. M. Forster warned of the many difficulties, both within oneself and within the country, that a newcomer must overcome to enjoy India. Forster himself had determined to surmount the roadblocks; he relied upon humor for a way around the obstructions, and when humor failed, he accepted the obstacles. "When obstacles cease to occur in my plans," he wrote, "it will be the surest proof that I have lost the East."

A short while in India, though, and Naipaul was in no mood for Forsterian goodwill. He recorded his first impressions after disembarking in Bombay: "And it was clear that here, and not in Greece, the East began: in this chaos of uneconomical movement, the self-stimulated din, the sudden feeling of insecurity, the conviction that all men were not brothers and that luggage was in danger." And added, in what could almost be an allusion to Forster, "How tired I am of the India-lovers, those who go on about 'beautiful India.'"

In Naipaul's *An Area of Darkness*, India is anything but beautiful. *Area* is the narrative of a young man not finding the India he expected and not liking the India he finds. Naipaul voiced his disappointments in an attractive dark wit, and even if one dislikes the book (in India it approaches being universally detested), it remains fresh in its defiance of the rule about travelers in India. For supposedly everyone meets the India he has prepared himself to find. If one anticipates discovering a holy land, as Paul Brunton did, then, once there, one moves among clouds of incense and miracle workers; if one inclines to the sybaritic, he will soon learn that Indians are the most sensual people on earth; etc.

That *etc.* includes, it could be charged, every figure so far discussed in this book. Madame Blavatsky parted the draperies of the otherworldly, with guru magicians as her guides. Annie Besant, champion of the underdog, located the country of the oppressed, which needed only her direction to oust the British brute. E. M. Forster connected with Indians emotionally warmer than the cool, stiff Englishmen back home. By contrast, Naipaul traveled not in the country of his—or his father's—dreams but in a nightmare, which is what India became for him.

Naipaul did not blame his father for having misled him; he blamed India for not living up to his father's vision. Naipaul's father, a failure on a remote Caribbean island, obviously has little in common with the energetic Gandhi in South Africa, fathering the Indian nationalist movement, and even less with the aristocratic Nehru, imbibing the best western education at Trinity College, Cambridge. Naipaul disagreed: each man had similarly espied from afar, through a long-distance telescope, a noble, coherent, ancient Indian civilization. Up close, Naipaul found no such civilization but caste against caste, ethnicity versus ethnicity, region opposing region, with no one ever sacrificing a particular selfish interest because he was, after all, an Indian, too. "India has been a shock for me," Naipaul recorded, "because—you know, you think of India as a very old and civilized land. One took this idea of an antique civilization for granted and thought that it contained the seed of growth in this century. . . . [But] India has nothing to contribute to the world, is contributing nothing."

A decade, several trips, and one book later, Naipaul was still compiling the same indictment. The reviewer in the *Times Literary Supplement* wrote of *A Wounded Civilization* (1977), "Although well over a decade has passed since *An Area of Darkness*, Naipaul's violent impression remains unaltered. Indeed, he repeats many of the [earlier] book's arguments and even phrases."

What, specifically, were Naipaul's grievances? First item on the docket, India smelled—and you could guess of what. On a hillside slope overlooking Dal Lake, one of the beauty spots of Srinagar, Naipaul chanced upon three women companionably defecating. Evidently the whole area served as an outdoor latrine. Outside the High Court in Madras, a man near Naipaul lifted his dhoti and defecated. "Indians defecate everywhere," Naipaul decided. "They defecate, mostly, beside the railway tracks. But they also defecate on the beaches; they defecate on the hills; they defecate on the river banks; they defecate on the streets; they never look for cover." The chamber pot, for Louis XIV, had served as a throne from which he enacted state business. But India was not Versailles, and Naipaul was in no humor for historical analogies. He was a fastidious man who had landed in a country with pretense to being an ancient civilization but instead was one huge outdoor water closet. A progressive reader of Naipaul may experience a shock, in which he awakens from his Enlightenment dream of improved conditions, a dream of a better life, and finds he is standing in a pile of turds.

Other travelers have experienced some fascination when they leave behind streamlined comforts and predictable conditions. But these travelers were often, like Forster or Ackerley, on a holiday from their comfortable security back home. Naipaul's life's project involved extricating himself, body and mind, from a poverty and backwardness that were once part of the very air he breathed. And there in India it was—his despicable, impoverished past masquerading as the present and promising to be the future. "The poverty of the Indian streets and the countryside was an affront and a threat," Naipaul wrote, "a scratching at my old neurosis. Two generations separated me from that kind of poverty: but I felt closer to it than most of the Indians I met." To create distance, Naipaul took to identifying himself in India as a journalist from Mexico.

When Naipaul could not appreciate beautiful Indian silk because emaciated wrists displayed it to him or admire noble ruins because of the child defecating among them, his sentiments were in tune with progressive intellectuals of the 1960s and '70s. Intellectual fashion dictated blaming the former colonialists, who plundered their colonies' resources and reduced the talented native-born to subservient menials. Only when he began to assign blame did Naipaul, the potential darling of leftists both in India and abroad, become anathema. Instead of the champion of India's downtrodden, he became their accuser. "Why is it that certain countries and certain peoples have allowed themselves to be exploited and abused?" he asked. "What is their flaw?" Like a clever prosecutor, he relentlessly pressed his indictment against the Indians themselves: "You will find that perhaps their flaws are still with them, that the flaws aren't always external."

The internal, fatal flaw of Indians was then—what? For Naipaul religion was once more the opiate of the people; having Hinduism in your veins was as harmful as having heroin. Hinduism, he argued, had not served its adherents well, addicting them to docility, fatalism, passivity. As a boy in Trinidad, he considered Hinduism as outside history, perpetuating a stagnant status quo indifferent to politics. Consequently, when he arrived in India, Naipaul did not chalk up the country's backwardness to a superseded premodern economic stage but saw it instead as a metaphysical condition, the disease of the Hindu meditative soul. And all the castes and classes within Hinduism usurped an Indian's loyalty, so that no greater rational principle could prevail for the erection of a modern, progressive nation. Naipaul cited Albert Camus's observation that the Inca and the Hindu were two people incapable of rebellion because suffering was built into their traditions and tradition was sacred. Thy enemy who defeated thee, India, wouldst thou see him? Look in the mirror.

Naipaul's arguments, intellectually, may seem rather old hat. In the nineteenth century Sir Alfred Lyall, in his *Asiatic Studies*, had attributed the absence of the nation-state in India to the caste system. Max Weber had argued that modern capitalism failed to develop on the subcontinent because all its kinship groups prevented an impersonal economic ethic from developing. Through literary alchemy, though, Naipaul charged his argument with a fresh new electricity.

The secret of some writers' power is that they annex an earlier writer's rarefied vision and take it out into the streets. As Naipaul penetrated the remote corners of the globe, observing men going to rot in the tropics and European ideals festering amid Third World corruption, a helpful shade hovered at his side. "I found Conrad—," Naipaul wrote, "sixty years before, in the time of a great peace—had been everywhere before me." Joseph Conrad wrote fiction, though, while Naipaul purports to give an objective description of real people. Kurtz and Decoud and Axel Heyst step off the imaginative page in Naipaul and jostle you on the crowded bus or wail into your ear about inflation and their lousy prospects.

In fact, Naipaul's so-called travelogues gain their power by riding the back of Conrad's "myth" of civilization under siege by barbarism. Civilization, in Naipaul's version of Conradianism, was in retreat when Indians shat in the open, like animals; and when Kashmiris whom he had trusted for months cheated him; and when, in response, Naipaul himself raged with an ugly, angry emotion he didn't know he had in him. *Heart of Darkness* has been relocated to the contemporary map, and the similarity of Naipaul's title, *An Area of Darkness*, is not accidental. Like Conrad, Naipaul was an émigré who counted upon an enlightened world citizenry as his only countrymen in a dark and alien time. When Naipaul warned about civilization under threat, he spoke, as it were, with the rope around his neck.

If *An Area of Darkness* and *A Wounded Civilization* were Naipaul's last word about India, he would himself resemble a character in a sad Conradian tale. In "An Outpost of Progress" (his favorite story by Conrad), two European buffoons prance off to the dark tropics, waving the banner of civilization; and there they perish, and the bush is their grave. Though certainly no buffoon, Naipaul fancied that in going to India he might find some carapace for his tentative self, but a part of him also seemed to perish there. In some insidious way India simultaneously swallowed him up and denied him. It undermined his sense of who he was to be in India: there was nothing in his appearance to distinguish him among those strange crowds eternally hurrying down every street. As he explained in *Area*:

> In Trinidad to be an Indian was to be distinctive. To be anything there was distinctive; difference was each man's attribute. To be an Indian in England was distinctive. . . . Now in Bombay I entered a shop or restaurant and awaited a special quality of response. And there was nothing. It was like being denied part of my reality. Again and

again I was caught. I was faceless. I might sink without a
trace into that Indian crowd. . . . I felt the need to impose
myself, and didn't know how.

India, Salman Rushdie claimed, was the sad ruin of Naipaul.
Before going, Naipaul had exuded affection and humor, Rushdie
said, but he returned from his Indian disappointment a detached,
embittered case. The sequence of Naipaul's books structures a
similar testimony: the four novels that precede his trip to India are
infused with a playful humor that, after India, never suffuses his
writing again. The Authority himself concurred: "It was a journey," he declares at the end of *An Area of Darkness*, "that ought not
to have been made."

But Naipaul was not a character in a story, not in one by Conrad,
not even in one by himself. His interests carried him far beyond
Conrad's verities about honor and valor, and his nonfiction poked
around corners Conrad's tales never investigated. And finally
India itself, even were it as despicable as Naipaul often presents it,
is infinitely more complicated than the bush. Naipaul's story
demands some continuation. As in Twain's witticism, the reports
of his spiritual death in India—and of India as the country of the
dead and the backward—may have been exaggerated.

⚜

In 1982 Naipaul met the bush head-on. That year he traveled to
the Ivory Coast, which, despite its relative prosperity, appeared
heaven-made for his satiric pen. The president of the Ivory Coast
had built at his native village of Yamoussoukro a gleaming new
metropolis, a showcase of ultramodernity. Avenues wide as run-
ways, high-rises shooting up in the air, deluxe hotels, a manicured
golf course, all testified to its founder's pharaonic daydream. For
*day*dream it was. When darkness fell on Yamoussoukro, an
African night-world of spirits and magic would reclaim the
city/village for its own, as its inhabitants swayed in tribal rituals
and chanted incantations. In Yamoussoukro the day repudiated

the night, and the night mocked the day, and the contrast between them appeared perfect for Naipaul, who, in the Third World, invariably mocked both.

But Naipaul had suddenly become tolerance itself, accepting everything, understanding all. He accepted Yamoussoukro's outright contradictions, the daytime rationality versus the nighttime superstitions, as effecting a healthy symbiosis. By living in a double world, the Ivorians had remained faithful to the African immediacy while their neighbors—Liberia, Guinea, Ghana—had chased foreign-bred schemes into "chaos or nullity." The alternation between modern and primitive in the Ivory Coast, Naipaul even suggested, merely enacted what people do everywhere who have their light and dark moods, one moment logical, the next irrational.

Had our hero been fed some witch's potion? Instead of satirizing the Ivorians, Naipaul engaged in the most un-Naipaulian act: he identified with them. "The people I found," he wrote in *Finding the Center* (1984), "the people I was attracted to, were not unlike myself. They too were trying to find order in their world, looking for the center." Earlier, the endurance of primitive elements in the Ivory Coast (he now genially called them "African completeness") would have caused him to dip his pen in scorn and write in mockery. But evidently no longer dreading the primitive within himself, he could placidly accept its outward manifestation.

The year Naipaul traveled to the Ivory Coast he turned fifty. So much work, so much accomplishment, was psychologically paying dividends. The terror that he had felt during his writing apprenticeship now lay, in calendar time, years past. That terror had its etiology in having witnessed his father's breakdown. Torn between golden myths and a shoddy present, between romances and journalism, his father had succumbed to divisions within himself that Naipaul once worried might destroy him, too. Wherever he had traveled in the Third World, his inner terror had taken the form of outward conditions, practically coming up on the street and greeting him. India wasn't the only place that tore an old scab open.

But Naipaul's travel narratives melded together the romantic mythmaking and the objective journalism that had tugged his father in opposing directions. Traveling and writing had not opened an old wound, as Naipaul thought, but rather allowed it to heal, without at first his noticing it. The experience of finding his own way through a chaos of obstacles, and then constructing a narrative that made sense of it, gradually matured him in confidence. Travel, he later said, "became the substitute for the mature social experience—the deepening knowledge of a society—which my background and the nature of my life denied me. My uncertainty about my role withered; a role was not necessary. I recognized my own instincts as a traveler and was content to be myself."

Contentment to be oneself is not an achievement to be underestimated. How, exactly, had Naipaul achieved it? Apparently, sometime between being in India and venturing to the Ivory Coast, he had done nothing less than redefine for himself what the self was. For the age-old identification of self with place, for its associations with house and home, he substituted the image of the self as traveler, the self in motion; instead of identity as an essence, identity created itself in the wheels of action. Once Naipaul, too, had believed in the necessity of home. (In *A House for Mr. Biswas* he had linked his father's inability to achieve a stable identity with his failure to secure any permanent housing.) In his quest for a "spiritual home" for himself, since Trinidad was unwanted and England too alien, Naipaul had no recourse but at least to try India, which from his father's stories had lodged in his mind "like a fantasy of home." *An Area of Darkness* recorded his disappointment and damned India as unfit for human habitation (how wrong about this Forster was). But later he began to have second thoughts that India's disabusing him of antiquated notions like home was actually useful. Naipaul's was a demarcating experiment in contemporary understanding: to turn identity out of doors, to dispense with reference points, no home in front and no home behind, the self become a modern nomad, a travel-writer.

Having dispensed with all fantasies of home, Naipaul now fancied he could be at ease anywhere. Although he identified with the Ivorians, he blithely declared, "I would have found equivalent connections with my past and myself, wherever I had gone." And since he no longer needed to feel at home, perhaps—perhaps— might he even be at home in India, finally?

So another visit to India was called for to see, changed himself, what he might find changed there. Perhaps such a trip would stabilize and secure his "content[ment] to be myself." And so began the journey that was to be called *A Million Mutinies Now*.

※

Way back when, in his twenties, Naipaul came to India already identifying that country with abjectness and shame. India was the miserable country, the defeated country that cast out its children, such as Naipaul's grandparents, to labor as indentured servants elsewhere. But "what I hadn't understood in 1962, or had taken too much for granted was the extent to which the country had been remade," Naipaul wrote a quarter century later, in *A Million Mutinies Now*. In his new book Naipaul determined to take the long view. "For 150 years or more," so Naipaul's poetry of the long view now went, India had known

> a remarkable series of leaders and teachers and wise men,
> exceeded by no country in Asia. It [that long period] had
> been part of India's slow adjustment to the outside world;
> and it had led to its intellectual liveliness in the late 20th
> century: a free press, a constitution, a concern for law and
> institutions, ideas of morality, good behavior and intellec-
> tual responsibility quite separate from the requirements of
> religion.

Naipaul's endorsement of India was so unexpected, yet still it unrolled, yard after yard, whole spools of it. "People [throughout India] everywhere had ideas now of who they are and what they owe themselves. The processes quickened with the economic development that came after independence; what was hidden in 1962 . . . had become clearer. . . . [It was] the truest kind of liberation."

In the last pages of *A Million Mutinies Now* Naipaul had become, finally, the defender of India. Indeed, it would have been perverse had he not tried vaguely to champion that country. The real masters of perversity in this regard may be the politicians like Richard Nixon, Henry Kissinger, and Georges Pompidou, who, when they looked toward Asia, admired China's order and industrial efficiency and deplored poor, messy India. China, so went the Nixon-Kissinger song of praise, should provide India, always on the edge of anarchy, its model, its textbook for development. But Mao Zedong's China achieved its order by brutally suppressing individual choice and freedom of thought and every nuanced restraint associated with civilized existence. In *A Million Mutinies Now* Naipaul belatedly recognizes that, despite civil unrest and economic catastrophes, though rocked by mutinies, India had not forfeited the bases that permit civilized life to exist.

A little revolution is good for a country, wrote Thomas Jefferson. Naipaul went Jefferson one, or one million, better: mutinies, instances of unrest everywhere, were signs of India's well-being. Albert Camus, thou shouldst be here now, to see the Hindus rebel. Specifically, Naipaul's argument went: when social groups cease to accept their backwardness and oppression, they begin to see themselves as an outsider might seem them. This objective view of their condition fills them with a rage, with mutinous rage. "And—strange irony—the mutinies were not to be wished away. They were part of the beginning of a new way for many millions, part of India's growth, part of its restoration."

In nineteenth-century novels the ending is often tacked on, unrelated to what had gone before. (*Cousin Bette* might inspire any woman to a career in vice, but to satisfy propriety, Balzac dutifully ruined his heroine in the last pages.) Naipaul's endorsement of India that closes *A Million Mutinies Now* appears likewise an afterthought. The vigorous India on the right track hardly resembles the suffering country that limps through the preceding sections of the book.

In the India Naipaul describes, you cannot drink a cup of tea, or if you do you won't enjoy it, because the bad water has soured the taste. You can hardly walk down the street in Calcutta, shoved by the crowd, tripping over broken footpaths, inhaling the sick brown auto exhaust. Everything that should be done, might be done, can't be done in *Mutinies*, and around the corner awaits more frustration. Naipaul ticks off a list of them: "the difficulty of travel by air or train or road; the crowded, dangerous city streets; the poisonous fumes; the difficulty of doing simple things; the difficulty of arranging the physical details of day to day living." Naipaul reports people who quit their jobs, defeated by all the obstacles in simply getting there. In *Mutinies*, ambitious fathers wake their children at four A.M. to do schoolwork, because by seven the noise and crowding will have made it impossible. At dinner one evening, a famous actor declaims, "Everyone is *suffering* here." "And that simple word," to Naipaul's ears, reverberated "like an illumination."

"I was far enough away from it to cease to be of it." So Naipaul explained his unique angle of vision, which allowed him to see the unremitting suffering that travel writers largely ignore. "But I was near enough to understand the passions; and near enough to feel that my own fate was bound up with the fate of the people of the country." Journalists perhaps, missionaries probably, social workers definitely, but no foreign author of Naipaul's stature ever ventured into the tenements, the poverty, the defeated lives, to reveal the particular India that Naipaul unveils to the outside world.

Naipaul's unique angle of vision, however, may have stranded him in a no-man's-land of critical interpretation. Indian novelists (and social scientists) writing about their own country usually focus on (1) family, (2) community, or (3) religion to show how Indian society ameliorates jarring realities into a bearable way of life. But family, community, and religion name the three things that bore, if not actually appall, Naipaul. These insider's keys to understanding India he ignored altogether. Other figures have made intuitive leaps of empathy to come to terms with India. But unlike Annie Besant, Naipaul did not concern himself with religion in India; unlike Forster, indulge in sexual fantasies; and unlike Curzon, he did not involve himself in political plans for communal improvement.

Nor, on the other hand, was Naipaul simply a traveler, determined (as, say, Forster was) to enjoy his trip. That sort of traveler requires—more even than a guidebook or antiseptic ointment—a sense of humor, a relish for individual quirkiness, and, above all, a devout little prayer for the pleasurable moment. Naipaul, though, has applied a scorched-earth policy to life's little pleasures. In *Mutinies*, one of his interviews runs overlong, which keeps his guide from attending the circus. Unbelievable!—there are actually circuses in Naipaul's India? An old taboo forbade high-caste Hindus' traveling abroad: that taboo may faintly linger on in Naipaul, who, though ricocheting over the globe, never associates travel with enjoyment. In *A Million Mutinies* a reader encounters no lust, not even lusty eating: neither the sensualist nor the mystic, neither the visionary nor the glutton, has any role to play here. The insider's preoccupations and the outsider's diversions are thus both effectively banned.

A Million Mutinies Now is fascinating in the way that documents that embody a genuine struggle are. Its perfunctory prose is animated by Naipaul's handsome intention to go beyond his predisposition to sound a new affirmation. He would reveal the country of his ancestors—which formed a dark knot within himself—to be healing, healthy, whole. Since he first went there twenty-seven years before, Naipaul gladly acknowledges, India had advanced, sundered ancient barriers, recorded impressive material progress. "Many people had risen," he observes, but then adds the damning qualification that "a good deal of that improvement had been swallowed up by the growth in the population." *Mutinies* is the story of a man with the sun behind him trying to outrace his own shadow:

in India overpopulation overshadows every advance. Despite Naipaul's fine intentions, and despite his showing that India is modernizing, indisputably so, the book concludes that modernity may be little akin to what was once thought its Siamese twin—a better life.

Possibly Naipaul's whole strategy in *Mutinies* was misconceived. He took with him a quality-control list of what a modern society was elsewhere, and he checked India off point by point to see whether it passed. In order to make his case for an India healthy and whole, he joined the British Raj and the forty years since independence together into a single era that had lifted India out of its Dark Age of Muslim invasions and eighteenth-century anarchy. He began his chronological ladder in the Hindu mire and portrayed each rung as an ascent—Enlightenment rationality; economic development; civic polity; the idea of individual responsibility—until India reached secular modern nationhood. But Naipaul recognizes his ladder is shaky, too narrow, for the masses of Indians to climb very high on. For the many unable to ascend, and for the many who fall off, he has no consolations to offer.

The balms that make the difficulties of ordinary life bearable—religion or intoxicants, community or eroticism—are not to be found in Naipaul's medicine cabinet. Even more important, the one item entirely lacking from that cabinet is empathy. Naipaul had never sympathized or identified with any group. ("I wished," he wrote in *A Way in the World* [1994], "to belong to myself. I couldn't support the idea of being a part of a group.") Now, when his whole project of affirming India depended on his sympathizing with a broad range of its people, his organs of receptivity were too atrophied, and he coldly left them to their fate, unconsoled and unmourned.

Besides, there was no one there to sympathize: what is missing from Naipaul's India in *A Million Mutinies Now* is mainly Naipaul. In *An Area of Darkness*, every page is informed by the presence of that young man who, equating self with home, struggles tragicomically to make India the homeland for himself it cannot be.

But in *Mutinies*, content to identify himself with the motions of travel, he feels no pressure to be emotionally present in India at all. His absenting himself creates in *Mutinies* its impersonal, mechanical atmosphere, which feels as if some social scientist has flipped on the "tape recorder" and let it do the imaginative work for him. The information gleaned from interviews is not shaped into drama. The interviewees are not fleshed into characters. They are names and occupations, declaring themselves in mono-tone voices that are all interchangeable. The machinelike whir of *Mutinies* drones on, drones about grievances, misfortunes, set-backs, unable ever to click off. In the very length and mass and sprawl of the book, in the author's reluctance to amend or end it, speaks the hidden passion that, in a quarter million words, Naipaul could never utter directly.

An Area of Darkness, three decades before, revealed not only an unsatisfactory first encounter with India but, even more, a young writer's pleasure in his art. In *Mutinies*, Naipaul has ceased caring for the pleasure of writing; India finally overwhelms even his con-cern for his craft. Perhaps, in his Conradian tour of the earth's cor-rupted places, Naipaul had gazed too long with cold eyes upon too much of human baseness. In the end he could only record the harsh particulars: literary flourish, like redemption, had trickled away over the rocky, parched, cracked course. Every avenue Naipaul ventured down turned into one more dead end.

After such a journey, after such knowledge—what aftermath?

The aftermath was to be a happy one. It takes place in that other India, the one the other Indians called Manhattan. After finish-ing *A Million Mutinies Now*, Naipaul delivered an address to the Manhattan Institute in New York. The speech is everything that *Mutinies* is not: compassionate, generous, visionary, beautifully written. Naipaul's recent experience in India haunts his talk, hovering between the lines, but the ghost has become a friendly one.

That Naipaul had to put time and distance between himself and India to appreciate the country was hardly surprising. He had determined to give two cheers for mutinies and rage, but his immersion in poverty and violence was hardly cheering. Only afterward, in Manhattan, was Naipaul urbane and at ease with a vision that had germinated under quite different circumstances in Bombay and Calcutta and Madras not so long before.

Naipaul titled his talk "Our Universal Civilization." This was the early 1990s, when no one used *civilization* to characterize the globe's geopolitical fragments all warring and competing with one another. But Naipaul, formerly a pessimist's pessimist, now declined to share in the general gloom. Naipaul's talk was inspired by a most un-Naipaulian idea: happiness. Naipaul used his mother as an example of the kind of person for whom happiness had been irrelevant, as she passively reproduced a set of inherited responses to every situation. Indeed all his ancestors, like most of mankind, Naipaul said, had lived before the ability to choose happiness became an option for them. By "happiness" Naipaul did not mean a subjective emotion but the felicitous historical convergence of "the idea of the individual, responsibility, choice, the life of the intellect, the idea of vocation and perfectability and achievement"—all of which together allowed an individual to take his inheritance of givens and reshape it to a happier end. This happiness "is an immense human idea," Naipaul concluded. "It is known to exist; and because of that, other more rigid systems in the end blow away."

Naipaul's New York audience was hearing the conclusion of *A Million Mutinies Now* restated, with all references to India deleted. His discovery of "happiness" had to be freed of its troublesome Indian context to hum, as it did in his talk now, with a purer sound. On his recent visit to India, Naipaul had discovered, to his surprise, that "Enlightenment" values were flourishing there—the values of individuality, responsibility, vocation, etc.—though at the time their existence had been all but drowned out by more depressing sights and sounds. That such values could exist in

India now formed the basis of his argument that a universal civilization able to underwrite individual happiness had come into being. Naipaul, of all people, was suddenly the voice of optimism, and that voice was declaring India the model for civilization. What madness, what "happiness," was his New York audience hearing?

Earlier, whenever Naipaul traveled the globe, he discovered the civilized remnant besieged by the forces of barbarism. His discovery tells as much, or more, about Naipaul as about the new terrain. For of course barbarism wins if one identifies, as Naipaul did, the barbaric with anything merely irrational and the primitive with emotion itself. Such a cold, polarized understanding came naturally to a man who by will alone had navigated his way from a backwater to a world capital and become a recognized writer by sheer intellect and determination. But now, several decades later, the frozen seas within him were breaking up. Naipaul was not a confessional writer, so he talked about the modernization of India or a universal civilization instead of making a confession about himself.

What was Naipaul so indirectly confessing? First of all, that it was on the road that he learned something new about what home and self now mean. Travel was once the antonym of home because boundaries were so resistant to penetration that only those who mastered languages and "went native" (like the Jesuit Roberto de Nobili in seventeenth-century India) fully navigated the passage. Naipaul shows that cultural borders are today porous enough that brilliant amateurs can be at home where scholars fear to tread. If any volume on India by that brilliant amateur Naipaul endures, likely it will be *An Area of Darkness*, where he knew *the least* about India. Written in the season of books like Alex Haley's *Roots*, *Area* narrates the sad picaresque comedy of a young man seeking his past and then backing off, appalled: "Oh no! it can't be this." People like Naipaul and Haley dug for tubers in strange lands because—so pervasive had democratic notions become— suddenly the disenfranchised ones of history might possess a past, a historical pedigree. Taken as a whole, Naipaul's books record the hidden journey of a man who went from being an illegal alien in his own psychology to becoming a first-class citizen in the great world. The "Indian-ness" within him changed, in the process, from an area of darkness to part of his universal citizenship.

When he was young, Naipaul believed he had nothing within him to write about, and a half century later, he had become one of the world's most respected authors. Along the way he discovered (and recorded in *The Enigma of Arrival*) that even the contemporary keepers of English tradition suffered from a displacement or lostness almost as bad as his. Naipaul staked out early a territory that more and more people recognized as they came to live amid circumstances for which their birth or upbringing had failed to prepare them. By the late 1990s, Naipaul's estranged explorations of uprootedness had won him every honor short of the Nobel Prize. It was a strange success story: a marginal man had contrived, by concentrating on marginality, to become Representative Man.

Secondly, Naipaul's confession reveals how literature, which once made a sublimated or substitute home for him, fell by the wayside as he made himself at ease in the world. Initially, Naipaul had pushed his artistry to the limit in writing about India because he was secretly endeavoring through it to redefine himself. If India were the genuine article, then there he might cease his mimicry of the English and become himself a genuine article, with a genuine identity. Only as that fine intention excruciatingly failed (or as, he thought, India failed him) did Naipaul retreat into the social scientist who, with nothing personal at stake, can approve of India, though as a literary craftsman he'd never allowed himself to. The indifferent sociological prose in *Mutinies* appeared to contribute to his reconciliation, for in its neutral drone Naipaul could accept India intellectually while distancing himself from it emotionally.

Finally, Naipaul confesses that his tragic encounter with India had been, at least, a necessary tragedy. In India—likely it could have happened nowhere else—Naipaul ceased his flirtation with comedy that characterized his early novels and entered into his deeper vision. The early fiction, like *Miguel Street* and *The Mystic Masseur*, had manufactured humor out of the distortion of European ideals in the Third World. But it was relatively easy to make comedy out of what one has left behind, as he had Trinidad; far harder to have to face what was ambiguous and threatening from within as from without, as India was. Naipaul's encounter with India exudes a poignancy, even heroism, as he compulsively returned again and again to the most disturbing place on earth for him.

Miguel Street had closed with the unnamed narrator leaving Trinidad, walking toward the airplane, "not looking back, looking only at my shadow before me, a dancing dwarf on the tarmac." In the wholeness of India he would outgrow his dwarfed identity— that was the illusion, Naipaul later said, he had to lose. But first he had to discount his father's gift to him, the golden myth of India as a beckoning home. Only many years after that illusion had died— and hope and idealism seemed to die with it—could Naipaul recognize that India might displease him and still be part of civilization. And only then could the compulsion that bobbed him back and back to India—in which he was damned if he went and damned if he stayed away—begin to dissolve. Each new abrasive trip there strengthened the dissolvent until he became less the ambiguous Indian or the Indian manqué and more the "universal man," at last perfectly poised to deliver a lecture on "Our Universal Civilization."

"Something inherent in the necessities of successful action," Conrad had written, "carried with it the moral degradation of the idea." Something in Naipaul's success had degraded, or withered away, the imaginative force that had carried him through his long apprenticeships and journeys. Though he had forfeited imaginative power, he had gained self-acceptance. It was, incidentally, *Sir* V. S. Naipaul, knighted by Queen Elizabeth, who stepped before the Manhattan Institute to announce that one could be happy after all. Even couching it in terms of a Universal Civilization could not quite conceal his amazement that he had experienced this revelation personally.

❊

Was Naipaul, then, happy at last? Students working on their theses or dissertations used to write him, or even phone, asking whether his books were a search for identity and then saying, "How's it going?" Going very well, would be his response—he'd abandoned it entirely. Naipaul's retort was flippant, dismissive, but it actually describes rather well how Naipaul finally scoured himself clean of that fantasy of finding a home for himself, associated with his father's tall tales of India, by ridding himself of fantasy altogether. It may have been time in the wilderness or desert, but if India dried up Naipaul's literary charms, it also succeeded in drying up the pools of his anxiety. He was, as we have seen, a man beginning to know contentment as he stepped before that New York audience to beguile them with his own romance about civilization, echoing his father's fable about India.

So it hadn't been a curse, after all—the dust from his ancestors' village he had disturbed and which had settled on his clothes, on that first trip now so long ago. What had begun then, when his jeep roared into that village, disrupting unknown relatives' lives and puncturing his own dream, had ended in a kind of reconciliation. Over the long decades his inexorable wrestling with India had both diminished and enlarged him, which is perhaps the most that can be asked of life. Yet can the ultimate reconciliation be imagined?

Suppose that village in Uttar Pradesh were to stage a celebration in honor of its most celebrated great-grandson today. Suppose, too, Naipaul had the curiosity—of which he is rarely in short supply—to attend in person. On the one side would be the slightly tedious festivities, and on the other, Naipaul with an embarrassed half-smile. The ceremony, tacky, homemade, would unfold through the long day without unpleasantness, congenially enough. But what if, toward the end, an ancient figure dressed in white approached him—for that boy who long ago begged a ride would be old now, too—and this old man requested, after the ceremony, a lift into the next town? Naipaul gives every indication he would be no more inclined now than then to give an "idler," that is, an ordinary Indian, a lift. Finally, in his determination to reach his destination, there had been too little room in his jeep.

PART III
Universe

Gandhi and the "American Gandhi": Like his Indian hero, Martin Luther King Jr. was a religious man who used religion to change politics in ways few politicians dreamed possible.
Bob Fitch Photo

Redefining Religion for the Future

That winter of 1939, as the ship steamed out of its English harbor, two passengers aboard felt as though they had caught the last barque of escape before the civilization behind them crumbled to extinction. Those passengers, one a novelist, the other a poet, had helped set the fashionable attitudes of the decade now ending: iconoclastic in the arts, aggressively secular toward religion, and above all, leftist-leaning in politics. But as the ship bore them past their customary milieu, long pent-up feelings, thoughts they hadn't realized they were thinking, suddenly blurted from their mouths, much to their surprise. Walking the deck one morning, Christopher Isherwood heard himself say, "You know, it just doesn't mean anything to me any more—the Popular Front, the party line, the anti-Fascist struggle. I suppose they're okay but something's wrong with me. I simply cannot swallow another mouthful." His friend, W. H. Auden, answered, "Neither can I."

After that admission, Isherwood never converted to any right-wing ideology. But that morning his leftist politics, the foundation of his intellectual life—and his camaraderie with all those who opposed Franco in Spain and the Conservatives at home; his knowing in advance what to think on every issue—collapsed. The entire world he knew, Europe itself, was about to plunge into the long dark night of World War II, and Isherwood to fall into his own dark night of the soul, having no way to orient or succor himself amid the impending death and destruction. When their ship landed in New York, Auden entered a period of flowering productivity, but what Isherwood entered was despair. Auden could retreat into his Christian beliefs, acquired in childhood and never fully abandoned, while Isherwood had nothing in which to believe. He despised the comfort Auden took from religion. Religion, to Isherwood, belonged in the nursery right beside the belief in Saint Nicholas and the tooth fairy. Religion belonged to the nursery stage of human history, along with other horrors like inquisitions and crusades.

Such opinions, which once would have branded Isherwood a heretic, were merely platitudes by the time he expressed them. Secularism Triumphant was the faith of right-thinking people everywhere during the mid-twentieth century. Even those tempted by the solace or beauty religion might possibly give considered it their duty to resist the temptation. Jean-Paul Sartre (born a year after Isherwood) argued that, granted God exists, we must reject him anyway, since the idea of a greater Power negates our freedom. In 1939, whatever Isherwood's predicament was, it was not the dilemma Sartre described: he knew God did not exist, and he felt no attraction to religion. Yet the expansive exhilaration Isherwood should have felt upon shedding the old religious corset had yielded, somehow, to an ever more constrictive sense of misery.

Isherwood is a good case study for students of twentieth-century religion. He ranted against "sin-obsessed, life-denying" Protestantism but using easy, ready-made formulas, as though not his own but his generation's biases were speaking through him. When he damned it to hell, he merely repeated the objections to religion as his era defined religion. And what exactly were those definitions of and objections to religion? Like Sartre, Isherwood protested the idea of God, a Boss in heaven, which then made him a junior employee in a firm doing questionable business. Like Marx, he denounced the social uses religion served, allowing the exploiters to have a good conscience and the exploited to acquiesce in their bad lot. Like D. H. Lawrence, he faulted the religious prohibitions against wholesome desires. But Isherwood's chief complaint was that religion required you to *believe* in far-fetched dogmas unrelated to experience. Isherwood never bothered to wonder if all religion was like his caricature of it or whether a faith without sin, dogmas, or even God might be possible. When Isherwood disembarked in New York that cold winter's morning, had anyone then suggested that in America he would acquire an Indian guru and become a religious devotee, surely he would have laughed: he was a novelist, and not even he wrote fiction that implausible.

The critic Edmund Wilson once proposed an experiment. Wilson observed that religious words like *God* had been worn down to near-meaninglessness and so proposed obliterating them and seeing what actual experience discovered under their pentimento. Isherwood's life in the New World came close to enacting Wilson's experiment, as a mind that had already dispensed with God got backed into a cul-de-sac from which a spiritual practice was one of the few ways out. Isherwood needed support in a world going up in flames; he required some justification for his embryonic pacifist feelings to counter the pervasive, patriotic war rhetoric. By chance he met a Hindu monk in Los Angeles who refuted most of Isherwood's stereotypes (all negative) of what religion was and supplied him a different vocabulary of faith that a sensual modern like himself could speak. Surprised as he was to have gotten involved with swamis and India, Isherwood tentatively began a spiritual life—one that the fierce preachers and fiery proselytizers of old would not have approved or even recognized—but a spiritual life nonetheless. In regard to religion, Isherwood felt like the awkward guest who arrives during the last hour of a party, knowing no one else there or what's gone on before. Only little by little did he realize he had arrived not during the last but nearer to the first hour, that he was in fact participating in one of the larger religious reinterpretations in history. Something unprecedented was being given birth to, and he was, so to speak, part of the labor pains.

❈

The same year Isherwood sailed for New York, the greatest living poet in the English language died. William Butler Yeats felt that he was by nature religious but that a materialist age had prevented that nature its fulfillment. Yeats never tackled the subject of religion directly, preoccupied as he was with poetry, the occult, and Irish rebel nationalism. Off to the side, though, he felt a peculiar attraction toward India. "India" became for Yeats what pure theory is to a mathematician: through it he could elaborate his thought unhampered, without all the ramification and qualification that complicated his poetics and his politics. In relation to India Yeats could reformulate his ideas about religion, doing as an exercise in thought what Isherwood had to live out by residing in a temple, journeying to India, and finding a guru.

Yeats had intended to travel to India, too—an intention never fully abandoned even after he grew too old and unfit for the journey. In 1937 a suitable invitation from India finally arrived. The seventy-two-year-old Yeats was tempted but at last declined, giving the most extraordinary excuse. He'd recently undergone a "Steinach operation" that supposedly restored sexual potency, and if he denied the sexual urge, even for an excursion to India, he claimed he might go mad, as the critic Ruskin had. The Dublin wits howled, calling Yeats the Gland Old Man. But just as the Steinach operation had reinvigorated him physically, so India might mentally, he hoped, renew him in imaginative vigor. (In that same year, 1937, Jung was preparing his trip to India, to similarly restore an ailing European mentality to greater psychological balance.)

India had fascinated Yeats at each stage in his life but for different reasons. In his youth, India meant fantasy. Around age twenty he met Madame Blavatsky's disciple Mohini Chatterjee, who, in between faking psychic experiments and being seduced by Theosophical ladies, taught Yeats a vapory cosmology "at once logical and boundless." Chatterjee's pantheistic religion infused Yeats's immature poetry—"The Indian upon His God," "Anashuya and Vijaya," "The Indian to His Love"—which allowed the young poet to mistake his fantasy for the world. Yeats's India, then, "far away [from] the unquiet lands," took its curious place in the Celtic Twilight, part of its fin-de-siècle inventory sandwiched between fairies and world-weary sighs.

In his middle age, Yeats's image of India solidified and became synonymous with reality, or at least his ideal of culture. In 1912 he met—a far cry from Mohini Chatterjee—the fabled poet Rabindranath Tagore, touring Europe in his majestical white beard and flowing robes, an Old Testament prophet come to life. Yeats was thrilled, for here was the model for the Irish bard he had long sought. Indian peasants supposedly sang Tagore's poetry as they worked and thus demonstrated that the poet and the people, art and religion, could be all one, as supposedly they had been in ancient Ireland. "I associate early Christian Ireland with India," Yeats improbably declared. Only he grew tired of declaring. He grew tired of Tagore, too, who despite corroborating his pet ideas, left Yeats's own imagination unchanged.

Only in his old age did India allow Yeats to express ideas that he could not have formulated just as well without it. It was only then, after he had ceased hoping for an Irish renaissance ("romantic Ireland is in the grave"), that he began to speculate what India might be in itself. He no longer wanted Indian religion to confirm his notions but to show him what lay beyond their furthest perimeter. All the *isms* of contemporary Europe—fascism, Futurism, communism, capitalism—appeared to him to strait-jacket the imagination. He scavenged for some perspective to allow him to see beyond the common assumptions of his genera-tion, even beyond his own intellectual limitations. One Indian critic, Shankar Mokashi-Punekar, observed, "Till 1930, Yeats appears to be standing amidst his thoughts. Suddenly after 1931, we see him stepping out and watching his philosophy as an out-sider, annexing new fields to replenish the shortcomings he per-ceived in his thought."

It was in 1931 that Yeats met the third Indian who was to play an important role in his life. Outwardly, Sri Purohit presented an unimpressive figure, short and dumpy, all wrapped in rose-colored robes. Irish wags observed Yeats was last seen in the company of a giant pink carnation. The pink carnation was in fact a serious scholar, though, with whom Yeats went to Majorca to translate the Upanishads. In Majorca Purohit would dawdle up the stairs so that behind him Yeats with his heart condition did not overexert him-self. But for Yeats this exertion in old age—translating the

Upanishads, with their different worldview—might propel European thought onto new and untried ground.

With Purohit as his informant, Yeats now composed essays—"An Indian Monk," "The Holy Mountain," "The Mandukya Upanishad"—that attempt to move onto this untried ground as he gropes his way beyond the typical thought processes of his era. He cites as the two representative postwar novels James Joyce's *Ulysses* and Virginia Woolf's *The Waves*, because they delineate the ordinary mind eddying through the flows of daily experience. Indian religion, as he learned about it from Purohit, just might be a way of surpassing the limited imaginative life that Joyce and Woolf had been content artistically to portray.

What did India offer intellectually, to pit against triumphant European logic? Reincarnation, for example, Yeats argued, would alter the bases on which western morality proceeds. That which would be immoral if a person lived but once—sins against society—would be replaced by sins against one's own soul, if that soul outlived many different societies. Yeats produced the example of Indian courtesans meditating without guilt, and of ascetics who shared their abodes, knowing in their next lives saint and sinner may switch roles. So much did reincarnation promise to turn utilitarian morality on its head that Yeats slipped amid his circumlocutions his assent: "Life, and all lives, would be unintelligible to me, *did I not think of them as an exfoliation prolonged from life to life.*"

Even meditation might effect a similar reversal of values. In his youth, Yeats had identified meditation with something like Joyce's or Woolf's stream of consciousness, but it had plunged him into a bewildering mental chaos. Purohit taught a different kind of meditation that suspended thoughts entirely, that created a mental state as empty as light is of contending ideas and *isms*. By descending to a level beneath desire and beyond logic, the mind opened, Yeats wrote, "not to its own but to the Divine purpose" or to what the old bards called inspiration. Indian epistemology thus allowed Yeats to insist there could still be poets and visionaries and prophets in an era that increasingly denied the legitimacy of all three.

Yeats's flirtation with Hinduism resulted in no conversion; it issued in no manifesto; and it made no appreciable public difference. And yet in those peripheral essays on a marginal subject, Yeats quietly converted what religion had once meant into something like its opposite. While the earlier Victorians had prided themselves on their tempered, reasonable faith, Yeats returned religion to an improbable divine scheme beyond logic. While they had believed in progress, Yeats's reincarnation looped time into cycles where what was once will be again. While the Victorians had taught self-denial in the name of religious duty, Yeats plunged into a personal quest for self-fulfillment. And finally, where his elders' religion was ascetic ("sin-obsessed," Isherwood would have called it), Yeats's was so infused with sensuality that, instructing his readers in Tantra, the sex act and the religious act became nearly interchangeable. Irrational, mythic, personal, and sensual—Yeats's writings on India, marginal though they might be, emptied out the Victorian cupboard of faith and restocked it with a different inventory.

Yeats never issued a manifesto, and really, the whole point was, one no longer *believed*. For centuries what a person believed, *Credo*, determined whether one was a Christian or heretic. But when Jung was asked if he believed there was a God, he would reply teasingly, "I don't believe. I know." Where belief once stood, Jung, like Yeats, wanted experience. Reading sacred texts, associating with a swami, possibly meditating, and translating the Upanishads constituted a religious life of sorts, whether Yeats called himself a believer or not. And by this *practice*—as opposed to *beliefs*—Yeats transferred religion from the rarefied plateau of dogma to the common plains of daily living. Such a change in religion may be what Isak Dinesen meant when she observed that, in contrast to the Jewish epoch of the Father and the Christian one of the Son, we are now entering the era of the Holy Ghost.

"I know nothing but the novels of Balzac, and the Aphorisms of Pantanjali. I once knew other things, but I am an old man with a poor memory," so Yeats wrote in his old age. It was a lie, but he told that lie for its symbolic truth. He hoped to infuse Balzac's bourgeois *comédie humaine*—something of an endangered species in 1930s Europe—with a different spiritual lifeblood, hence the reference to the Indian philosopher Patanjali. His own Indian studies had given him, through techniques like meditation, a different way of knowing and, with ideas like reincarnation, a different standard by which to judge what was known. His imagination stirred and his perspective broadened, Yeats resumed writing poetry that suffered no diminution, and he enjoyed the most productive old age in the history of English poetry. "Things fall apart; the centre cannot hold," he had written earlier in "The Second Coming." Through Balzac *plus* Patanjali, he began to envision a new center, metaphorically east of Dublin and west of Delhi where, just conceivably, the center might hold after all.

※

"He was silly like us," Auden wrote of Yeats, though privately he suspected the great Yeats was not like us but even sillier. "Silly"— escapist, inconsequential—has rendered the common verdict on those who go chasing spiritual wild geese in the East. When Isherwood published *My Guru and His Disciple* (1980), the reviewer in *The Economist* lectured that Isherwood might amuse himself with his Swami, but it was not religion and was in fact of no public consequence. When Allen Ginsberg sought out holy men in India (invariably inquiring: "Care to take some drugs?"), he was mocked as a figure of fun. If only they had been importing Russian communism instead of Indian religion to America, the charge would have been not silliness, but sedition.

The Trojan Horse was not innocent, though, and more got smuggled in disguised under Eastern spirituality than those of a political bent noticed. The modern political order, the social sphere itself, depends upon carefully constructed distinctions that types like Yeats and Isherwood, in their exotic enthusiasms, tended to blur. Early in the century, mainline churches had been a prop and reinforcement of the public order, but Yeats turned religion into a private affair. As for Isherwood's religion, *The Economist* charged, it was too nearsighted to tell the difference between a subjective feeling and an objective significance or even between what was religious and what secular. If these distinctions—public versus private, subjective versus objective, secular versus religious—all collapsed, then a delicate social balance might topple over into every-man-for-himself anarchy.

For centuries, Europeans had believed that Indian religion was just such an anarchy. Religion in India was everywhere, and nowhere: a seeming infinity of faiths was practiced there, and yet, until recently, there was no word for *faith*, no word for *religion*, and in all the many languages no word even to suggest "Hinduism." Evidently religion was so messed in with politics and economics that (except for the Muhammadans) it did not merit a separate name for itself. Industrious Victorian scholars began, on behalf of India, to organize the myriad bizarre practices into a single, tidy faith that a great religion should be. Sir Monier Monier-Williams's popular handbook *Hinduism* (1877) gave that national religion a name, so that Hindus were no longer simply the people living on the far side of the Indus River. But Monier-Williams's *Hinduism* had its problems. It described a mighty two-branched religion—a majestic creed, Brahmanism, and its popular expression, Hinduism—where his predecessors had seen something more than religion (philosophy) and something less (superstition). Monier-Williams had to acknowledge, in fact, that Brahmanism and Hinduism "are not names recognized by the natives." Despite such obstacles, by the end of the nineteenth century Oxford professors like Monier-Williams and the great Max Müller had established a Hinduism to neatly parallel Christianity, and Indian leaders like Ram Mohun Roy began promoting it as a spur to national consciousness. Yet this official Hinduism concealed an older outlook wildly dissimilar from the Christian worldview, and western discontents were magnetically attracted to its "functioning anarchy" (as John Kenneth Galbraith later described India itself) to counter an overregulated existence back home.

India's religious appeal to people like Yeats and Isherwood was exactly this, that experience in it appeared organized and categorized in ways different from Christianity and in the West at large. Christian theology categorizes one as either orthodox or heretical, but in India Madame Blavatsky could be happily both and neither. Europe's politicized geography divides between important centers and the negligible periphery, but in provincial southeast India Mirra Richard could imagine herself at the center of a world drama. Once past the West's distinction between the active male and the domestic female, Madeleine Slade could cease being a misfit and become a public figure in India. Of course, these people were privileged foreigners, exempt from the rules in India, but the rules were also different. Subjective or objective? Center or periphery? Masculine or feminine? Jung phrased India's appeal to a westerner in a bon mot: "Not the niggardly western *either/or*, but the eastern *both/and*." Indian religion's combination of philosophy and superstition did seem to present disaffected westerners with a new door when all the old ones had become stuck shut.

※

Yet upon all those western distinctions between public and private rests an even more crucial one—the separation between politics and religion. *Both/and*? If religion were joined to politics, surely that would signal now, as in the past, that fanaticism, jihads, and persecution would soon begin.

Yeats's and Isherwood's detour into Hinduism predates that late-twentieth-century bombshell explosion—the "return" of fundamentalism, the relinking of politics with religion—that caught a generation of intellectuals off guard. In Isherwood's era, most intellectuals confidently expected the sea of faith to dry up and themselves to reclaim the empty lakebeds. Gilles Kepel, of the Institute of Political Studies in Paris, has described this mid-century attitude of secularism triumphant:

At that time it was thought—mistakenly—that secularization was a straightforward, unstoppable process in the
Muslim world as elsewhere. . . . [Religions like Islam or
Hinduism were] regarded as an outmoded belief held only
by rural dotards and backward reactionaries. While this
impression may have had some basis in reality, it owed
much to the fact that certain secularized intellectuals had a
virtual monopoly on opinion forming, and projected on to
society as a whole the changes that had taken place in themselves.

Kepel titled his book, aptly, *The Revenge of God* (1994).
Secularized intellectuals could err about the fundamentalists, of
course, but they could hardly be mistaken about themselves.
Progressive, well-educated Americans or Europeans reinvolving
themselves in religion belongs to a surreal scenario—something
out of *Rhinoceros* or *The Night of the Living Dead*, where the haters
of a thing become its exponents. Yet from an unusual perspective,
from a parade of sophisticated westerners like Besant, Yeats,
Forster, and Isherwood drawn toward India (a country that has
never been secular, though Nehru tried his damnedest), do we
glimpse something nobody anticipated: a revived, liberal interest
in a religiously undergirded society. Eventually that interest
would ramify politically nearly as much as the fundamentalists'
so-called return did.

Since midcentury, nonpoliticians have influenced American
politics by applying religious ideals to the civic realm, thereby
confusing the utilitarian and the utopian. In the 1960s civil rights
leaders like the Reverend Martin Luther King Jr. put Gandhi's non-
parliamentary, religious model to political use here. Similarly, not
in Congress but through a personal morality applied to the policies
of a nation, did the anti–Vietnam War opposition originate. (One
antiwar poster, confusing the private and the public, showed
female singers like Joan Baez urging other women to "Say Yes to
Boys Who Say No [to the draft].") Outside America, the "velvet rev-

olution" in Czechoslovakia or Mandela's victory in South Africa illustrate how moral and even Gandhian considerations have rewritten politics. All this is far away from and yet oddly reenacts what Yeats and Isherwood did in their Indian religious studies when they substituted for the *either/or* divisions of secular/religious, public/private, and serious/pleasurable a *both/and.*

Gandhi surely would have approved of Yeats and Isherwood, had he heard of them. The *either/or*s of modern culture they disliked he considered the intellectual equivalent of England's divide-and-rule policy in India. Gandhi was more "Hindu" in his desire to join opposites and to reconcile the irreconcilable. His list of the "Seven Social Sins," for example—

> politics without principle,
> wealth without work,
> commerce without morality,
> pleasure without conscience,
> education without character,
> science without humanity,
> and worship without sacrifice

—is a religious challenge to the clear-cut secular understanding of modern society. After all, the point of politics is to maneuver without "theological" constraints; the point of financial success is to unshackle one from manual labor (which is what Gandhi meant by work); the point of modern economics is to operate by rational logic; etc. Gandhi was as much a revolutionary against the conventions of modern thought as he was against British rule, which in the end made him all the more slippery as an opponent. The English knew how to deal with an insurrectionist armed to the teeth but not with someone claiming the weapon he carried was his love for them. Indeed, what is any westerner schooled in Locke and Jefferson to make of Gandhi's claim that his political activities merely furthered his quest for religious salvation? Gandhi redefined spiritual faith, though, to include even atheists who make a Truth of their atheism, and so widened religion to include the whole secular realm, which challenged the British who claimed to rule it through a disinterested, neutral logic.

At first nobody understood what Gandhi was doing—nobody. When G. K. Gokhale, his political mentor, read Gandhi's Home Rule pamphlet *Hind Swaraj* (1909)—with its rejection of newspapers, machinery, and even doctors in favor of a return to the Simple Life—Gokhale shook his head: "This," he declared, "reads like the work of a fool." Likewise Lord Ampthill received what seemed a fool's missive when Gandhi proposed that since English capitalists exploited India, England should simply abandon capitalism. The better part of a century later, after King's, Mandela's, and scores of others' emulating it, Gandhi's foolishness stands revealed for what it was. If the oppressor—in this case, the British—controls the government, the army, and the economy, then do an end run around them through what they cannot control: spirituality, the claim to a higher truth. Before Gandhi, religious leaders like Swami Vivekenanda and Sri Aurobindo had argued that, though the English governed the country, Indians true to their religious traditions were masters of the subcontinent in the ways that mattered most. But Gandhi dared to reinterpret religion—his version was too Christian to be entirely Hindu and too Hindu to be Christian— to incorporate westernized politics, and in doing so, made the Indians masters of the subcontinent, period.

Yeats's and Isherwood's spiritual quests in "India"—when multiplied by the tens of thousands who shared their interests—helped open the political sphere in the West to nonpolitical considerations. Gandhi's version of Hindu *moksha*, or salvation, required a westernized political involvement in a social cause. Something peculiar appears at work here: as religious and political ideologies traveled west to east and back again, they often mutated into each other. In America, the same religious-into-political twist occurred when Martin Luther King Jr. took up the spiritual example of the Mahatma: a preacher in the South invokes a religious saint from

India, and it lights a stick of political dynamite in America. Was there a glitch in the translation?

Smugglers know better than scholars that to pass contraband over the border, it must be made to appear innocuous. In the modern West, where political considerations are all-important, Yeats and Isherwood could hobnob with Swamis and translate Hindu gospels precisely because it didn't matter. How much more danger King would have risked had he been smuggling into America not the Mahatma but Marx or Mao. In India, by contrast, the political has traditionally occupied a poor second place, behind the religious. Or rather, politics operated within its own self-contained amoral sphere, which allowed Indians to copy foreigners politically without—so they believed—its polluting their other social interactions. From a Hindu viewpoint, Gandhi could promulgate western political reforms to his heart's content, so long as he wasn't smuggling Christianity in with them. Yet in both cases—with religion in America; with politics in India—the back door indirectly led into the main parlor of action.

When Yeats translated the Upanishads, just as when Gandhi brought Marx or Ruskin into the subcontinent, they snuck in plain wrapping more explosive materials than the West's political authorities or India's religious guardians would knowingly have let enter. For as Yeats, Isherwood, and King carried on their "innocuous" conversation with India, the meaning of religion in the West subtly changed. And sometimes, unexpectedly, the meaning of politics changed along with it.

And so the dream of an East-West coupling of the spirit concludes, with unanticipated political ramifications. It had first dawned on that crystalline winter's morning, a century and a half ago. The original dreamer of the dream had sallied out into the woods, to enjoy a retreat of quiet and seclusion, only to have his tranquillity abruptly imposed upon. He looked up startled, for there—in the middle of Massachusetts!—were Indian coolies, breaking up the ice on the pond. The stirrings of a global economy had interrupted his calm, for those chunks of ice would travel in insulated merchant ships to Madras and Bombay and Calcutta, to refreshen the torpid summer there. Watching this interruption, the man reflected that he had beat those workers to this crossing of cultures, for the book at his side was India's great religious classic. And reflecting thus, Henry David Thoreau scribbled in his journal:

> In the morning I bathe my intellect in the stupendous and cosmological philosophy of the Bhagvat Geeta. . . . I lay down the book and go to my well for water, and lo! there I met the servant of the Brahman . . . come to draw water for his master, and our buckets as it were grate together in the same well. The pure Walden water is mingled with the sacred water of the Ganges.

CHAPTER 5
Spirituality's Back Door

Hollywood recycles its successes, retreading its movie classics into new box office attractions. The remake follows the basic story line, but the actors are different, the settings changed, and the moral updated to suit fashion. Remember E. M. Forster's confession to the maharajah, in which he stuttered and stammered and finally revealed his homosexuality? Nearly two decades later Hollywood restaged that scene—not in a movie this time, but in actual life—where an English novelist confesses to a Hindu authority figure things he would hardly say to his closest friends. In the early '20s, an Englishman like Forster was shy and embarrassed to reveal his sexual interests. By the late '30s, though, the Englishman in Hollywood hesitated, embarrassed to confess that what interested him was, well, religion.

Christopher Isherwood's "confession" took place on August 4, 1939. The setting was a pleasant house in a cozy neighborhood in Hollywood. That bungalow at 1946 Ivar Avenue was so American wholesome-clean that apple pies should have been popping out of the oven and kids trooping in to do homework and father returning from work whistling. Not exactly the setting one would expect for a famous English novelist's visiting an Indian holy man. In the yard a small incongruous Hindu temple, complete with an onion-shaped dome, indicated, though, that the bungalow housed the Vedanta Society. More out of place than that Oriental onion dome, Isherwood thought, was his being there.

At thirty-five Isherwood, so critics said, represented the future of the English novel. All his attitudes, his every position, was à la mode: he was a leftist in politics, satirical and avant-garde in the arts; and dismissive in matters religious for which he had no use, thank you very much. Other celebrated English intellectuals had preceded him to Swami Prabhavananda's door: Aldous Huxley and Gerald Heard and now Isherwood were demanding answers to questions that, in a tranquil age, would never have occurred to them. But the age was not tranquil, with Europe tumbling head-long into war. Isherwood felt terribly uncomfortable, though, approaching his interview with Swami P. (as Prabhavananda was affectionately called). He could hear his friends back in England snickering, "Chris has gone to Hollywood to be a yogi." But his friends, though perplexed, would have trusted that Isherwood was acting honorably, even in investigating religion, which he had hitherto disdained. The person sneering at him, Isherwood realized, was himself.

As he entered Prabhavananda's study, Isherwood was struck by its air of quiet calm. He loathed it; give him the tumultuous real world any day. Swami's appearance was at least reassuring, though. He looked quite boyish at forty-six; Isherwood, eleven years his junior, took pride in his own boyish-looking appearance. In height Swami P. was quite short, which was to the good. Isherwood, short himself (Virginia Woolf likened him to a jockey), felt avuncular whenever he met anyone even shorter. Swami smoked cigarettes, and Isherwood, a chain-smoker, felt put at ease by the unchurchiness of Swami's tobacco-clouded study. (Cigarettes dangled from everyone's lips then; the first half of the twentieth century was almost invisible, veiled in a bluish blur of tobacco smoke.)

A social meeting, in Isherwood's experience, was a congenial battle—a battle of wits. One was a little vain and the other person was a little vain, and by quietly, cleverly stepping on his vanity, you felt your own superiority as he let out an ouch. But this Swami Prabhavananda was so uncompetitive, so unmindful of his position, that he made Isherwood feel vain, like an overdressed woman wrapped in boas. Whenever he felt uncomfortable in a social situation, Isherwood playacted some scene, and now as the movie unreeled in his head, he imagined himself in the role of a contrite seeker approaching a holy man. Isherwood started the interview by doubting whether he could follow any religious path, because the life he led was. . . . He trailed off, leaving the vague sense that there are dark things Swamis know not of.

Prabhavananda had encountered the same false contrition a hundred times before. He offered a metaphor about compromised existence and the soul's purity despite it, which was as new to Isherwood as it was trite in Hinduism: "You must be like the lotus that floats on dirty water. The lotus flower is never wet."

Okay, round one for the Swami. Isherwood then objected, suppose religion demands too much? Suppose he tried and failed and became discouraged. Wouldn't he be worse off than if he had never begun?

"There is no failure in the search for God," Prabhavananda answered. "Every step you take is a positive advance."

God! There was that word. Isherwood, his mask of the contrite sinner slipping, said he simply detested the word *God*.

"You can just as well say 'The Self' or 'Nature,'" Swami P. suggested, luxuriating in another drag on his cigarette. The smoke slowly dissolving seemed like doubts fading in air.

Damn it, the interview was proceeding too smoothly. Isherwood blurted out, tactlessly, that Hinduism had always struck him as silly, superstitious nonsense.

Prabhavananda broke out laughing. "And now you have fallen into the trap?"

Isherwood's earlier reference to "the life he was leading" carried conventional undertones of worldly ambition, of materialism, and of compromises—with maybe a whiff of alcoholic vapors from the occasional drink or two. That is what Isherwood meant, but he also meant something more specific. He posed his next question cautiously and waited to hear whether the Swami's answer would be satisfactory. Of course it would *not* be. In which case there would be no point in their ever seeing each other again. Isherwood asked: can one lead a spiritual life if, that is, uh—while having a sexual relationship with a young man?

He awaited the icy blast. But Prabhavananda failed even to appear decently shocked. He simply said, "You must try to see him [the young man] as the young Krishna."

Krishna who? But Isherwood didn't need to know who Krishna was exactly (maybe a sort of Hindu Jesus?). What was important was that the monk's response had not damned his kind of relationship. The earthly beauty that attracted Isherwood to the boy was related to, and might even lead into, the divine beauty of what's his name—Krishna. Isherwood, far from discouraged, found Swami's answer exhilarating, not at all like the sour puritanism he'd anticipated. And Prabhavananda had only said *try*. When they weren't in bed together, that would be the time to try. Isherwood departed from his interview thinking, "Well, why not?"

The answer to that question seems obvious. A person should be loved for his own sake, not because he is the doppelgänger of some deity. But in Isherwood's case there was a better reason why not. From adolescence on, he had been violently antireligious. As for Hinduism, he hardly considered it a religion at all but some primitive superstition. Sensible people (e.g., himself) did not waste their time thinking about—about Krishna. If he followed the Swami's advice and tried it, he was sure to succeed in one thing—in making himself an object of ridicule to sensible people, including himself. *Chris has gone to Hollywood to become a yogi?*

Now, some threescore years later, it is hard to understand why Isherwood felt such trepidation at expressing a little curiosity about Hinduism. Everybody at the end of the twentieth century knows something about eastern religions and has a friend like Isherwood who dabbles in them. The best-known religious figure in the West, besides the pope, is probably the Dalai Lama; Zen has become nearly as American as apple pie. The leap into the abyss Isherwood felt he was making would seem today hardly more startling than taking a stroll around the corner.

Threescore years ago, though, Isherwood's "conversion"—if that's what it was—provoked shock and, mainly, disapproval. That a Bright Young Talent of the '30s should turn religious was incomprehensible. It would have been bad enough had he become (horrors!) a Catholic, but to become (horrors multiplied!) a yogi-man was sheer insanity. A few years later, after England went to war with Germany, Parliament deliberated what punitive action to impose upon its delinquent yogi-man basking in the California sunshine. One parliamentary motion proposed banning any movie for which Isherwood wrote the script from showing in the United Kingdom. Even his friends who should have understood did not sympathize. Auden, with his own deepening Catholicism, declared when Isherwood disclosed about Swami P. and Vedanta: "All this heathen mumbo jumbo—I'm sorry, my dear, but it just *won't do.*" Forster, with his own passage to India, was pleased Isherwood had discovered Indian culture but puzzled by what he had plucked from it: religion? Nobody saw that Isherwood was not in fact converting to a bizarre faith but fumbling and feeling his way through despair and in the process redefining what religion was.

⌖

Religion? Isherwood was more astonished than Forster ever could be to find himself dabbling in religion. When he was growing up, merely the mention of certain words—*God, savior, heaven, soul, redemption, love*—would cause young Christopher to grind his teeth in rage. Religion to him was Blake's Nobodaddy, God as a tyrannical father figure in heaven whose sole redeeming feature was that he did not exist. Religion was the ten-times-Ten Commandments of *thou shall not.* Everything anybody might conceivably want to do was a sin to do. Christopher delighted in stories about misbehaving clergymen copulating like rabbits.

Where did such loathing come from? Isherwood, born in 1904, came of age as the Great War ended, too young to have fought, old enough to witness the subsequent dreary disillusionment. He heard only the leaden echo of the golden echo, of the politicians' and clergymen's patriotic rhetoric that had sung young men to their graves. Among the dead on the battlefield was Christopher's own father, slain in 1914, near Ypres. Isherwood passed considerable time during his youth holed up writing stories about an imaginary world he called Mortmere, creating a fantasy-shelter from the world of war and war rhetoric in which his father had perished. Later, in his autobiography *Lions and Shadows*, he described this fantasy world at length but, curiously, never acknowledged what the word itself meant. *Mort* in French is death, *mère* is mother, and in fact Isherwood had an ambivalent, troubled relationship with his mother. His father was dead, he secretly wished his mother the same, and he inhabited a world of fantasy. Had Jung met this troubled adolescent expressing such animosity to Christianity, he might well have predicted the boy was destined to become strangely religious. If Mortmere named Christopher's private universe, he also had a name for the so-called real world of soldiers, politicians, clergymen: the Enemy.

Even Cambridge University, in which he enrolled in 1923—Forster's beloved Cambridge—was part of the Enemy, too. Only after Isherwood left Cambridge, though, did his real trouble begin. Mortmere evaporated into air as he was forced to live and support himself in the real world—could he but figure out how to. We were young then, Isherwood said of himself and his literary friends, and we thought the answer to every problem was *le mot juste*. But *le mot juste* did not pay anything, unless one were a writer. Isherwood wrote his novel *All the Conspirators* (1928), and it sold approximately three hundred copies. So much for supporting oneself by writing. In desperation, he enrolled in medical school, where he couldn't distinguish among the Pharyngo-, the Epi-, the Cerato-, and the Hypo-bronchials, or make a decent dissection, or prepare a good slide, and he was, he suspected, the stupidest member of the class. Medical school was Cambridge all over again, only worse. The Enemy had won.

In the corner into which Isherwood had painted himself, his sexuality suddenly pointed to an exit sign. He had a wealthy gay uncle, and he began hinting to this uncle that his own tastes were perhaps not so different. In exchange for listening to his uncle's stories—one concerned a guardsman paid not to bathe for a month before they had sex—Isherwood received a small monthly allowance from him. No sooner did the allowance begin than Auden invited him to join him in Berlin. Berlin in the 1920s was the avant-garde arts capital of Europe; no less important to Isherwood, homosexual life was the freest there (though the young men sometimes charged). Isherwood liked the blond boys, but the Blond Beast appalled him. Living through the Nazis' rise to power sobered him, and his new novels set against that background—*Mr. Norris Changes Trains* (1935) and *Goodbye to Berlin* (1939)—sold far more than three hundred copies. Twenty years later, *Goodbye to Berlin* would be made into a successful play, *I Am a Camera*, and twenty years after that into as successful a movie, *Cabaret*, in which Liza Minnelli dangles her red fingernails and lisps, "Decadence." Herr Issyvoo, as his Berlin landlady calls Isherwood in the novel, was to find himself famous in the real world. When Somerset Maugham introduced Isherwood to Virginia Woolf, he announced: this young man holds the future of the English novel in his hands.

With that apotheosis before Queen Virginia, a brief synopsis of Isherwood's formation might conveniently conclude. But history does not conclude and was in those years anything but convenient. History, for Isherwood, was the fact that by the late 1930s Berlin was a place where he could no longer live. History was also the fact that if he joined the British Army he might kill his German lover, who had been drafted into the German Army. The alternative to possibly killing the person you loved—and almost everyone is the person someone loves, Isherwood, no great reasoner, reasoned—was to become a pacifist. Unable to live under the Nazi regime he detested and unwilling to live amid the English establishment he disliked, Isherwood immigrated to America. Had "history" not intervened, Isherwood might like Forster before him have become a literary fixture in England, a grand old man of letters in spite of himself. Instead . . .

Instead, by 1939 he was a not-so-young man in despair and destined to become more so. Arriving in America in that year he discovered he was unable to write and he lacked any other professional skill. Having emigrated permanently from England, he was a man without a country, while fascism and war threatened to extinguish the civilized norms by which he lived. As he was preparing to leave England, Czechoslovakia was partitioned, and a friend remarked, "That's the end of Europe as we wanted it." Isherwood agreed, "Yes. That's all behind me now." Everything was, in fact, behind him, and nothing seemed in front. Soon after Isherwood first arrived, one New Yorker hearing his English accent told him, "Here you'll find sympathy in the dictionary and everything else you need at the drugstore." When, after months of talks with Swami Prabhavananda, Isherwood decided to move into the Vedanta Center, it was a last straw to clutch at before being blown like dust across the desolate wastes.

Experiencing both longing and loathing, he felt drugged, as the willpower to escape ebbed from him. Somnambulantly he crossed the Temple courtyard and pulled the bell chain. Slowly the forbidding door opened. Lurking in the shadows inside, shadows themselves in their cowls, were the Hindu monks. It took only a moment for them to strip him of his clothes and forcibly robe him. He stammered the irrevocable vows and, now a monk himself, he could never leave the Temple grounds—never live free again.

Such was the comic fantasy Isherwood amused himself with that February day in 1943, as he moved into the Swami's temple complex on Ivar Avenue. The reality, though, would fail to live up, or down, to Isherwood's grade-B movie fantasy.

Hardly a fortresslike monastery, the Vedanta complex spread itself over the lawn—cheerful, Southern California eclectic. Three neighboring bungalows, built in different styles and bought at different times, wedded Hinduism to Hollywood. The domed temple Prabhavananda had erected abutted a Spanish-style hacienda. During the war, two soldiers stumbling past it thought they were even drunker than they were. One soldier turned to the other, exclaiming, "Boy! The guy who built that thing sure had one screwy wife!"

Inside, the human ambience recalled to Isherwood the Quakers with whom he'd worked just before the war: the same considerate tone in conversation, the same politeness, the same attempts at wholesome humor. The dozen or so men and women who lived there would furnish Isherwood his most continuous relationships over the next forty years while, after moving out of the center two and a half years later, he careened from one house, lover, job, to another. Isherwood had stumbled into not only the faith he never wanted but also the family stability he'd always hoped to escape.

Isherwood was the life of that little Vedanta family. Washing up the dishes after supper at the center, he'd improvise some inane limerick—

With many a mudra and mantra, with mutterings
and mouthings and moans,
The rishi flew into a tantrum, and rattled the
avatar's bones.
After reams of ridiculous ritual, after offerings
of ointments and eggs,
The cripples were kissed by Rasputin, and recovered
the use of their legs.

—that had the women in the kitchen (an easy audience) teary with laughter. As to what Isherwood actually did in the temple, besides the dishes, the silly jingle describes it rather well. He did reams of ridiculous ritual; he recited his mantra; he performed mudras (ritualized hand gestures to focus concentration); he meditated. In addition, he worked on translating the Bhagavad Gita with Prabhavananda, edited the Vedanta Society publication, wrote Somerset Maugham about his misuse of the Upanishads in *The Razor's Edge*, and took on errands like burning the trash and driving into Los Angeles to get Prabhavananda's watch repaired. Exhausted after one such day, Isherwood complained to his diary, "This is what they call an escape from the world!"

What did Isherwood, the accomplished sensualist, find appealing in it? We know the answer. He filled column after column of the center's magazine explaining what an ordinary American may gain from Vedanta (as Prabhavananda's variety of Hinduism is called). Every action, even washing the dishes, can become a sacred ritual if done in the right spirit, Isherwood pointed out; every task, even burning the trash, can either pass in a sleepy daydream or heighten awareness, depending on the person's attitude doing it. When Gerald Heard introduced Isherwood to Vedanta, he called it "intentional living." In intentional living, Heard explained, you maintain a moment-to-moment vigilance over your every action, even over every thought, since each one will either retard or advance your relationship to "this thing." By "this thing" Heard meant, more or less, what D. H. Lawrence had meant by "the X" (and what bumpkins who are not afraid of the word mean by God). Isherwood was fascinated. Intentional living is to everyday life what plot is to the novel: each provides a larger schema that hyper-charges the ordinary details that fit in it. Of course the novelist labors at his plot only for a limited number of hours; the "intentional liver," the Vedantist, would need to be conscious and alert every waking moment of every single day. That prospect both appealed to and appalled Isherwood.

In 1943 Isherwood had moved into the Vedanta Center on Ivar Avenue for the usual reasons one is moved to do such things. He hoped that working at intentional living all day long, in the company of like-minded souls, would enable him to do what he could never do on his own. Isherwood was called a monk during this period, inaccurately, since he wore no robes and took no vows; yet not inappropriately, since he was attempting what monks attempt, including sexual abstinence. The effort did not agree with him—though spiritual exercises are not necessarily meant to be agreeable. As for the rituals at the temple, the truth was, they bored him. Yet even as he filled his diary jotting, "Boredom. Blankness . . . resentment," something ineffable, unnameable about the temple life compelled him.

After he moved out of the Vedanta Center in 1945, whole days might pass, even weeks, when Isherwood scarcely thought of the temple or Prabhavananda. But then suddenly he would jump into his car and drive straight to Ivar Avenue. Though the distance in miles was insignificant, he felt himself crossing a border into another country. The temple added another realm to his existence—the way dreams are another realm, even if forgotten in the morning. When Isherwood suffered a catastrophe, usually amorous, he had sympathetic friends, but their sympathy seemed only to make it worse. Instead, he would go to Swami P., with whom he did not discuss his sexual problems, and there, in his consoling presence, endure or outlive difficulties that no direct remedy could cure.

Isherwood's departure from the temple in 1945 can look, from the outside, like a smooth downward slide from divinity to decadence. During the late '40s, Huxley and Heard thought it their duty to inform Swami about Isherwood's alcoholic-drenched promiscuity. But Prabhavananda merely rebuked the tattletales. "Why don't you pray for him?" When other devotees complained about Isherwood's "naughty" novels, Prabhavananda roared in his Bengali accent, "Is it *warse* than Shakespeare?" In Prabhavananda Isherwood had found the friendly, protective father he'd barely known. Isherwood valued the Swami, for being in his presence was almost like a form of belief for him. It hardly mattered whether he lived at the temple or not; as long as he enjoyed the

Swami's company, Isherwood absorbed subliminally what he needed from religion without having to name that need.

Vedanta was, however, but half Isherwood's story during the '40s and '50s, and the other half was of such a glittering surface that some people may wonder why he bothered with Vedanta at all. Isherwood was also writing for the major movie studios and, otherwise, speeding merrily down the fast lane. Earlier he had fantasized about meeting Greta Garbo, but she now came visiting so often Isherwood hid under the kitchen table to avoid her interruptions. Earlier Charlie Chaplin had seemed a figure out of mythology, but in Hollywood Isherwood was a regular at Chaplin's house (at least until, too drunk, he urinated on Chaplin's sofa; their friendship had to dry out, too). His artistic friends in Hollywood numbered Bertolt Brecht and Thomas Mann and Igor Stravinsky. Isherwood's time in Southern California looks, from the outside, like one long picnic. One actual picnic may suggest, symbolically, that half of his life to which his writings on Vedanta (or elsewhere) never allude.

Isherwood's hostile critics in England should have had this ammo: Madrid had just fallen, Hitler occupied Czechoslovakia, and in Hollywood Isherwood was going on a picnic. The movie-star contingent of the picnic included Garbo, with raw carrots for her vegetarian diet tied to her trousers, Charlie Chaplin, and the beautiful Paulette Goddard in a south-of-the-border outfit. The picnic's brains were Isherwood, Huxley, and the philosopher Bertrand Russell. India was represented by Annie Besant's godson, Krishnamurti, surrounded by ladies arrayed in elegant saris. As Krishnamurti's group began boiling rice, they suddenly froze. A strange man was pointing a gun at them. The gun pointer, evidently some sort of sheriff, barked, "What the hell's going on here?" He glared at Bertrand Russell and Isherwood, demanding, "Don't anybody in this gang know how to read?" Well, yes and no, since they had failed to read the NO TRESPASSING sign. Aldous Huxley, cool and composed, introduced the sheriff to Greta Garbo, Paulette Goddard, and Mr. Charlie Chaplin, and waited for the galoot to stutter his apologies and beg for autographs. The sheriff's little eyes squinted suspiciously. "Is that so? Well, I've seen every movie they ever made, and none of them stars belong in this outfit. Get out of here, you tramps," he snarled. Only after sheepishly repacking their gear and slinking away did they regain enough composure to joke about the newspaper splash it could have made:

MASS ARREST IN HOLLYWOOD

Greta Garbo, Paulette Goddard, Charlie Chaplin, Aldous Huxley, Lord Bertrand Russell, Krishnamurti, and Christopher Isherwood Taken into Custody.

Fame, fortune, and fun—and yet how little they ultimately satisfied Isherwood. He more often consorted with earnest seekers and scrubbed souls asking the meaning of life, drab companions that in England the sophisticated young Isherwood would have shunned like the plague. What virus had he caught in California?

At moments of dejection, when bored or baffled by the Hindu "mumbo jumbo," Isherwood would hearten himself by thinking that he stood on a human frontier. "To live the synthesis of East and West is the most valuable kind of pioneer work I can imagine," he confided to his diary. To go, intellectually, where few of his cultural background had ever gone; to live, emotionally, in the white area of unmarked experience—that was the brave challenge Isherwood imagined himself accepting, and set next to it, dull cocktail parties with starlets sank to nothingness.

And then, too, perhaps Isherwood had no choice. Arriving in America, he had suffered a writer's block about the size of the Empire State Building. He blamed it on having lost his political faith. In 1942, he applied for conscientious-objector status, but as he filled out the 4E application form, he felt he was a liar. He needed to present himself as an idealist with clear-cut principles, whereas he merely intuited that pacifism might be right for him personally. Unlike the exemplary Mrs. Besant, who though she might change her mind daily had always known her mind, he felt an uncertainty about his position that propelled him into that uncharted territory where western intellectual confidence ends. More than Annie ever did, he desperately needed to find new ground in the Wild East. After Arthur Koestler lost his faith in Marxism, he traveled to India to mine new values—and extracted nothing, false gold. But if Isherwood found in Vedanta or Hinduism only bogus treasure, he would be in bad shape.

Descartes's experiment in the seventeenth century of doubting everything had never extended beyond an intellectual exercise. Three centuries later Isherwood was living out Descartes's experiment in broad daylight. Doubt was his meat and uncertainty was his drink, and he was in a strange land. It may well have required three centuries of Cartesian doubt turning in on itself to produce a person like Isherwood, so cultivated and yet so directionless, who had clutched at Vedanta with determination and desperation without even knowing what it was.

※

And what exactly is Vedanta? Take the ancient *Vedic* scriptures and add *anta,* the Sanskrit word for *end,* and you get Vedanta. At the end of the Vedas you come to the Upanishads, Hinduism at its most "philosophic." The Vedanta exported to the West was thus a Hinduism cleansed of superstition and most rituals, with the camphor and coconuts removed (and thus a Hinduism many Hindus might not recognize). The Vedanta Order, of which Prabhavananda was a monk and Isherwood a follower, dates back not to the ancient Vedic scriptures as its name might suggest, but only to the late nineteenth century, when it was founded by disciples of Sri Ramakrishna.

Ramakrishna (1836–1886) suggests to many Westerners a sort of Hindu Saint Francis, half child and half sage. To his followers he evokes something more, and many believe he was an avatar, a human embodiment of divinity on earth. In the nineteenth century when two celebrated Indian sages cross-examined him and first announced he was the godhead, Ramakrishna replied humorously, "Just fancy. Well, I'm glad it's not a disease." In his biography of him, *Ramakrishna and His Disciples* (1965), Isherwood hems and haws and skirts this vexing question but finally states, "I believe, or am at least strongly inclined to believe, that he was what his disciples declared that he was." Really? Was the worldly author of the Berlin Stories declaring that a man who had died a mere eighteen years before Isherwood was born had been God puttering about on earth?

Isherwood was obviously uncomfortable making the kind of assertion that Madame Blavatsky casually tossed off between puffs on her cigarette. What a pity that she had not known of Ramakrishna, for he might have validated her wild thesis about living, divine Mahatmas. Ramakrishna, however, had heard of Madame Blavatsky. He observed of the Theosophists that those "who go about making disciples belong to a very inferior level. So also do those who want occult powers . . . to report what a person says in a far-off land [Madame Blavatsky's favorite clairvoyant trick]. It is very hard for such people to have pure love for God." If Ramakrishna was a divinity, he spoke very sensibly; Madame Blavatsky, if she was a mere person (she liked to hint otherwise), proclaimed in the deep voice of an oracle. It does seem ironical that Madame Blavatsky's Theosophists, educated and worldly, combined western and eastern religions into such a childish, magical concoction that it fell through the crevices of the modern world. By contrast, the naive, uneducated Ramakrishna forged a version of Hinduism so independent of the miraculous that it could be exported successfully to the West.

Isherwood's book about his own dear Swami, *My Guru and His Disciple* (1980), requires no more suspension of everyday credibility than does the newspaper. Indeed, only one extraordinary incident occurs in it. Prabhavananda gave an ailing disciple, once, a drop of Ganges water to aid her indigestion. Devoid of supernatural extravaganzas, Isherwood's beliefs are thus relatively easy to describe.

Vedanta won over the skeptical Isherwood by transporting religion from heaven, from clouds and majesty, down to earth, where he could finger and inspect it. Instead of beliefs one must either accept or reject, Vedanta supplied a working hypothesis, namely, that the godhead is knowable, in fact no different from one's deepest, truest nature. Vedanta then required a would-be disciple like Isherwood to get some spiritual experience, using techniques like meditation, to test that hypothesis. Prabhavananda taught that what the disciple discovered for himself was his truth, even if that truth was that Vedanta was hokum. Brought up on English puritanism, Isherwood was particularly struck, beguiled, by Vedanta's lack of preoccupation with sin. The Vedantic idea of karma meant that cause and effect and not a theology of damnation determines whether someone suffers or not. Religion for Isherwood ceased to be an outré matter of times (Sundays and holidays), of special places (churches and confessionals), of special beings (a Father-God and archangels), and special metaphysics (sin and expiation): he no longer felt he would have to exit himself to attend services. Probably these points, and Vedanta itself, have lost their novelty for westerners today, but in the '40s they suddenly illumined religion for Isherwood in an unexpectedly positive light. He said of the message of Vedanta, "I heard it with an almost incredulous joy."

Isherwood was also pleased that Ramakrishna had lived not all that long ago. He knew three people who had known Ramakrishna's chief disciple, the great Vivekenanda (1863–1902), personally. He asked an old lady at the center what Vivekenanda had been like in person. "Oh, he was like a great cat," she answered, "so graceful." Christ and Buddha, Mohammed and Lao-tzu are obscured in myths, in misty antiquities. But there exist photographs of Ramakrishna and documentary records of what he daily said and did. Max Weber's description of civilization over the long ages, progressing from magic rituals to charismatic heroes to bureaucratic rules, seemed compressed into the three short generations separating Ramakrishna from Isherwood. Ramakrishna's divinity had yielded to Vivekenanda's charismatic charm, which in turn had condensed into Prabhavananda's organizational competence—but Isherwood felt himself living in the fading light of wonder reborn. With just a faint hint of a new millennium, he concluded his biography of Ramakrishna: "How should one interpret it [the phenomenon of Ramakrishna]? How react to it? . . . Should it be taken as the starting point of a change in one's own ideas and life?" Was this what a Christian convert might have asked, living in the first century A.D.?

Isherwood, the Vedantist in Hollywood, made an odd, incongruous picture. He was a sex-crazed screenwriter working at a major studio, and yet at some level also the godhead. He was a sophisticated alumnus of Cambridge University, and the disciple of an eastern Swami. He was an agnostic, unable to profess or believe anything with certainty, and yet obsessed with religion. Perhaps his occasional allusion to the frontier, to the pioneer, was *le mot juste* after all, for never had such a combination exactly occurred before. What would come of it—what would come of him?

Most westerners know a Sanskrit word: *Om*. The sound supposedly embodies the divine as a hum rises sonorously from the throat and elongates through three syllables: *Ah-oo-mm*. Out of sheer perversity Isherwood would sometimes pronounce it *om* like *Tom* in *Uncle Tom*. He would make it a comic noise, less the chant of sages than Winnie-the-Pooh humming om-tiddily-om-pom.

Something was wrong. The truth, the awful truth, was that though Vedanta was the noble life, Isherwood suspected he was the wrong person to lead it. After he moved from the Vedanta Center, there would be mornings when he was nursing a hangover and Sinatra was crooning on the radio and Isherwood would feel waves of longing for the simple, clean life at the temple. But at least he was feeling something, he realized, while at the center he often felt nothing at all. Then his thoughts might take a dark turn. Suppose there was no greater Truth after all? Oh, would the tedious division within him never, never end? While he lived at the Vedanta Center, he had envied his friends their heedless life of the senses. Now, when he lived in Hollywood or Santa Monica, carousing at night and hungover the next morning, he often longed for the center's tranquil calm. He grew weary of arguing within himself and scribbled in his journal, "In a stormy sea there's no point in doing anything but continuing to swim. Keep going through the motions—nothing more."

To be credible, Isherwood should have been in India. His marriage of Hinduism and Hollywood was too bizarre. One fine June evening in 1945, Isherwood took Prabhavananda to a party given by the director George Cukor. Cukor was attempting to film Somerset Maugham's novel *The Razor's Edge* about a young American's quest in India, and Prabhavananda was Cukor's technical consultant on Spirit, so to speak. The beautiful actresses there were friendly to Prabhavananda, treating him like a minor colleague in show business. Their behavior changed, becoming simple and humble in his presence as they began acting the role of virtuous women who disdain artifices and vanity. They couldn't have known that in the Bengal of Prabhavananda's youth actresses were considered no better than prostitutes. Prabhavananda may have treated those famous actresses so politely because he considered them harlots, and he wanted to show that even whores were embodiments of the Divine Mother. Had they realized this, they might have exclaimed, "Why, isn't that the cutest thing you ever heard!"

Isherwood felt out of place. His sexual history should have ensured him a rightful place among the prostitutes, and here he was, more or less a damned monk. After Cukor's party, Isherwood confessed to Swami that he was having trouble with sexual abstinence. Prabhavananda patted Isherwood sympathetically. "It's a hard life," he said. "Just pray for strength, pray to become pure."

Swami Prabhavananda was so sympathetic, so nonjudgmental.

A man he and Isherwood knew was arrested for sexual solicitation in a men's john, and Prabhavananda's reaction was, "Oh, Chris, if only he hadn't got caught! Why didn't he go to some bar?" Isherwood laughed aloud at the Swami's unworldly worldliness. But tolerant though he might be, Prabhavananda still held that *all* sex must be eventually given up. He explained that one surrendered sexual activity not because it was sinful but because sexual energy (or *kundalini*), if not discharged in orgasm, can rise through the body to awaken greater awareness. "This will happen naturally as you make progress in the spiritual life," he reassured Isherwood. "The more you travel toward the north, the farther you are from the south."

The trouble was, south was where Isherwood wanted to be. Can one be too clever for his own good? By his roundabout Indian route Isherwood had reached the same tormented division that had vexed his European puritanical ancestors. When Isherwood decided to write his autobiography, he had to write it twice, *Christopher and His Kind* for the sexual memories and *My Guru and His Disciple* for the spiritual ones. He had become an internal segregationist: sexual and religious experiences were not permitted to eat and drink under the same roof. When he quit living at Ivar Avenue in 1945, he did so, he said, "for a reason which had nothing to do with the Vedanta Society." He'd met a man and wanted a relationship. But that reason had everything to do with the Vedanta Society. Vedanta satisfied only half of him, which meant that one part of himself was forever moving out and leaving the other part behind.

People often behave in a certain way because they believe that is what behavior is. Unconsciously Isherwood was enacting a new paradigm of human behavior. In Berlin he had met a well-known psychotherapist who told him, "There is only one sin: disobedience to the inner law of our own nature." Isherwood took the lesson to heart; he became Freudian Man. Indeed, the pattern of his existence came to resemble nothing so much as the psychiatric session writ large. During the psychiatric hour the patient may cry, rage, utter the unspeakable: so likewise, during periods of promiscuity, Isherwood allowed his desires to rampage uninhibited, unchecked. But just as after fifty minutes is up, the analysand abruptly composes himself and exits into the ordered world, so, after a certain time, Isherwood inhibited his sexual escapades and returned to the Vedanta Center. Isherwood's back-and-forth conduct, his alternation between Vedanta and debaucheries, mirrors the basic Freudian division of human nature, torn between moralistic superego and libidinal desires.

Isherwood prided himself that he had shed Victorian guilt, had left behind sickly remorse over what one did sexually. But had he? In his novel *A Meeting by the River* (1976) Isherwood personifies his divided temperament in two brothers—one a would-be Hindu convert, the other a homosexual literatus—but the vehemence with which Isherwood condemns the homosexual brother as selfish, caddish, and deceptive indirectly condemns that side of his own character. The critic Carolyn Heilbrun has pointed out that in Isherwood's novels the homosexual protagonists are usually betrayed by their young partners, while the characters capable of love are women. Yet this world of sad gaiety did not correspond to Isherwood's own experience, which included several fulfilling relationships and one that lasted over thirty years. Isherwood recklessly began that relationship when he was forty-six and the boy, Don Bachardy, was in his teens, as though he were living in Socrates' Athens and not America, where relations with a minor are criminal offenses. But what Isherwood did in deed, he dared not do in writing. Though he poached everything else for his novels, Isherwood evidently concluded that the longest, happiest relationship of his life was off-limits for his writing. He could live with Don Bachardy for thirty years, but he could not repeat that successful "marriage" as an aesthetic construct or ideal.

Freud had observed that many people admire one sort of person or ideal but sexually desire the opposite, and he called this division "the most prevalent form of degradation in the erotic life" (in an essay of the same name). Isherwood's Vedanta and Isherwood's sexuality never in a sense ceased degrading each other. In stepped Prabhavananda to assure Isherwood that erotic desire and spiritual striving necessarily led in opposite directions. Somewhere along the way Isherwood had forgotten his original conversation with Prabhavananda, where his love of a young man existed on the same continuum with the love of Krishna. In Isherwood's biography of him, Ramakrishna may be a god or he may be a man, but unlike all men and most gods, he was one unbothered by sexual thoughts. Isherwood as biographical narrator was hardly different from a Sunday school teacher who could not possibly think improper thoughts while in proximity to the holy. It did not occur to him to take a hint from the Master, Ramakrishna himself.

Some disciples had once decided to shock Ramakrishna. As a prank, they told him in hushed, scandalized tones about Tantric practitioners who performed sexual rites instead of religious rituals to advance their spirituality. Nothing, the pranksters thought, could be more calculated to horrify Ramakrishna than the physical body indulged in all its eroticism as a path to God. Ramakrishna reflected awhile and then said, "It is a back door. But it is a door."

It was a door Isherwood did not dare walk through. Through Swami, Isherwood had overcome a great deal, most notably his repugnance to anything to do with religion. Vedanta was like a plank that had allowed him to cross those Cartesian chasms that abjectly separate subjective and objective and one's intellect and emotions, and thus Isherwood healed within himself these splits in the personality that had troubled westerners for centuries, at least since Descartes's era. Was he doomed then to perpetuate that final division—the last duality: spirituality versus sexuality— which he needed personally to end? Perhaps instead of hovering at Prabhavananda's neat, onion-domed temple in Hollywood, Isherwood should have suffered the disorientations and reorientations of India proper. After all, in India Shiva, the god of asceticism, happens also to be the god of fertility, knowing sixty-four thousand positions for carnal intercourse.

⚜

But then in late 1963 Isherwood did take the plunge. The prospect of going to India made him so queasy he took Librium to steady his nerves.

The occasion for the trip was the centenary of Vivekenanda's birth, which Calcutta was celebrating by holding a World Parliament of Religions. Early in 1963, Prabhavananda began waging a subtle campaign to persuade Isherwood to attend, and Isherwood waged a countercampaign of evasion. But in September, his defenses momentarily weakened, he consented, which gave him three whole months to start popping pills in anticipation.

Finally the dreaded day arrived. The narrow seats on the Japan Air Lines flight to Calcutta clamped his wide western hips into a soft vise that left him practically sitting on top of Prabhavananda. Swami P. stared dreamily out the windows at the clouds, remarking, "To think that all this is Brahma and nobody realizes it!" Isherwood's thoughts were of a slightly different order as he recollected a sexual escapade he'd had the day before. His obsessing on that erotic adventure constituted a mental rebellion against the mission toward which the plane was speeding him.

He was scheduled to lecture at the Parliament of Religions and give talks to the Vedanta Society in India. The prospect of delivering "God lectures" (as he called them) sickened him. It was like George Cukor's party all over again, where he was one of the Sunday virtuous, which made him feel like a whore in bad drag. "As long as I quite unashamedly get drunk, have promiscuous sex, and write books like *A Single Man*," he thought, "I simply cannot appear before people as a sort of lay monk." For his lecture topic he chose Girish Ghosh, who had been a disciple of Ramakrishna as well as a noted dramatist, actor, and lush. When drunk, Ghosh would drive out to see Ramakrishna, and Ramakrishna, recognizing Ghosh's inebriated high spirits, would lapse into an ecstatic trance. "I wouldn't dare to claim to have one quarter of Girish's devotion," Isherwood said in his lecture, playing it for laughs. "I would not even claim to have half his capacity for drinking." The joke fell flat before the Parliament.

When all else fails, one course of action remains. Isherwood observed that the proof of a westerner's liking India was he did not get sick. Isherwood got sick. On New Year's Eve, he started shivering with the grippe. All night long he shivered, unable to sleep. Sick and alone in his room at the Vedanta Mission, he felt resentment sweep over him. He hated the Mission, he hated India, and he almost hated Prabhavananda for bringing him there. Sometimes the religious life is less than beautiful.

But even the longest night ends, and in the dawn Isherwood decided what he must do. He even rehearsed it and, having rehearsed it, was already feeling much improved when he approached Prabhavananda. "Swami—it isn't just that I'm sick. I feel awful about everything," Isherwood began. "I've made up my mind: I can't ever talk about God and religion in public again. It's impossible." Having begun, he might as well go the whole show. He questioned whether he should have anything further to do with the Vedanta Society: "I can't belong to any kind of institution—because I'm not respectable—"

Prabhavananda was bewildered. "But, Chris, how can you say that? You're almost too good. You are so frank, so good, you never tell any lie."

Isherwood continued his rehearsed speech, ignoring Swami's sympathy. "I can't stand up on Sundays in nice clothes and talk about God. I feel like a prostitute. . . . I should never have agreed to come to India. After I'd promised you I'd come, I used to wake up every morning and dread it—"

"Oh, Chris, I'm *sorry*. I shouldn't have asked you."

Isherwood was playacting, but the look in Swami's eyes was enough to break his heart. "I don't want to lose you, Chris," Prabhavananda said. Hearing this, Isherwood cheered up. He *knew* that Swami *knew* he wouldn't lose him, no matter what. Swami must be playacting too, calling his bluff.

Having thrown his tantrum, Isherwood relaxed. Later that same day, when his car stalled for a mini-eternity in a traffic jam, he displayed the patience of an angel. As Calcuttans shouted at one another in angry voices that seemed to express no real anger, he felt something like love for them. India was a most charming country after all.

Isherwood playacted his way through India. At the Vedanta Mission he would bow to even the most junior Swami. The junior Swamis were terribly embarrassed. Some tried bowing to him, but Isherwood would execute a standing jump backward, to avoid it. It was all rather comic and charming in its playacted way. But then, out of the corner of his eyes, he spied the real thing. One old Swami attracted his attention by the fervor of his chanting. As Isherwood studied him, he imagined the old Swami as a boy, just entering the monastery, and here he was an old man with his nose nearly meeting his chin. And that old man, Isherwood thought, had done a total of one thing in his life—taken Ramakrishna's teaching absolutely literally—and the result was that he had no children, no money, no fame, and was afraid of nothing in this world or the next. The old Swami's purity presented him an ideal, a possibility, but one that was, Isherwood knew, no longer possible for him.

No, Hinduism or Vedanta could not be the end of his journey. Sometimes Isherwood retired to his room at the Vedanta Mission and masturbated, not out of horniness but spite. "I feel nothing," he noted in his journal on January 5, "but the dull senseless urge to get the hell out of here. Such is my longing for escape that I'm not even nervous about the flight." Later, he reflected that his best experience in India had been reading a novel by Willa Cather.

His trip to India was a failure (so he judged). Yet one onlooker, studying Isherwood's behavior, saw in that supposed failure a quiet success. Prabhavananda observed that Isherwood failed to have a great life-changing experience in India because in him India and America, East and West, were no longer separate worlds. And, in truth, if Isherwood was not at home in India, nor was he at home in his birth-land England. He was most at ease, perhaps, not *at* but on the drive *to* the Vedanta Temple on Ivar Avenue, while the car radio blared, horns honked, and a Hindu and an Enlightenment world-view swirled together in his head. Beguiling charlatans like Madame Blavatsky or Paul Brunton could feel at home in India, for they had only to open their mouths and out spouted eastern wisdom. Isherwood's whining discomfort in India, if its syntax is straightened out, was saying something more complex and more original. His was the new voice of an almost visionary ambivalence that could hover between opposing viewpoints and combine a religious and a secular outlook. The question that had vexed Isherwood as he had exited a Europe toppling into destruction and ruin—"How does one live now?"—had eked out a response somewhere in alien India. How live? By willing to, even when you don't want to; by fudging nothing about yourself, not even what is distasteful; by holding on, if by the thinnest, barest thread, to some ideal; by accepting the discovery that Prabhavananda's spiritual goodwill to others and his own lustful attractions were two sides of the only coin you can pay for the privilege of being in the world—that's how Isherwood did it in India.

But he was in no mood while in India to recognize that his stay there had reconciled him to the difficult. The friend who drove Isherwood to the Calcutta airport grinned and said, "I suppose you'll be writing that diary all night." Isherwood did write the night through; the plane was bitterly cold, and some drunken Australians were hollering during most of the flight. Anyway, Isherwood wanted to record his impressions before they all faded away, maya, a dream. In the ghostly middle of that night, something unanticipated happened: India gave him a belated present. Later, he would joke that Vivekenanda—grateful, no doubt, for Isherwood's help in celebrating his centenary—had presented him a thank-you gift. On the airplane, out of the blue, an idea for a new novel came to him. That novel, as it turned out, would be Isherwood's final work of fiction.

On the plane the plot of the novel unfolded itself. A westerner goes to India to become a Hindu monk. The would-be monk has a literary brother, a secret homosexual whose erotic appetites are gargantuan. The two brothers meet, collide, and make their peace by a river in India. As for who the real-life models for the two brothers were, obviously they were Christopher Isherwood and Christopher Isherwood. Immediately after India, and with India as the setting, he was able to translate the two sides of his personality into the realm of art. And there they could live side by side, holy monk and gay libertine, happy together at last.

⌖

A Meeting by the River (1967) was not the first novel about a western seeker in India. In terms of popularity and sales, it pales beside Somerset Maugham's earlier *The Razor's Edge* (1944). Maugham (1874–1965), with his acute sense of the literary marketplace, intuited that after World War II audiences would lap up a novel about a spiritual quest.

The original for Maugham's hero in *The Razor's Edge*, *Time* magazine reported, was none other than Christopher Isherwood. Maugham's young hero, disoriented by modern life, and the real-life Isherwood do to some extent resemble each other: both represented a new type of individual, disaffected but idealistic, who would populate the latter twentieth century. In *The Razor's Edge*, having sped his new sort of hero to India, Maugham had trouble imagining what to do with him next. He wrote to Swami Prabhavananda inquiring, what in fact do a guru and seeker chat about? Maugham's *Razor's Edge* is a wooden work, full of shopworn hocus-pocus and wordy raptures about nirvana. Yet a general audience gobbled it up, for its first exciting taste of eastern mysticism.

Two decades later, the clouds of incense over the mystical East have dispersed and the sleights of hand disappeared in *A Meeting by the River*. The novel nonetheless falls short of Isherwood's best work, unsurprisingly, because mysticism (subjective religious interiority, that is, as opposed to Dostoevsky's or say Flannery O'Connor's depiction of religion in society) is the worst subject for drama. Isherwood's novel is interesting less for its fictional intrigue than for the new tone it strikes in representing this interior religious life.

Indeed, Isherwood can seem more mundane than any other mystic in history. Saint John of the Cross's Dark Night of the Soul has become in him broad daylight. Maugham had not really believed in the hero's "enlightenment" or nirvana on a mountaintop, which accounts for The Razor's Edge sounding so wooden now. Isherwood did not believe in them either, but he also did not believe in a religious life where such things play a part. Isherwood's achievement—startling then, less so today—was to bring mystical religion down an octave, so that it spoke in an ordinary voice. So ordinary that the difference between belief and doubt was almost indistinguishable—which is why secular moderns like himself could believe or nearly do so.

Of course all religions have lax and blasé followers, even as their ministers (rabbis, imams) exhort them to strive harder. Prabhavananda's genius was to recognize in his western devotees that everyday emotions and even absentmindedness have a place, like a pause for rest, in their religious life. Swami's easy, nonauthoritarian presence allowed Isherwood to vent his frustrations in India, and back in Los Angeles he didn't bother to hide from Prabhavananda that the Vedanta Center was really getting on his nerves. The earnest questions after the lectures irritated him; the innocuous jokes around the dinner table fell flat with a wholesome thud. The temple ceremonies too bored him with all their alien rituals—made worse by the western substitutions. (For Ramakrishna's birthday, the women of the temple presented his image a breakfast offering of bacon and eggs and left a cigarette burning in an ashtray for him.)

Irritated, bored, Isherwood decided he simply must say something. He sought out Prabhavananda and let his complaints fly. All the rules he had to follow—

There are no rules you have to follow, Swami interrupted him.

But the endless ritual services. Isherwood said that he only attended them as a duty—

"Well then, don't come to them."

That simply, Swami rubbed out the ten-times-Ten Commandments of *Thou shall* and *Thou shall not*. Isherwood felt the oppressiveness of religion lift. But unlike most people who throw out the commandments, Isherwood did not throw out religion with them. When the last thing he felt like doing was meditating, he would still meditate. When he woke up with a hangover worse than death and the sensible thing to do was die, he recited his mantra instead. In his approach to religion, Isherwood navigated a narrow course between dogma (which he couldn't subscribe to) and complete agnosticism (which would have left him unsatisfied). He thus entered the middle ground—a place that Madame Blavatsky or Annie Besant would have found too ordinary and reinvented as something more fanatical and fantastical.

Isherwood didn't have to declare himself a fanatical believer because he believed vicariously through Swami Prabhavananda's believing. Lawrence refers vaguely to "the *X*" and Gerald Heard equally vaguely to "this thing," but Isherwood could say, matter-of-factly instead, "my friend." He did not need to swear that Prabhavananda's statements were true for them to satisfy something quite real within himself. And, in fact, in believing that his friend, his teacher, embodied a higher insight, Isherwood made his leap of faith after all. He became a believer of sorts, though when he looked in the mirror the mirror reflected back an ordinary, sensual, secular man.

And secularism itself was changing. In the mid-1950s Heard and Huxley discovered a shortcut to "this thing," and tens of thousands would soon follow them down it. In May 1953, as a volunteer in a psychiatric experiment, Huxley took four-tenths of a gram of mescaline. Huxley and Heard were soon meeting regularly to take mescaline or lysergic acid (LSD) and discuss their god-in-a-pill revelations. When Isherwood asked to join them, they explained that his emotional instability ruled him out as a suitable subject.

Isherwood acquired some mescaline on his own and during a trip to England swallowed it. At once he hailed a taxi to take him to a Catholic church and afterward to Westminster Abbey, "to see if God is there." He couldn't stop laughing. That God would be in those churchy carcasses of dead whales struck him as so hilarious that he retreated into a dark corner to try to control his giggling. Earlier, though, when he had moved out of the Vedanta Center, Swami had told him that God wasn't particularly there either. If Prabhavananda was right, Isherwood could neither make a pilgrimage to religion or dodge to get out of its way, for it was wherever he happened to be. Isherwood was thus one of the first to stake out boldly a position that, over the next half century, would become nearly a cliché: religious holidays, churches, and miracles are superfluous because every day, anyplace, and life itself were close enough facsimiles. For the rest of his life, Huxley periodically took mescaline—it let him out of the steel cage of his hyperintellectualism—but Isherwood desisted. Drugs were unnecessary, just as miracles were. By believing vicariously through Swami's believing, Isherwood obtained the consolation of there being something more, without having to profess *Credo*. It was rather as in a novel, where style and ambience determined not what the protagonist does but what it means. By immersing himself in Vedanta's atmosphere, Isherwood gave to his ordinary actions, thoughts, and even his doubts a resonance beyond themselves.

How often it had seemed a nuisance, to have to drive up to the Vedanta Center; and tiresome, to have to meditate when he was otherwise busy. But such tiresome nuisances, in the long run, had built up a field of meaning for him. It had widened the margins of Isherwood's world and opened him to a different order of happenings. Unlike T. S. Eliot, who, for all his Anglican faith, depicted old age as a bleak and desiccated abandonment, Isherwood grew steadily more curious and accepting as he grew older. No depression nor artistic sterility marred the happiness of Isherwood's last years. And since he spent those years writing about

Swami P. and Vedanta, and since his last book was *My Guru and His Disciple*, the faith that he doubted doubtlessly abetted his triumph in and over age.

❊

On May 29, 1976, Swami Prabhavananda suffered a slight stroke and was taken to Cedars-Sinai Hospital in Los Angeles. The nurses treated him like a movie star, arranging his bed by the window so he could gaze out on the Hollywood hills. But Swami had not come to the hospital for diversion. "I've seen the Himalayas, I've seen the Alps," he grumbled, "so what do I need this view for." When a nurse leaving his room said "Good-bye," he snapped back, "Okay"—as though to say good-bye was precisely the reason he'd come to the hospital. "*Okay's* the only word they know here," he explained. He began chanting his mantra aloud, which is a customary practice as a Hindu monk approaches death. Prabhavananda made the nurses chant it along with him, waving his arms like a conductor directing a choir. When into this surreal spectacle a disciple barged, he was startled by how radiant Prabhavananda appeared. "How beautiful you look!" "Yes," Prabhavananda answered, "I look beautiful in my death."

A good day to die, he determined, would be the Fourth of July. On July 4 in 1902, the great Vivekenanda had died. Seventy-four years later, as the minutes of the evening of July third ticked toward midnight, Prabhavananda inquired the time. When told that it was around eleven, he shook his head, "No, too soon—it must be midnight." Immediately after twelve o'clock, his breathing ceased and his vital signs stopped.

Isherwood was bereft. For so long his religious life had been lived vicariously through Swami. Prabhavananda had been his Bible (even when unopened), his minister (often unheeded), and his church (though his attendance had been bad of late). Now, for the first time Prabhavananda had let him down by being so inconsiderate as to die. How could he do that, Isherwood fretted, when Swami knew he could not carry on alone. To make matters more perplexing, before he died Prabhavananda had baffled Isherwood by telling him, "I think you have the makings of a saint."

Isherwood's response to that lollapalooza was to laugh awkwardly. He knew how much promiscuous sex he'd consummated and the quantities of alcohol downed and the ambition toadied to. All right, a saint, but a saint where—in hell? "No," Prabhavananda said, "I mean it. You have devotion. You have the driving power. And you are sincere. What else is there?"

Prabhavananda was not simply being flattering—an encouraging pat on the head. Isherwood's life project, outside of literature, had in a sense been to narrow the age-old western separation between saintly and human, between divine and profane. As England and the world he knew had slipped into the inferno, Isherwood was in his own hell when he wrote—in fact, he wrote very little during World War II. Through Vedanta he attempted psychologically to colonize the earth into greater habitability again. But try as he might through all his waking hours, he could not stop setting up as a pair of opposites the sexual and the spiritual, a dichotomy that harmed mainly him. His night dreams, however, tell an oddly different story. Waking, Isherwood complained that the whole pantheon of Hindu gods and goddesses faded from his mind as soon as Prabhavananda died. But in his dream life Prabhavananda's own guru—the great Brahmananda, Ramakrishna's spiritual heir—now visited him. In those dreams Isherwood seemed to accept Prabhavananda's intuition that he had the driving power, the necessary spark, to achieve the final reconciliation.

Isherwood asleep: in one dream, for example, the great Brahmananda prostrates himself before him. Within the dream, the dreaming Isherwood interprets this act negatively: Brahmananda is prostrating before me, the way Father Zosima bowed down before Dmitri Karamazov, bowing to the suffering that is my lot. But, after waking, Isherwood realized that such an idea might belong to Dostoevsky but not to Vedanta. Even if Isherwood's karma was as bad as Dmitri's, Brahmananda would have been bowing to the divine Atman in Isherwood. If, as Vedanta holds, everything that lives is sacred, that sacredness had finally to include Isherwood, too.

And include him sexually. There was one peculiar dream in particular, a dream of taboos overwritten. Isherwood had never discussed his intimate erotic life with Swami. In that dream, though, he and Swami Prabhavananda are sharing the same bed. Isherwood is respectful as always to Swami; but the bed does sit smack in the middle of a male whorehouse. That dream of their bedding together in the whorehouse broke the last taboo that had always segregated the spiritual and sexual aspects of his life. "I've got a new mantra for you, Chris," Prabhavananda tells him in the dream. "It is: *Always dance.*" "What a strange mantra!" Isherwood replies. "Yes, it surprised me, too," Swami says, laughing. "But I found it in the scriptures."

After he awoke, Isherwood remembered reading stories of Ramakrishna dancing with drunkards in the streets, whom he mistook for holy men whirling in ecstasy. He also recalled stories of Ramakrishna encouraging Girish Ghosh, when he was drunk but inspired, to go on drinking. Isherwood chided himself for lacking the courage of Ghosh, for fueled with liquor, Ghosh still visited Ramakrishna, and the two sides of Ghosh's personality were thus not schizophrenically quarantined. Regretfully, Isherwood realized that not once in their long relationship had he dared venture into Swami's presence while merrily drunk. He strained to picture a tipsy confrontation with Swami and decided, "Something wonderful might have happened." But as he brooded, the regret melted in air: for something wonderful had happened anyway. A "sinner" for thirty-seven years had enjoyed the company of a saint, and Isherwood and Prabhavananda's friendship had brought the light and dark sides of human character face-to-face.

Thus it ended, what had begun nearly half a century before, as the French liner *Champlain* had sailed into New York one frozen January morning. After a blizzard off Newfoundland the *Champlain* was so covered in ice and icicles it resembled a mammoth wedding cake floating into New York harbor. At its rail one chilly immigrant peered, nervously, through the snow and mists, as though straining to see what the new country held in store for him. On the pier, practically from the very first step, Isherwood had to shove his way and shout to make himself heard. Here was the New World, turning, churning, its engines revving twenty-four hours a day. All the commotion seemed to admonish him, "Don't you come snooting us with your European traditions—we know the mess that you've got into. Do things our way or take the next boat back." That morning he felt as vulnerable as the *Champlain* had seemed slithering over the huge Atlantic swells under an ominous sky. Onto the pier he stepped, to start a new life in a new land, and possibly he lacked the inner resources, the courage, for the enterprise.

It worked out differently from what Isherwood could have envisioned that white January morning. Indeed, to follow him over his next forty-seven years is to encounter a United States that has itself worked out differently from what anyone would have then predicted. A few years after he stepped ashore the Depression ended, and America was again the Land of Opportunity, run by a WASP establishment, governed by Christian morality, where the American Dream promised material improvement to a better life. In 1986, Isherwood died in a land radically changed, where houses could be prohibitively expensive and jobs insecure, but minorities more easily claimed their integrity; where Christianity had melted into a world pot of spiritual possibilities, and the American Dream had become dreams, permitting different pursuits and definitions of happiness. Christopher Isherwood, the Englishman who inhabited America and thought Hinduism, played a minor part in creating this new New World.

The journey was not ending as the *Champlain* docked, only

beginning. On that journey Isherwood reversed the preposterous error an earlier voyager to America had perpetuated. Columbus, landing here, supposed he was in India. Four hundred and fifty years later, Isherwood disembarked in New York, rounded the corner, and there it suddenly was—Prabhavananda's India waiting for him.

CHAPTER 6

The Gandhian Century

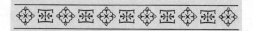

V. S. Naipaul had the perfect illustration of how pathetically limited—in a word, how very Indian—Mahatma Gandhi was. The example concerned a white suit. In October 1888, when the nineteen-year-old Gandhi arrived in England to study law, he disembarked from the ship wearing a suit of white flannel. Like Gandhi, Naipaul also would first arrive in England during his late teens, and he knew what it was to be a young provincial overwhelmed in a world capital, dazzled, seeing and trying to comprehend the unfamiliar at every turn. But Gandhi had seen nothing, Naipaul charged; he might as well have been blind. The only fact Gandhi recorded in his autobiography about his arrival was the narcissistic one that he himself was wearing a white suit. You can take the boy out of the Indian morass, Naipaul implied, but why bother. The boy—Gandhi—was the Indian morass walking on two feet, indifferent to anything except that white suit—that is, blind to everything outside itself.

But the white suit Gandhi recalled is not insignificant. Any dramatist might have pounced upon that suit for its symbolic value. Gandhi arrived in the fall, and the season when the English gentry sported about in white was well past, and thus his entry into the English scene was, fashionably, socially, a blunder. At his London hotel, it being the Sabbath, he could not get at his baggage, and being the only person there in white, he stuck out like a sore thumb.

As determined as Curzon or Annie Besant had been to reach India, so young Gandhi—in a reverse mirror image—had been to come to England. Before resolving on England, Gandhi had for nineteen years shown no particular promise. Lackadaisical, apparently far from bright, he got poor marks at school and at everything else he tried. But anticipating England—"the land of philosophers and poets, the very centre of civilization," to quote his words at the time—he remade himself overnight into a dynamo that no obstacle could deter. He was ready to travel without his widowed mother's blessing, but she reluctantly consented, providing he forswore the triple evils of alcohol, women, and meat. He contemplated not only leaving his young wife behind (as he did) but also selling her jewelry to pay for his passage. Gandhi broke the interdiction against Hindus traveling abroad, and he suffered excommunication from his caste in Bombay, which threatened never to assist him again.

Lest some further hindrances arise, Gandhi booked his passage prematurely, traveling at the worst time of the year. Day after day the S. S. *Clyde* inched its leisurely progress over the Arabian Sea. Though this was the golden era of the passenger ship, Gandhi was miserable aboard his. Inept with a knife and a fork, he avoided the dining room out of embarrassment. Besides, he had his vegetarian's vow to uphold, so alone in his cabin he picked at the fruits and sweets bought before embarking. Inept as well with English, he took so long to decipher any fellow passenger's remark that, by the time he understood it, the conversation had progressed down other byways. When he could make out what his kind shipmates were saying, often it was this: in England's cold climate, unless he devoured quantities of beef and downed vats of beer, he would not survive. For the eight-week mini-eternity that the trip lasted, Gandhi dressed in a plain black suit and hovered inconspicuously, a shadow on the deck. In his trunks, though, awaiting the moment of arrival, lay that immaculate white suit—to be donned when it would transform its wearer into a fashionable young Anglo-Indian gentleman stepping ashore.

So much for flannel suits and white dreams. After that first mistake, Gandhi continued for some months to experiment with clothing himself in the modern West. He paraded about London in silk top hat, spats, and silver-knobbed cane. Impeccably attired, he strolled to his French lessons or to pirouette in his dancing lessons. Soon, though, Gandhi tabulated his expenses and concluded he couldn't afford such a dandified existence. In truth, it suited his temperament even less than his pocketbook. Forty-three years later, when he met King George V at Buckingham Palace, he would wear a loincloth. Already on that autumn day in 1888, however, his ill-advised white costume signaled Gandhi would never don successfully the fashions of the England—of the "centre of civilization"—that he had idealized from his reading.

And discarding that white suit, Gandhi began his immersion in an England he had not read about or suspected existed—in those little-known alleyways of a different Europe just then coming into existence. Reeling about London half-famished from his dietary restrictions, by luck Gandhi chanced upon—nobody had alerted him that there were such establishments—a vegetarian restaurant in Farringdon Street. Upon entering, he purchased at the door a pamphlet, Henry Salt's *A Plea for Vegetarianism* (1886). Here was a lightning bolt! At the very moment progressive Hindus in India were taking up meat eating, progressive Englishmen, it appeared, were turning vegetarian. Among the daredevil Hindus who had sunk so abysmally low as to taste the flesh of the cow had been young Gandhi. At school he had felt compelled to discover whether carnivorism told the secret of the Englishman's power. In his schoolboy's ears had run the jingle:

> Behold the mighty Englishman,
> He rules the Indian small,

Because being a meat eater
He is five cubits tall.

Gandhi's meat eating had been but a brief experiment, foolish youth's trial and error. If Gandhi remained a vegetarian in India, though, it was by the sheer force of custom, unthinkingly. His stay in England converted him into something quite different—a vegetarian by choice.

As with vegetarianism, so with much else. Many of the reforms that Gandhi would later introduce within Hinduism he first encountered during those student days in London. Salt's pamphlet discussed avant-garde thinkers, Thoreau and Ruskin and Tolstoy, the very writers who came to inform Gandhi's thinking. As Salt's pamphlet suggested, vegetarianism was entangled, in that fin de siècle hothouse atmosphere, with every other fad and reform—social, sexual, and religious. Salt was a Fabian socialist, and here began Gandhi's introduction to and instruction in socialism. Some vegetarians favored free love, others chastity, while most denounced restrictive Victorian marriage: one was free to question and experiment with erotic mores, which in later life Gandhi would freely do. Some Theosophist vegetarians queried Gandhi about religion, asking what he thought about the Bhagavad Gita. When he confessed to having never read it, they pressed an English translation upon him. Gandhi was startled to read in Annie Besant's *Why I Became a Theosophist* that secularism might not be the key to the future, after all. From Madame Blavatsky's *Key to Theosophy* he encountered the even more shocking notion that Hinduism—dismissed by the British as a barbaric relic—was of all religions the most profound. The English education Gandhi had journeyed halfway around the world for turned him into an Indian, though an Indian such as there had never been before. A lifetime of defending Indian rights in South Africa and fighting for independence in India still lay before him, but at the end of it, the Hindu extremist who assassinated him would snarl his furious complaint about Gandhi: "All his reforms were at the expenses [*sic*] of Hindus."

That Gandhi corrupted Hinduism with his western notions is the exact opposite of Naipaul's indictment that Gandhi betrayed western progress by turning himself into a holy mahatma who had exchanged the civilized world for mystical vapors. And both the assassin's and Naipaul's accusations have a grain of truth to them. Were Gandhi not one of the twentieth century's most famous men, he surely would be reckoned one of its oddest. Easier to throw one's hands up in dismay, as Naipaul did, than to fit all the discordant Indian and European pieces together that made up Gandhi. One person could be both a political Father of the Nation and a religious *saddhu*? The same psyche could combine a search for secular salvation, full of Emersonian self-reliance and Shavian diet fads, with a Hindu holy man's longing for the godhead? Even the physical descriptions of Gandhi don't tally: one disciple depicted a hunched-over old man, while the next described an upright figure radiating health and vitality. The one certainty about Gandhi's life is his long, unfaltering fight for Indian independence, but set next to other wild-eyed revolutionaries, he is mighty peculiar.

Gandhi, for example, would interrupt a political campaign on the eve of success and devote himself instead to questions that, to critics like Naipaul, must have seemed sheer lunacy. By the early 1920s, Gandhi's policy of Non-cooperation had shaken British rule in India to the foundations, but just as victory first came within his reach, he volunteered to call off Non-cooperation. In 1921 he conveyed to the Viceroy that if only the British government would (1) promote home spinning and weaving in the villages and (2) suppress alcohol and opium, Non-cooperation would end. Evidently a nation of self-reliant spinners and sober weavers made irrelevant who governed that nation. Two decades later, when negotiations over independence had reached a crucial stage, Gandhi took precious time off to write articles about his troubling sexual dreams and to announce that he would test his spiritual purity by sleeping with a young woman. Evidently the dream of national independence became compromised if you yourself were having bad dreams. Here, for disenfranchised westerners, was certainly politics by another name, even if they couldn't be sure what that name was.

Many Europeans and Americans made pilgrimages to India, as Martin Luther King Jr. did, searching for Gandhian political inspiration. Others, such as a British admiral's daughter, sought Gandhi out because they detected in him Beethoven's ineffable music of the spheres. This is a book about how different hopes for the West—visions of another kind of West—were glimpsed, of all unlikely places, on the Indian subcontinent. Gandhi's social and personal experiments in India became in time repeated in hundreds of "laboratories" throughout Europe and America.

Though he was not a westerner, Gandhi nonetheless spoke to Europeans and Americans in ways that resonated for them, as intimately and strangely as their own dreams. His equation of microcosm with macrocosm—of personal conduct with the political life of the nation—reclaimed the public sphere from impersonal powers. His belief that one's own actions can be as sacred as worship redeemed the private sphere from vacuity. There was once a time when religion and politics and personal life had all overlapped in the West, too, but at the cost of religious wars, persecution, and inquisitions. Gandhi's making devotion, social duty, and private conduct all one, by contrast, glowed with a new light, the promise of a fresh dawn. For many westerners, both the noblest and the nuttiest, Gandhi appeared the last best hope, if hope there still was.

※

After decades in England and South Africa, in 1914 Gandhi returned to India, at the midpoint in his life. The most important thing he did there, in his own opinion, was to establish a series of ashrams—Sabarmati outside Ahmedabad and Sevagram in the then Central Provinces being the best known—to serve as models for the larger society. These ashrams were an odd, new kind of laboratory, and the "research" they conducted was to discover the social formula for a better future. "The umbilical cord of India," some Indians called the ashrams, and even secular westerners considered them holy sites of pilgrimages. Into the ashrams streamed curious European and American visitors, summoning a reverence rarely found outside a Dostoevsky novel. Here, this side of heaven, was an attempt to build heaven on earth.

Had the visitors prolonged their stays, however, these little heavens might have turned before their eyes into—not hell—but something like a minimal security reformatory. Gandhi's sons could have told an ashram visitor about the dark side, the iron oppressiveness of ashram life, that went under the name of idealism. In 1915 Gandhi's middle son, Manilal, lent some money to his older brother, who had gotten into a scrape in Calcutta. Although the money came out of Manilal's own savings, Gandhi practically accused his son of embezzling, on the grounds that an ashramite's private property should be considered the property of all. Already in disfavor because of a liaison with a married woman, Manilal was expelled from the ashram. His father banished him to work elsewhere *under an alias* for a year and then to live permanently in South Africa. Gandhi's dealing with his sons at the ashram combined lofty words with an iron hand, but then he had a name for that combination: "plain living and high thinking."

High thinking, yes! At Gandhi's ashrams one's thoughts should not descend so low as to food or sex or comfort. Try to imagine what it would have been like to live in such a place. "Abandon the Senses, All Ye Who Enter Here" could have been the motto posted over the entrance. Once, when asked to bless a young couple at their wedding, Gandhi happily did so and then told them, "Now go and live as brother and sister." The human species must preserve itself, which meant that even an ashramite couple might engage in the procreative act—twice or thrice in the course of a long marriage. The more fortunate unmarried person could be spared this debauchery of passion.

The second taboo at a Gandhian ashram: food, or rather enjoying it. There was a good deal more eating than copulating at a

Gandhian ashram, but—relatively speaking—not all that much. Food was to be swallowed the way medicine is, to support the health of the body. All sorts of edibles were all but ruled out: milk, for instance, might dangerously inflame the passions. Meat was, of course, the source of protein that dare not speak its name. Although Gandhi always gave the person the choice, there were at least three occasions when he seemed prepared to let his wife or children die rather than serve them the animal food product the doctor had prescribed. "There must be some limit to what we will do in order to remain alive," George Orwell observed, and for Gandhi, "the limit is well on this side of chicken broth."

Even close friendships were in effect a taboo at a Gandhian ashram. Gandhian philosophy is based on love, but not on the love for one person over another. Preferential friendships meant taking sides and could lead one, out of loyalty, into wrongdoing like Manilal's or even wishing an enemy harm. E. M. Forster famously declared, circa World War II, that if he had to betray his country or his friend, he hoped to have the guts to betray his country. Gandhi, in similar circumstances, might have prayed not to betray his enemy.

"No doubt alcohol, tobacco, and so forth, are things that a saint must avoid," George Orwell wrote in his essay on Gandhi (1949), "but sainthood is also a thing that human beings must avoid." Orwell found Gandhi unquestionably noble, but what he did not find—if one can put it this way—was that nobility itself was noble: "The essence of being human is that one does not seek perfection, that one is sometimes willing to commit sins for the sake of loyalty, that one does not push asceticism to the point where it makes friendly intercourse impossible, and that one is prepared in the end to be defeated and broken up by life, which is the inevitable price of fastening one's love upon other human individuals."

Thus Orwell faulted the great human being Gandhi on humanitarian grounds, arguing that at the heart, in the very laboratories, of Gandhism lay something humanly stultifying. Yet what was stultifying in Gandhi's ashrams pointed to something hidden that was desirable. After all, no one joined an ashram simply to avoid yummy dinners and preserve his svelte figure. No one abjured friendship or physical comforts, except on the quid pro quo of obtaining greater comfort emotionally. Gandhi's exorcism of sex may not have overly troubled ashramites already troubled by their sexuality, but even they bartered hypothetical erotic satisfaction only for something potentially more satisfying than sex. The high purpose in being a Gandhian transformed the bare, hard routines there, and in the ashramites' eyes, their ugly-duckling lives had all the nobility of swans.

In 1929 a young Englishman named Reginald Reynolds joined the Sabarmarti ashram. He was struggling to orient himself to an atmosphere unlike anything he had known and learning to spin, when Gandhi came up behind him. Gandhi laughed. "Well, stranger," he said, and then asked him—first thing, straight off the bat—how his bowel movements were. Later Gandhi shocked Reynolds by expressing dogmatic opinions but expecting nobody to agree with them. "Many things were taboo at Sabarmati, but there was no taboo," Reynolds realized, "on discussing them, or on the discussion of any subject whatsoever." The Sabarmati ashram was like a man who wears business suits and adopts conventional behavior (Wallace Stevens and Rainer Maria Rilke come to mind), precisely because his thoughts are unconventional and unconstrained in the extreme. There were a number of regulations governing the ashram, but beneath them, the rules of the game had changed. Things that did not happen outside in society could happen freely inside the ashram. Muslims and Untouchables did not openly mix in Hindu society but were readily admitted to Gandhi's ashrams; a leper applied for admission and Gandhi not only admitted him but insisted on giving him massages personally. Gandhi, the most famous man in India, did chores in the kitchen and merrily cleaned the latrines. The western ashramites working beside him in the latrines felt themselves changed, why or how they never quite understood.

Gandhi's admiring biographer Louis Fischer has offered an explanation: "He often changed human beings by regarding them not as what they were but as though they were what they wished to be." What "strangers" like Reynolds often wished, not surprisingly, was simply not to live the damaged or inconsequential lives Life had apparently assigned to them. And so, while Martin Luther King Jr. and Nelson Mandela studied Gandhi for political inspiration, people like Reynolds attempted to emulate Gandhi personally. They said to themselves, in effect, let me try Gandhi's way of life, and see whether I don't come out on unexpected terrain. What constituted a motive, an action, and a success in Gandhi's ashrams often little resembled what Reynolds had known as such back in London, and the difference intoxicated him. He and hundreds like him fought Gandhi's political battles, but often for reasons that were not entirely political, having more to do with the promise of another, changed mode of existence.

❖

"Generations to come, it may be, will scarce believe that such a one as this ever in flesh and blood walked upon this earth," Albert Einstein wrote shortly after Gandhi's assassination. A half century later the question is not whether Gandhi walked on earth but why he bothered. As the twentieth century ends amid worsening conditions and violence, Gandhi's idealism can seem like a fly's wing brushing against a tough-hided beast. One frequently hears talk about Gandhi's failure—a verdict voiced by Gandhi himself. His life's work was to evict the English from India, but today colonial administrations, colonies themselves, are all but extinct, and Gandhi or no Gandhi, the British would have had to relinquish their imperial prize. Gandhi, seen through the distorting spectacles of hindsight, was the beautiful but unnecessary flower that bloomed in the harsh soil of revolution.

The retort to that hindsight is not that the British left India at midnight, August 15, 1947, but that they left peacefully, with acrimony minimized between the two countries. Into the anti-imperialist struggle, Gandhi introduced a strategy or approach so unlikely as to seem surreal. He proposed fighting the imperial overlords by empathizing with them. Unlike the Marxists, to whose analyses of imperialism he largely subscribed, Gandhi refused to reduce the contest in British India to class warfare or hopelessly antagonistic self-interests. In his view, colonialism and economic exploitation took their toll on both the oppressed *and* the oppressor. A master who degrades a servant by that action hardens and distorts himself. Likewise, when the British sahib dismissed native Indians as ineffectual, effeminate, or childish, he could not but imply he himself was a no-nonsense, hypermasculine adult—a self-image that worked to stifle and suppress his own emotions and human faculties. Gandhi was battling for India's independence, but he was also fighting to liberate the British from their own stunted psychology of colonialism. Victory on both fronts would restore a "softer" image of humanity to its proper place.

Gandhi thus reformulated the anticolonial struggle in terms carrying universal significance. The British colonized minds as well as bodies, he recognized, and the West, once a geographical region, was rapidly turning into an intellectual one that no boundaries could confine. Gandhi could demonstrate that *politically* the Viceroy was not ruling the country for Indians' benefit and that *economically* the indigenous industries were made subservient to British interests. Yet politics and economics mattered little, he felt, if the *moral* character of Indian civilization quietly vanished in the advance of (Western) progress. "Gandhi was convinced," the political scientist Bhikhu Parekh has written, "that the 'rule' of British *civilization* could continue even if the British *government* were to stop ruling over India and British *capital* to cease exploiting it." For Gandhi, if all independence won was a change in the nationality and pigmentation of the elite personnel, that would hardly merit the word *victory*.

What was needed, so Gandhi believed, was to challenge not only British rule but also the rationale of modernity that justified it. The Indian struggle for Home Rule was thus a battlefield for an even more epic contest—the battle between ancient and modern. Curiously, in Gandhi's lexicon *ancient* was the good term, *modern* the pejorative. In all previous ages, so he argued, Asian and European civilizations had shared the same basic values. Quite recently, though, a Europe infected with a despiritualized hyper-materialism had whirled off on its own destructive tangent, imperiling human dignity and even survival. Such an interpretation of ancient versus modern was flattering to the Indians, whose self-esteem had suffered badly under the British. India became the upholder of sane tradition against (and for) a bunch of Johnny-come-latelies gone berserk.

But modernity is not so easily wished away. So omnipotent are modern institutions that they even dictate what constitutes a legitimate (as opposed to a "Luddite") protest against themselves; the omnipresence of modern thought delegitimates (or co-opts) all other forms of thoughts. Gandhi's staggering challenge, while having a philosophical aspect, was beyond anything that philosophers had ever attempted: he had to *unthink* modernity. Can it be done? Can modern politics be imagined without the key terms of power and conflict? Can modern economics be conceived except on a grid of material progress? Can a modern society be understood except through its historic development? Perhaps a conference convened of Kafka, Borges, Calvino, and I. B. Singer could devise such a world, but it would be located on another planet or in fable. Yet Gandhi organized in this world, in this century, a national independence movement without resorting to the power vocabulary of nationalism. He envisioned a prosperous India without the technological hoopla associated with industrial modernity. Gandhi's revolutionary agenda would have been a victory of the imagination, if it had been nothing more.

As a critic of modern civilization, though, Gandhi often ends up strangely sounding like a modern critic. His "Indian" arguments rejecting the West's ways echoed western thinkers before him. Before Gandhi, Henry David Thoreau had seen man as part of his environment, not its proud overlord. Leo Tolstoy had already differentiated ancient from modern, as Gandhi would, by the latter's increase of violence. Likewise, Karl Marx had earlier formulated Gandhi's complaint that industrialism alienated the laborer from his labor. Such resemblances and antecedents were no accident, since, when living in the West, Gandhi had read these thinkers and been influenced by all of them.

But Gandhi had several advantages (*disadvantages* might be the correct word) over his western counterparts. They fretted about injustices from a Russian country estate or by a pond in New England. As a wog in England or a colored Sammy in South Africa, Gandhi experienced firsthand, by his being in the street, on public transportation, and, of course, in prison, the injustices they simply speculated about. And while Tolstoy and Marx proposed remedies through reasoning about the problems, Gandhi had the storehouse of Indian culture to borrow from, when it was convenient, to locate alternative solutions. His vision of a more just society could not help sounding, to western sympathizers, more original.

Perhaps too original. Western liberals, leftists, progressives, revolutionaries, have all admired Gandhi . . . up to a point. That point is where Gandhi declares, "For me there is no distinction between politics and religion." Religion married to politics? Isn't that the reactionary recipe for intolerance, for hate? Didn't Gandhi know about the Crusades, the Protestant-Catholic wars in Reformation Germany, the Inquisition in Spain, the missionary-supported ethnocides in the New World? No wonder the sole non-Muslim political figure the Ayatollah Khomeini expressed great admiration for was Gandhi. Western liberals have tended either to ignore Gandhi's religious obsession or to believe that when Gandhi conjoined politics and religion, it was a clever strategic ploy.

It was no ploy. Gandhi advanced a novel thesis—that each era demands its own unique form of religious observance, and for the present age that form must be political:

> Whenever the religious spirit is on the decline, it is
> revived through such an effort in tune with the times. In

this age, our degradation reveals itself through our political condition. . . . In other words, one who aspires to a truly religious life cannot fail to undertake public service as his mission, and we are today so much caught up in the political machine that service of the people is impossible without taking part in politics.

Gandhi's polluting his political realism with religious nonsense was, to critics like Naipaul, an Indian aberration, deplorable within the Hindu context, ignorable outside of it. Gandhi's politico-religious mishmash did not emerge out of Hindu traditions, however, but ran counter to them. "Moral politics" belongs to a line of thinking that runs from Aristotle through John Locke to John Stuart Mill, and not to one that includes Ramakrishna, Ramana Maharshi, and Sri Aurobindo. Hinduism traditionally took a low view of politics. Gandhi's taking a high view of it played havoc with many long-accepted practices of Indian society. Once morality was grafted onto politics, it was no longer so easy, for example, to disregard the wretched status of women or the pariah lives of the Untouchables.

Here was a new kind of politician in India (or, possibly, anywhere). One year Gandhi would devote himself to national politics, debating whether India should break completely with Britain. The next year, with the same dedication and fervency, he would deliberate whether the ashram should have a communal kitchen. "Political life is to Gandhi," M. R. Jayakar exclaimed around 1920, "only an extension of domestic life, governed by the same ideals of truth, justice . . . love, generosity, and refinement." Gandhi's strange mixture of political preoccupations and the search for *moksha*, spiritual liberation, resulted in an unquestionably noble vision: sympathy should replace the social contract; a sense of extended family replace a police-monitored system balancing rights and duties; and community replace the sterile wrangling of parliaments and congresses. The question was, how could such a vision be realized in practice? How, Gandhi puzzled endlessly, was he to touch with this vision the great masses of his country-men, who lived in poverty, uneducated and dumb to politics?

Indian religion offered a clue. Gandhi's faith taught that within each individual is Brahman, or the godhead, and the more one cleanses himself of impurities, the more access he has to its infinite power. In Indian folklore, sexual activity is a terrible depleter of power: one discharge of semen expends the energy of twenty-four hours of mental activity or seventy-two hours of physical labor. Suppose that a desexualized or spiritualized erotic energy were allowed to flow through social interactions? In *The Symposium* Plato proposed that a small band of lovers might defeat all the armies in the world. Conversely, Gandhi appeared to believe that a few dozen *brahmacharyis* (those swearing a vow of celibacy), if pure enough, could arouse India from centuries of defeat and stagnation.

Gandhi understood how next to impossible it was to rechannel a powerful libidinal drive. Of all things he had triumphed over, he confessed, "sexual passion was the hardest to overcome in my case." Gandhi determined during his thirties to so purify himself of sexually tainted thought that it would even be irrelevant whether he was considered a man or a woman. Others, such as Freud in middle age, have taken "secular" vows of chastity to spare themselves the distraction and obsession that Gandhi associated with sexuality. But Gandhi's celibacy was undertaken so he might evolve into a spiritually developed person with the powers to influence the political struggle. He despised fakirs and their mag-ical hocus-pocus, but he himself would stop at nothing to gather the inner force necessary to stir his countrymen into action. "All power comes from the preservation and sublimation of the vitality that is responsible for the creation of life," he wrote, and he claimed that only by conserving his sexual force had he "derived such power as I possess for working in the political field."

Was this a Faustian bargain, bartering libido in exchange for social charisma? If so, then like all Faustian bargains, it rested on delusion. Gandhi could conserve every drop of semen and be asexual as a stone and pure as Himalayan snow, and he would still not levitate the Indian state into freedom and prosperity.

And yet. He did perform—not miracles, not magic—but things not lacking in wonder. Consider Gandhi's scrawny body, little more than a stick wrapped round with a loincloth. It practically dispensed with sleep and worked twenty hours at a stretch and on an amount of food scarcely sufficient to satisfy a squirrel. Gandhi was rarely sick, rarely moody, and he displayed tremendous powers of concentration. His body should have been debilitated through all his numerous fasts, but at the time of his assassination, approaching age eighty, Gandhi had recovered from one more near-fatal fast and was on the eve of another political march through the country, as though he were a youth of eighteen. Not all the magi and maharishis of Indian legends—those who ascended ropes into the ether and healed by psychic touch and materialized simultaneously at two places leagues apart—could match what Gandhi accomplished in fact. Except he dispensed with the supernatural supporting wires. At the time of Independence, Gandhi entered, on foot and nearly alone, regions in flames and blood, and quietly restored them to peace and sanity. The Viceroy, Lord Mountbatten, observed that Gandhi single-handedly quelled riots when Mountbatten's own soldiers, though mounting into the thousands, were helpless to affect anything. "In the Punjab we have fifty-five thousand soldiers and large-scale rioting is on our hands," Mountbatten reported back to the government in England. "In Bengal our forces consist of one man [Gandhi] and there is no rioting."

But did ever a man tread a thinner line? Gandhi was convinced "an indissoluble connection [exists] between private, personal life and public." But equating public and private, in Shakespearean comedies, is a formula for irony and backfire, and, outside the theater, it turns oddities of private behavior into public scandals. In Gandhi's case, the irony is that he who wanted to make his ego nothing indulged in a humility difficult to distinguish from hubris. He saw India at Independence poised on the edge of unspeakable new disasters, and instead of blaming historical conditions beyond anyone's control, he blamed himself. The country he loved was set for partition—to his mind, a vivisection; his countrymen, Hindu and Muslim, whom he had taught the ways of nonviolence, were slaughtering one another. "What shall I do? What shall I do?" he was heard muttering to himself. Violence inevitably ceased in the presence of pure love, he believed, and the greater force of good invariably dissolved the lesser force of evil. If only he were pure, pure absolutely, rid of the last vestigial drop of desire and selfishness, then he might radiate an energy that could transform the madness. "If I were a perfect man," Gandhi believed, he would be able to note social wrongs and "prescribe a remedy, and *compel* adoption by the *force* of unchallengeable *Truth* in me." And, thinking thus, Gandhi embarked on perhaps the most radical of his experiments, which it is tempting to say no westerner can understand, though in truth no Indian really understood it either.

The seventy-seven-year-old Gandhi conceived the experiment thus: he would sleep in his own bed, and in the bed beside him would sleep a young woman. On December 20, 1946, Manu, the nineteen-year-old granddaughter of a cousin, joined him in his bed, and the experiment properly began. If neither of them felt any disturbance or sexual desire, then lascivious eros had been conquered and his spirit was blemishless. Gandhi considered himself a "scientist" in *brahmacharya*, and like a good scientist he would let nothing deter the advance of his science. Nor does a good scientist hide the results of his researches, and Gandhi publicized what he was doing for the benefit of mankind.

And then the brouhaha began. Old associates refused to speak with him; the editors of his newspaper resigned; his son Devadas wrote him a severely reproachful letter; Nehru added his disapproval. One friend delicately explained Freud's theory that, though we do one thing consciously, we may be prompted by other motives unconsciously. Gandhi said he had developed his own methods for detecting his unconscious impulses but added— and this is endearing in an old man—he must read this Freud.

Others warned that, even if his experiment was innocent, it would alienate his admirers. "I must confess," Gandhi replied, "the prospect of being so debunked greatly pleases me." Never before—when he went to England to study or championed the Untouchables or befriended Muslims—had public censure deterred him. "The whole world may forsake me," he said, "but I dare not leave what is the truth for me." When Manu had an appendectomy, Gandhi requested to be present during the operation. Nearby he sat, with gauze over his face, contemplating the body of his "spiritual mistress" (the term is probably not right, but then no term would be), opened and operated upon. In that operating room, witnessing love and decay, affection and detachment all so nearly one, worked in Gandhi the final epiphany or liberation. "Sixty years of striving have at last enabled me to realize the ideal of truth and purity which I have ever set before myself."

Before undertaking the experiment, Gandhi had made a peculiar request of Manu: she should think of him as her mother. *Bapu*, Father, was what Gandhi's associates called him, but *father* had too rough a masculine sound for him now. Masculinity smacked of self-assertion, domination, aggression, whereas the feminine connoted the soft and the giving. "I have suggested that woman is the incarnation of *ahimsa* [loving nonviolence]," he wrote. "I have hugged the hope that woman will be the unquestioned leader." Until that better matriarchy dawned, if Gandhi shed all violent passion and masculine sexuality, he would manifest that feminine tenderness himself. If he could sleep with Manu "purely," he would have become as a mother to her. (When Manu published her memoirs, she titled them *Bapu, My Mother*.) Gandhi's experiment with Manu was for him the equivalent of a sex-change operation, minus the back alley in Casablanca and surgeon's knife. And the operation or experiment, if unprecedented, was called for by unprecedented circumstances. Amid the violence of India in partition, at the center of the bloodshed and hatred, would be one soul bleached of passion assuming responsibility, willing to suffer it, and emanating in return selfless love and goodwill.

Gandhi had come so far, to the outer boundaries of human possibility. In a lifetime of experimentation, his arrival at this destination seems an act of defiance of nature. The common needs that underwrite being human on earth—sufficient food and housing, adequate clothing, medical care when sick, and defense upon attack—Gandhi had come as close as is physically possible to dispensing with altogether. Everything he owned at the time of his death—two pairs of sandals, a pair of spectacles, a loincloth—could have been purchased, Orwell estimated, for five pounds. Gandhi had pacified his fiery temper until he felt affection even for those who hated him. The fear of death he had eradicated, too, and alone and unprotected he braved threats and assassins and merely declared that, were he to die comfortably in his bed, he should never have been called a mahatma. Even food, which forms a central orientation to every human's (and animal's) day, meant nothing to him beyond a fuel to keep the machine running. Thus he mastered the most basic needs and annihilated desire until, finally, to declare he was an ordinary mortal, a divine soul, a man, or imaginatively a woman was to fuss over distinctions he had left behind.

And it was not enough. Failed, failed—he had failed! Gandhi surveyed his long decades of struggle, when every fiber of his being had strained to the breaking point, and concluded it had served nothing, had been to no avail. Muslims were butchering Hindus, Hindus butchering Muslims, and in the streets one's nostrils filled with the rank smell of smoke and blood. Toward the end he lived in Delhi, in a cell among the Untouchables, and from it he could hear Hindu storm troopers drilling and training to kill Muslims. Gandhi's ally and political heir, Nehru, was threatening to restore order in the various provinces by aerial bombing—the detested method the English had used. In the politest terms, Nehru also let Gandhi know that his vision of transfigured villages at the heart of independent India had no place in a country requiring heavy industry to improve its standard of living. On Independence Day, August 15, the BBC begged Gandhi for a message. Everything considered, what message should he send? On that long-awaited day, after years of encouragement, decades of exhortation, words failed him and Gandhi fell mute.

Yet though outward events disheartened him, in his own being he had passed beyond anxiety and despair. In January 1948, Margaret Bourke-White photographed Gandhi for *Life* magazine, and she queried him: Didn't the prospect of atomic bombs falling, she asked, alter the utility of *ahimsa* or nonviolence? Well, Gandhi replied, if the bombs were actually falling on a city, *ahimsa* was the one thing in it they could not destroy. As the bombs fell, Gandhi suggested, followers of *ahimsa* should not dive for cover but look up bravely and pray for the welfare of the plane's pilot. The sacrifice, he assured her, would not be in vain. He then arose to address a five o'clock gathering assembled on the lawn. And there on the grass was waiting the "pilot" as it were—the assassin—who fired three bullets into his body, and within minutes Gandhi was dead.

Many Muslims grieved his assassination as much as most Hindus did, realizing that Gandhi's advocacy of their cause had brought his martyrdom. Gandhi's assassination achieved what possibly no life could have: afterward the situation began to stabilize, talk of war between India and Pakistan faded away, and the two countries settled into their uneasy coexistence. Gandhi's verdict of failure may thus be premature about efforts whose peculiar nature make them difficult to assess anyway. He had sometimes driven Nehru nearly insane because, just when some protest seemed to rout the British, Gandhi would suspend it because the means employed had become tainted with violence. His insistence on means over ends has attracted even people largely unconcerned with India's fate. He never liked the title Mahatma and said there was no such thing as Gandhism, but in America, in Europe, on every continent, "Mahatma Gandhi" has been seized on to advance causes Gandhi barely or never heard of. The assassination ended Gandhi's life but not his story, which continues elsewhere.

The Gandhian Century

⌖

> Let not the twelve million Negroes be ashamed of the fact
> that they are the grandchildren of slaves. There is dishonor
> in being slave owners.

In the year 1929 Gandhi composed those words for an American audience. The National Association for the Advancement of Colored People (NAACP) had deliberated whether to invite Gandhi to America but concluded, W. E. B. Du Bois said, "that this land was not civilized enough to receive a Colored man as an honored guest." Instead, Du Bois pressed Gandhi to write a message for his magazine *Crisis* (the beginning of which is quoted above). "It may well be," Du Bois mused, that "real human equality and brotherhood in the United States will come only under the leadership of another Gandhi." Nineteen hundred and twenty-nine was the year Martin Luther King Jr. was born.

When King came to learn of Gandhi, he liked the fact that Gandhi was an Indian. But he also appreciated this Indian's having been so influenced by an American, Thoreau, and in turn Thoreau's having appropriated Indian sources, the Bhagavad Gita and the Upanishads. The exchanges between East and West evidently ran along a fruitful corridor. King, who had little time for scholarly research, hardly realized how intricate that conduit was. *Ahimsa*, for example, is usually translated as nonviolence (or non-injury, noncoercion), but Gandhi disliked definitions with an *anti-* or a *non-*. So he borrowed the concept of Christian love to color in the translation positively. *Love* evokes turbulent passion, though, so Gandhi re-redefined *ahimsa*, using Hindu concepts of eros transfigured to qualify the Christian notion of love that was coloring in the Indian ideal of *ahimsa*. Most of Gandhi's key concepts are derived from a polyglot dictionary where the West redefines East and the East redefines West.

Redefinitions aside, King's intellectual encounter with Gandhi is well known—a stock piece in American civil rights history. In

the standard version, the black struggle prior to King was floundering for lack of a means by which to budge the white American
majority. King, a graduate student at Pennsylvania's Crozer
Seminary in the late '40s, was also floundering. He had come to
doubt whether Christian love had ever been or could ever work as
an effective tool for social change. Then one Sunday King heard the
president of Howard University, just returned from India, lecture
on Mahatma Gandhi. Here was revelation! King rushed out and
bought a half dozen books by and about this Gandhi who had used
the force of love and nonviolent resistance to bring the most powerful empire on earth to its knees. And the rest, so the phrase goes,
is history—the history of civil rights triumphant. King endorsed this
official version with his often-quoted remark, "Christ furnished the
spirit and motivation, while Gandhi furnished the method."

The actual King-Gandhi "encounter" lacks such neat, succinct
drama. For more than three decades, Afro-American leaders had
tried to adapt Gandhi's model into a viable method in America.
Nearly every black political figure of note before King—A. Philip
Randolph, James Farmer, Bayard Rustin—had puzzled the riddle
of how Gandhian techniques could be naturalized to the American
scene. Flip back through the black press of those decades: news of
Gandhi fills column after column, making him seem all but
omnipresent in the Afro-American consciousness. In June 1934,
for example, the *Baltimore Afro-American*'s front page ran three
separate stories:

GANDHI HITS U.S. BAR

and

GANDHI DENIES HE OPPOSES INTERMARRIAGE

and

INDIAN LEADER BRANDS JIM CROW AS NEGATION OF CIVILIZATION.

The year 1934 was the height of the Scottsboro Affair, and the
black press might have been thought to have space or attention for
little else. But in 1934, as Arna Bontemps remembers in *Black
Thunder*, "two stories dominated the news as well as the day-
dreams of the people I met. One had to do with the demonstra-

tions of Mahatma Gandhi and his followers in India; the other, the trials of the Scottsboro boys then in progress in Decatur, Alabama." Although Du Bois concluded Gandhi could not be invited to the United States, a succession of other prominent Afro-Americans—Dr. Channing Tobias, Dr. Benjamin Mays, Dr. Howard Thurman, Bayard Rustin—made the pilgrimage to India in the hopes of luring him to American shores. To all Gandhi demurred, on the grounds that he could not preach in America until his message had borne fruition in India. In lieu of visiting America, he gave to each the encouragement, "With right which is on their side and the choice of nonviolence as their only weapon, if they [American Negroes] will make it such, a bright future is assured." He even prophesied that "it may be through the Negroes that the unadulterated message of nonviolence will be delivered to the world." The lines were already there, before there was a Martin Luther King Jr. to utter them.

As Randolph, Farmer, or Rustin tracked Gandhi's setbacks and successes in India, it was his politics that concerned them and it was as a political figure they appropriated him. They were all, as was Du Bois, largely divorced in their own personal lives from religious concerns. Though they appreciated the communal functions of the Afro-American church, they hardly saw it playing much role in advancing social change. When they transposed Gandhi into an American context, it was into a bed of secularism—and it didn't take. King's singularity, as Lerone Bennett wrote in *What Manner of Man* (1964), "was not in the application of Gandhism to the Negro struggle but in the transmuting of Gandhism by grafting it onto the only thing that could give it relevance and force in the Negro community, the Negro religious tradition." If Gandhi was to play any role on American shores, King intuited, he was likely to have more political impact ironically as a religious figure. When, two generations before, Gandhi had imported his search for a moral politics into India, he had dressed it up as religion so it could acceptably pass there. King now performed this masquerade in reverse. He recognized the religious soul in Gandhi, and he brought Gandhi's message to possibly the most religious places in America, the black churches, but the result was a political explosion.

Before his encounter with Gandhi, King had become depressed, believing that the social gospel, "love in action," was futile for countering any evil. It had not ended slavery, it hadn't stopped Hitler, and it certainly wasn't eradicating racial segregation in the United States. Reading Nietzsche, King felt tempted to accept his argument that Christianity with its "slave morality" fostered social impotence. Yet if an oppressed minority, so outnumbered, abandoned the social gospel to protest by force of arms, was that not suicide? Reading Gandhi, King now saw how he might redefine minority into majority. Echoing Gandhi's line of reasoning, King began to argue that in America the real struggle was "not between Negro and white, but between justice and injustice." Those fighting for civil rights were waging a fight not on the color line but on the soul line of America—and every hue of citizen stood to win.

In late 1955, King assumed leadership of the Montgomery bus boycott, and Gandhian theory suddenly had to prove itself in practice. Some accounts of that struggle, notably Taylor Branch's in *Parting the Waters* (1988), have claimed that King was not much of a Gandhian but only found it convenient to appear so, as it made him a less threatening commodity in American politics. Yet to reread the rhetoric of the Montgomery boycott is to find Gandhi quoted and talked about and held up as an example throughout. At mass meetings during the boycott King quoted Gandhi's brave declaration: "Rivers of blood may have to flow before we gain our freedom, but it must be our blood." Quoting it, King urged his audience to despair not, because "unearned suffering is redemptive." As Gandhi had not hated the British as an enemy but rather embraced them, so we too, King preached in his sermons, must avoid creating a legacy of bitterness that can reduce victory to ashes.

The Montgomery bus boycott catapulted King into a national and international spotlight. By the end of the decade, fifty awards and honorary degrees decorated the walls of his home. King's taste ran to the finer things, and he was now earning sufficient money to purchase them. (In a good year his honoraria and royalties approached a quarter million dollars.) With Gandhi's example before him, though, he turned over his royalties to the Southern Christian Leadership Conference and, in exchange, received a salary of one dollar a year. Through the 1950s, his annual earnings as a pastor remained well under ten thousand dollars, and he continued to drive an old Chevrolet.

As the decade of the 1960s approached, the "American Gandhi," as some had taken to calling him, wanted to deepen his message and broaden its appeal. To do so, what could be more fitting than a pilgrimage to the source? Gandhi was not alive, but King could still meet people in India who had worked with him and investigate firsthand his legacy. When Gandhi attended the London Round Table Conference in 1931, he brought almost no baggage and, complaining of his companions' materialism, had most of their luggage sent back when the ship stopped at Aden. Twenty-eight years later, the Kings' trip to India commenced with the stiff excessive baggage fee they paid for all the trunks stuffed with elegant suits and fine dresses. A loincloth may be fine if you are Gandhi; otherwise wear appropriate dress when searching for a spiritual legacy.

Gandhi's legacy, King discovered, was divided in India into two parts—the political and the spiritual—or had fallen into the cracks somewhere between the two. Gandhi's political mantle had descended, he already knew, upon Jawaharlal Nehru, then prime minister of India. King got off to a bad start in India: because of a botched plane connection in Zurich, he arrived too late for his state dinner with the great Nehru. So famous by now was the thirty-year-old King, however, that, diplomatic protocol be damned, Nehru rescheduled a state occasion for a person of no official position. At dinner King besieged Nehru with questions about Gandhi's philosophy, Gandhi's idealism, Gandhi's non-violence. Such was Nehru's charm that it all but concealed the fact the questions were falling on deaf ears. Nehru kept referring to Gandhi the shrewd politician and assured King that, were Gandhi alive today, his response to India's problems would entirely be practical and utilitarian.

Gandhi's spiritual mantle had been inherited by Vinoba Bhave, the "walking saint" of India. With no fixed home, Bhave continually crisscrossed India on foot, and with no organization or authority other than his own moral force, he asked rich landowners to donate one-fifth of their acreage to the landless poor. In that way, Bhave's redistribution campaign had accumulated large numbers of acres, though not always of the most arable kind. King finally caught up with Bhave at the remote northern village of Kishangarh. Bhave was as vague as Nehru was practical-minded. Posing riddles and answering questions with questions, Bhave was like the caricature of an Indian guru. King's reaction to him was: kook. One feature of the Bhave experience, obligatory for a pilgrim, was to join the saint on his "morning walk." Bhave started at 3 A.M., in order to cover nine miles before his prayers and meetings began at seven. King opted for an "American version" of the walk: he overtook Bhave at the end in an automobile.

Confident from the success of the Montgomery bus boycott, King dreamed of extending its spirit into a rebirth of national and international politics. He confided to Bhave his inspiration. Might not India, conceived in Gandhian nonviolence, become the first nation to disarm itself unilaterally and thus set the model for the world to follow? Unilateral disarmament is hardly less a utopian idea than Gandhi's anti-industrial village-nation, but it was an uncluttered message of universal pacifism that King felt he could preach. Bhave responded sympathetically, and suddenly the mystical zany turned before King's eyes into a most sensible fellow. Returning to Delhi, King presented at a press conference "a suggestion that came to me during the course of our conversation with Vinoba"—namely, unilateral disarmament. One country, in a world racing toward nuclear destruction, should have the "faith and moral courage" to end the arms race. The audience responded enthusiastically, for denouncing superpower militarism was standard crowd-pleasing rhetoric in India. But when it became clear that the country so to disarm was not America but India, the crowd turned hostile. Did King want India overrun by Pakistan? What nonsense was King spouting?

King's month in India, from early February to early March, sped by in a blur of dinners, speeches, meetings, and talk and more talks. Labor leaders, Muslim mystics, African students on fellowships—King met with everybody, with everybody exchanged ideas. Yet when he left India in March, there was no evidence that his "message" had in any way broadened. When he mounted the pulpit in Atlanta, though, his sermon sounded a new note. He cited Gandhi's denouncing the practice of Untouchability to show that, while it is easy to criticize our enemies, it is more valuable to criticize ourselves. After India, the injustices King protested extended beyond the Afro-American community and included all America's poor and disadvantaged as fellow victims in the same tent. King went on to become one of the first Americans of prominence to oppose the Vietnam War. If King was the American Gandhi, then by analogy the American Viceroy, Lyndon Johnson, and his lieutenant governors, such as J. Edgar Hoover, were not amused.

In India, King's pilgrimage included a visit to Ahmedabad, where Gandhi had started his Salt March in 1930. That march had haunted black leaders like Bayard Rustin, who pondered how to adapt the idea to an American context. They conceived a similar march in America in the early '30s, but it was three decades later when King brought the idea to fruition. Gandhi's Salt March thus ended, after many a winding detour, in Washington, D.C., in 1963, where King made his most memorable speech: "I have a dream." After the march, King was invited to the White House, where John Kennedy greeted him, "I have a dream, too." The Washington March thus makes a handy, even happy conclusion to the Gandhi-King story. Only it did not conclude there: the parallels had still to deepen, to darken. On April 3, 1968, King said publicly what he had been telling friends privately, that uncertain providence had forfeited its power to frighten him, for he no longer feared death. The next day, on April 4, he was shot fatally. King's brave statement echoes Gandhi's remark after a botched assassination attempt, only ten days before the one that killed him. "If I am to die by the bullet of a madman, I must do so smiling," Gandhi said. "Should such a thing happen, you are not to shed one tear."

King was thirty-nine years old, half Gandhi's age, when he was shot. If Gandhi had died at thirty-nine, he would be little remembered today. Those intrigued by historical *if*'s may speculate what King might have done with a life span doubled. The principle of growth was obviously in him. King's assassination became coupled in many Americans' minds with John Kennedy's, so fresh in memory, so elusively connected in meaning. But the more distant parallel did not pass without comment. Bill Mauldin's syndicated cartoon, for example, depicted King entering heaven and there meeting Gandhi. The caption had Gandhi saying, "The odd thing about assassins, Dr. King, is that they think they've killed you."

※

Mauldin's cartoon set a precedent: henceforth Gandhi could not go anywhere alone. In the American imagination Gandhi's name was linked with King's as in some posthumous, mystical marriage. The marriage in turn produced progeny, the most famous being Cesar Chavez (1927–1994). Whenever asked what a lifetime of nonviolent struggle had taught him, Chavez would modestly reply that nothing could he add to what Mahatma Gandhi and Dr. King had already said. The year King died Chavez was engaged in a Gandhian pastime. As head of the United Farm Workers (UFW), he undertook a twenty-five-day fast to focus attention on the plight of the California grape harvesters. Gandhi would not have been Gandhi without a cause to fight for, and Chavez had made his own *la causa* so well known that, as he completed his fast, Senator Robert Kennedy was there to give him his first morsel of food. When Chavez started the UFW in 1962, it seemed that the migrant grape harvesters had not a friend in the world, but by the time he completed his fast, seventeen million American shoppers were boycotting the purchase of grapes. In 1970, under the glare of adverse national publicity, California agribusinessmen who had vowed to crush his pip-squeak union sat down and negotiated with Chavez.

Chavez did not begin life on the hard migrant road. His father owned a farmstead in Arizona, but when Cesar was ten the farm was foreclosed, and as befell the Joads in *The Grapes of Wrath*, a harsh Depression wind blew them to the unpromised land, California. The Chavez family lived there, in good times, in one-room tenant shacks and, in bad, out of their old Studebaker. His mother would dispatch the children—it was rather a Gandhian gesture—to see if there were hoboes or others hungry with whom they should share the little food they had. Chavez's vivid youthful memories were not of school, which ended by the eighth grade, but of crawling beneath twisted, scratchy vines to reach difficult-to-get-at grapes, breathing in hot dust and choking on the chemical pesticides. (His childhood of picking grapes bequeathed him lifelong, chronic back pain.) When Chavez was twenty-one, Gandhi died; the local movie newsreels revealed a frail man in a loincloth climbing some palatial stairs and announced that this humble man had defeated the mighty British Empire without firing a gun. Young Chavez sat in his seat puzzling: how was that possible? He managed to get his hands on Gandhi's *The Story of My Experiment with Truth*, which changed his life and history, too. Chavez's adaptation of Gandhian nonviolent methods (fasting, pickets, boycotts) led to recognition of the UFW and his becoming something of a national hero. "Gandhi" is evidently alive and well in America.

Or was, in that long ago of 1970. For the remainder of his life, Chavez could never repeat that early success. Fasting proved harder for Chavez than for Gandhi, and after two or three days he often had to call off an announced fast. But in 1988 he pushed his body to the limit—thirty-six days without food—to protest the millions of pounds of pesticides used to dust California grape fields. The 300 million pounds of pesticides dumped on California crops annually had made picking and harvesting in that state the most dangerous occupation in America. But in 1988 Chavez might as well have been eating steak for all the media attention that his fasting attracted. People who happened to hear of his fast often were surprised he was still alive, as though hearing of some long-forgotten movie star famous in their youth. Chavez's frustrations after 1970 are the tale of how Gandhian methods went from effectiveness in King's time to futility in America today.

Gandhi had at least opposed a recognizable foe, the British Empire, whose injustices, like the Amritsar massacre, were only too visible or, like the salt tax, could be made so. In the grape boycotts from 1965 to 1970, pickets were also visible, a "photo-op": the poor conditions in which harvesters lived and worked arrayed a human tableau, one with an emotional appeal. Gone now are those *Grapes of Wrath* days of obvious villains and observable victims. Although pesticides harm the pickers *and* consumers in the long run, it is the long run. In the short run, pesticides lack the evil iconography of fat-cat bosses and downtrodden toilers, and an "abstract" evil fades from view.

And then, while Gandhian-style activists matured slowly, the sophistication of their opponents progressed by leaps and bounds. Victories won by the United Farm Workers were turned, through their opponents' deft maneuverings, into defeat. Under Jerry Brown, sympathetic to the farmworkers, an Agricultural Labor Relations Board was established to ensure fair arbitration for the pickers. But Brown was succeeded as governor by George Deukmejian and then by Pete Wilson, both backed by California agribusiness, and their political appointments to the Agricultural Labor Relations Board made it the growers' best friend. When farmworkers have managed to strike successfully, growers have sued them for the loss of the unharvested crops. In one suit alone, the courts awarded the grower $5.6 million as well as setting "bail" at $5.6 million during any period while the decision was under appeal. The UFW's treasury did not have $5.6 million. Even when the farmworkers got a ruling reversed, their resources were depleted in endless legalistic wrangling.

Finally, society has developed a strain resistant to Gandhism. In 1947 when Gandhi undertook his fast to avert a Hindu-Muslim bloodbath in Calcutta, most Calcuttans were not in sympathy initially. But they heard updates on his conditions daily, which imperceptibly involved them with his fast, and gradually their tempers changed. To fast or boycott or immolate yourself to awaken the nation's conscience requires the national consciousness to be spotlighted on you. Fasting has lost its novelty, there have been too many fasts; protest has lost its novelty, there have been too many protests. In 1988 Chavez's month without food could not compete for the attention Elizabeth Taylor's or Oprah's being on a diet got. The world's supply of ethical indignation is evidently a limited resource. Since 1970 the United Farm Workers' moral appeal has dimmed, unheard amid the clamor of other just moral causes. A Gandhian fast has become, so to speak, one more hungry Indian.

And Gandhi foresaw this, too. He expressed a peculiar wish. His unstinting pen left over a hundred volumes of collected writings, and Gandhi proposed that all those words, all those pages, be placed on a pyre and burned. This bibliographical auto-da-fé would make clear that his answers, though an honorable response at the time, would one day cease to be answers. His own story of *My Experiment with Truth* was meant as a legacy not of truths but of experimentation. Political truths were the most ephemeral of all, with the life span of a butterfly. For Gandhi, it was fitting that his mode of struggle (or substitute King's or Chavez's) could seem true and right during the heat of the contest, and then become a puzzle to those who came after. Thus those who undertake political work, he believed, must take into account both its relative effect on society and its unconditional effect on their own soul. Chavez and King changed America, indisputably, but in doing so they changed themselves and became larger figures. From a

Gandhian perspective, the degree of personal transformation also measures success in an "experiment with truth."

⌗

As a boy, Anwar Sadat would wrap himself in what amounted to a diaper and pretend he was Gandhi in a loincloth driving the British out of Egypt. Sadat, like King and Chavez, fell under the spell of the political Gandhi, hoping to make the sun set on the imperial powers that oppressed his country. For others, though, Gandhi's politics was only the label on the bottle containing an elixir that might change their lives wondrously, if only they could partake of it.

When Gandhi attended the Round Table Conference in London in 1931, the people who wanted to see him, talk with him, touch the hem of his garment, might have formed a line stretching halfway from England to India. George Bernard Shaw, who called Gandhi Mahatma Major and himself Mahatma Minor, assumed the world's prospects would brighten significantly if the two of them enjoyed a tête-à-tête. Charlie Chaplin—though Gandhi had never heard of him—simply had to meet him. Of all the unheard-of Europeans and Americans who believed Gandhi was the one soul alive to unconfuse their confusions, none was drawn to him with a wilder fervency than Madeleine Slade had been. The force of gravity was nothing compared to the magnetic force field that attracted her to him. Rather like people who feel trapped in the wrong sex and surgically rectify the error, Miss Slade felt trapped in English society, and she had to right the mistake and to move her very essence to its true home, which was at Gandhi's side.

Madeleine Slade (1892–1982) was the daughter of an English admiral—the admiral of the English fleet in India, no less—who thus abandoned her superior birthright to squat at the feet of the Mahatma. The symbolism can appear a bit heavy-handed, as though England or the West, availing itself of Madeleine Slade's body, were atoning for wrongs done in India. Gandhi, who lived intuitively in a world of symbols, had her accompany him to the Round Table Conference in London. For a few months in 1931—

months of ecstasy for her—she was never far from his side, photographed everywhere with him, and the cheaper tabloids reported she was his mistress. By now she was no longer Madeleine Slade but Mira behn (sometimes spelled as one word), for Gandhi had given her, if not a new birth, a new name. On a speaking tour in England to win support for Gandhi, Miss Slade, or rather Mira, was badgered constantly with political and social questions. But on her American tour, audiences appeared not to give a hoot about politics. "Gandhi the man, the Teacher, the Apostle of Truth," she was amazed to discover, "was what they sought, and with such thirst and earnestness!" These Yanks were her truer countrymen, for they wanted what she also hoped for from Gandhi: a new dispensation.

Madeleine Slade and Gandhi—here was a romance for the ages, viewed, that is, from her side. Romance may be too wan a word, though, to evoke a passion that dwarfed in intensity mere sexual passion. As a young woman, Miss Slade had focused obsessively on Beethoven's music, and she devoured Romain Rolland's famous novel *Jean-Christophe* (10 vols., 1904–12), based in part on Beethoven's life. When she met Rolland in person, he had just completed a different kind of book about, he told her, "another Christ." As soon as this book, *Mahatma Gandhi* (1924), appeared in the bookstores, Madeleine dutifully purchased a copy. She read it in one sitting, hypnotized, entranced. Afterward, she booked immediate passage to India. Recovering herself, she realized she wasn't prepared—she wasn't worthy—to go to *him*, not yet. She rebooked her ticket for exactly a year to the day later. That interminable year, late 1924 and extending into 1925, she turned to profit, hardening her body by sleeping on the floor, learning to spin, and studying Urdu (unfortunately, not the language she would need in India).

Even the longest twelve months in the history of time eventually passed. At last aboard ship, she gazed at night dreamily at the moonlight on the water and saw a silvery path transporting her ever nearer to *him*. Upon arriving in India, she refused to tarry even a night in Bombay. Gandhi, whom she had written to, had arranged for her to be met in Ahmedabad, but of the kind men who met her train, all she could think to ask was, How far away is the ashram? As the jalopy bumped over the road, her conversation consisted of "Are we nearly there?" The moment the car braked, she jumped out and at once hurried into the building where Gandhi was. Her eyes couldn't focus him, though; she was conscious of nothing but a white light, and she fell to her knees before it. Gandhi lifted her up and said, gently, "You shall be my daughter."

To few daughters have befallen a harder lot. Gandhi would inquire, for instance, how acute her faculty of smell was and then send her off to sniff whether the latrines were working well. But such ordeals, which occurred by the thousand, were trivial compared to the Ordeal. Gandhi recognized Mira's attachment to him was feverish and personal, so he packed her off to work in other ashrams or remote villages. In those villages she gave instruction in sanitation and hygiene and endured a minimal existence without friendship, much less intimacy. Interruptions in this bleak routine consisted of (1) malaria, when she became so sick that someone had to come to take care of her and (2) prison, to which she was sentenced for her Gandhian activities. Inwardly she may have rebelled—all that waste of time apart from *him*—but her one object was to fulfill without complaint his every wish and word. In prison she was offered the choice of receiving either visitors or mail. She forsook having company so she could receive notes from Gandhi, who, amid a thousand pressing activities, never failed to write regularly. She chose solitude, but her solitude peculiarly resembled her conception of marriage. "My idea of marriage has always been something very sacred," she said, "an ideal of utter dedication . . . through oneness with the beloved." Mira resembled one of the poet Rilke's Great Lovers, those who love beyond themselves and grow large and finally transparent, vanishing into the beloved.

What, if one may put it so crudely, was the attraction? Gandhi's enemies dropped suggestive, naughty hints, but not even they believed those hints. The ideal harmonies that Mira had once heard in a fugue of Beethoven (coincidentally, one of the first Europeans to be influenced by Hindu thought) she now heard in Gandhi. A proper education might have restrained her free-fall fantasy, but girls of her time did not receive a proper education. Although her childhood had been privileged, even charmed, imaginative solitude had ringed it round with animal pets and trees invested with personalities as her best friends. As a young adult, she continued to hug trees and to roam in Wordsworthian wonder. She scarcely would have believed possible there was another person—namely, Gandhi—professing he would like to hug even a snake. When she first read Rolland's account of Gandhi, she experienced an ineffable, cloudy sensation that transported her from a man-centered to a nature-centered universe. This Gandhi she was reading about did not contrast the human to the nonhuman, or set man apart from animals and trees, but overlapped all beings in an interconnected net of great kinship. And Mira felt kin to it. History, her own position in history as an English admiral's daughter, should have made her a daughter of the Enlightenment skeptical about Gandhi's political mysticism. Her formative education had bypassed history lessons, though, in favor of romantic and mythic tales, which, she now learned reading about Gandhi, were truer than history. Viewed through a strict historic lens, Mira behn lived in India often abjectly and fairly alone; through a mythic lens, though, she dwelt in the midst of a populated struggle and enacted heroic deeds. No English beau could have asked so much of her, nor made so bounteous a return.

Gandhi became for her that different principle of existence that many Europeans, living in an increasingly industrialized, rationalistic, and bureaucratic society, had come to desire. But after Gandhi died in 1948, Mira was stopped in her tracks, at a loss what to do. She tried to carry on the work, promoting animal husbandry and lecturing in the villages in her broken Hindi, but she lived ever more alone and steadily higher up in the Himalayas. Although previously she had denied it, she had not been truly living in India, nor in the struggle for Independence, but rather in Gandhi's heroic vision of them.

After Gandhi died, Rolland kindly sent her some of his books, but she put them aside, thinking she could no longer read French. At an odd moment she snatched one up and discovered she could read it, and so reading Rolland's *Beethoven—Les grandes époques créatrices*, she discovered what she must do. She returned to Europe, resumed old habits (such as eating meat), and devoted herself to Beethoven. Gandhi's political fire, which raged across India and torched British goods and which he could barely contain—and which she had once shared—dimmed down to a private lamp by which she listened to Beethoven's symphonies and sonatas. As that wittiest of Indologists, Lee Siegel, remarked, "She went back to her high school boyfriend."

Gandhi—the political battles and her own exceptional labors and the years in prison and even India itself—all gradually faded from Mira's mind. For a centennial volume on Gandhi's hundredth birthday, to which the most famous names vied to contribute, she grudgingly scribbled a few paragraphs, evidently in a bad temper. "Gandhian workers need to be not missionaries but REVOLUTIONARIES," she harrumphed. At other times when people pestered her for recollections of Gandhi, she was vague and resorted to stock comparisons with Christ or Socrates—or with Beethoven! "How is it that you were so readily able to substitute Gandhi for Beethoven and Beethoven for Gandhi?" one interviewer dared ask her.

"They were much more alike than anyone supposes," she answered. And with that she closed the discussion: "Please don't ask me any more about Bapu [Gandhi]. I now belong to Beethoven."

Mira and hundreds like her, forgotten now and occasionally foolish in their own time, form an essential part—in a way, a test case—in the unfolding of the Gandhian story. Gandhi did not expect political regeneration to come strictly through political means, nor his economic vision to be realized through five-year plans imposed from above. The political and economic revolution needed to be preceded first by individuals who underwent a personal moral revolution. People like Mira who appropriated Gandhi personally may thus provide, even more than the political King or Chavez, a bellwether indicating what chance his vision has for a viable future. For they homed to him, offering up their bodies and their minds as sites of the most fundamental revolution of all.

And in that dawn how happy it seemed, the possibility of a Gandhian new beginning. Their association with the Mahatma gave their life meaning, their days a purpose. Madeleine Slade had held back, shy, hesitant, the odd girl out. But as Mira behn, she met with Lloyd George in England and in America with Mrs. Roosevelt, and now a good Gandhian, this neither caused her alarm nor turned her head. Gandhi was for western Gandhians a wishing well at which they obtained, if not their ultimate dreams, then sustenance, renewal. In Gandhi Mira found, for a while, a spiritual home on earth.

Yet after he died (or outside his presence), that sense of a new dispensation dissipated and ordinary life resumed. Why? Gandhi lived on a high plain, at a harsh altitude—a veritable Himalayas of moral rigor—where western disciples like Mira appeared to breathe in an air too rarefied for them. (Visitors to Gandhi's ashrams commented upon that harshness as they observed that vegetables were grown there but no flowers.) Mira appeared to match Gandhi in stoicism, her body to withstand the austerities every bit as much as his did, but only because her head was filled with unaustere, compensatory fantasies that she dared not admit even to herself. Mira's frustrations indirectly raise a question whether Gandhi's lofty but severe example can imprint itself in a softer emotional material—which it apparently must do if it is to have any future in Europe or America.

When Gandhi was praised for his sacrifices and all he was doing for India, he would reply, "No. I am doing it for myself." But when Mira was praised for her sacrifices for India, she in effect answered, "No. I am doing it for Gandhi." But by forcing an identity with him, she distorted the model. While she desired her soul to be like or one with Gandhi's, he by contrast wanted his to be transparent—absorbed by social and metaphysical truths largely outside her ken. Above all, he wanted a new human land—and so much the better if that land was independent India—where the spiritual and the material, inner and outer, would finally reconcile and become one. By taking Gandhi and not herself as her starting point, Mira lived inwardly too much on one side, the spiritual side, of the very divide Gandhi was struggling to close. If a Gandhian seed has taken permanent root in the West, it shall likely have sprouted in less obvious places than Mira's narrowly conceived dream of Gandhi, and something other than *Flora gandhiana* will be its name.

❈

Finally, there is no one better to explain Gandhi's appeal to the West than Charlie Andrews. Certainly none of Gandhi's western co-workers was more famous in his time than—to give him his proper title—the Reverend C. F. Andrews (1871–1940). He came to India as a missionary, resigned his post in 1914, and stayed on for the next quarter century devoting himself to the country's welfare. Forgotten in his native England, he is well remembered in India still. Go to the Gandhi National Memorial Museum in Delhi; upstairs one room re-creates, as though it were a stage set, an old-time veranda. There, among the rattan chairs and potted palms, Gandhi is talking for all time with two people (in wax effigies): the Nobel Prize–winning writer Rabindranath Tagore and Charlie Andrews. Exceedingly homely, Andrews was hardly the ethereally lovely Englishman of Richard Attenborough's *Gandhi*, but the film, picturing Andrews continually at Gandhi's side, scarcely exaggerates his importance. When Gandhi fasted, Andrews sat nearby. When in despair Gandhi penned his darkest letters, to Andrews they were addressed. Andrews acted as Gandhi's alter ego conferring with viceroys and high officials, and on trips back home he was, Gandhi said, "the voice of India" in Europe.

Forster's *A Passage to India* ends as a sympathetic Indian and Englishman acknowledge that, across the cultural divide, they cannot be friends. Gandhi and Andrews could. "We met simply as brothers, and remained as such to the end," Gandhi said. "I don't think I can claim a deeper attachment to anyone." Their friendship proved to Gandhi that Indians and English were naturally allies, once outside modern political confines. A few years after Andrews died, Gandhi was conferring with the new Viceroy, Lord Mountbatten, and he interrupted the complicated negotiations to ask Mountbatten if he had by chance heard of "an Englishman called Andrews who had decided to devote his life to the service of India." "He then astounded me by asking," so Mountbatten recalled, would I be prepared "to do the same myself, not as a British Viceroy but . . . appointed and paid for by the Indian Government?" Andrews had so demonstrated the true Englishman was an Indian at heart that Gandhi was prepared to pay Mountbatten to reenact the demonstration.

Andrews, from his side, needed Gandhi and needed him for more than friendship, dear as friendship was. For all his efficiency and industry, Andrews was too gentle a creature to find on his own a niche in competitive politics or commerce. Andrews's sheltered childhood—not so different from Mira's—was steeped in Christian and classical mythology and formed, he said, "a kind of backwater into which the current of modern thought has not been allowed to enter." It is not difficult to conjecture what a modern psychiatrist might say about Andrews. He, and for that matter Mira, never had sexual relationships. (Typical boarding school homosexuality had terrified young Andrews, precisely because it did *not* repel him.) A psychobiographical explanation of Andrews's and Mira's attraction to Gandhi might well postulate repressed sexuality and unconscious transference.

A psychobiographical explanation would be insufficient, though, since so many other Englishmen shared Andrews's receptivity to Gandhi and felt the same electrical excitement on hearing his name. The Great War and its disillusioned aftermath prepared them to see in Gandhi an idea whose time had come. Politics, Walter Lippman wrote, can never be conducted by the Sermon on the Mount, and yet to the ex-minister Andrews and other questioning Christians, the Mahatma was apparently doing just that. Gandhi's message sounded in their ears an antimilitant march by which they could reject war, reject jingoist nationalism, and still keep step in a great historical processional for human betterment. For many like Andrews, their world, which had lost its way after World War I, regained its bearings through Gandhi.

Other idealistic and heroic figures—such as Sun Yat-sen in China—worked no such spell. The sociologist Ashis Nandy hazarded a reason why Gandhi attracted high-caliber Americans and Europeans in such number. "Albeit a non-Westerner," Nandy suggested, "Gandhi always tried to be a living symbol of the other West." Gandhi was not at all like Madame Blavatsky's disembodied Mahatmas, beyond anything the West had ever known; he was the Mahatma the West could know. What could have been more reassuring to educated westerners than Gandhi's saying, "Every one of the Indians who has achieved anything worth mentioning in any direction is the fruit, directly or indirectly, of western education." And when Gandhi sent important letters to the Viceroy, he often did not use the mail or regular channels but had young Englishmen like Reginald Reynolds or Andrews deliver them— precisely to show that his message expressed viewpoints with which moderate western minds were in accord.

Yet with his New Age dietary nostrums, his "fads" like homespun, and his dhoti in place of a business suit, Gandhi was a public leader or political model who could not have existed in Europe or America. If Andrews could not stand shoulders back, on the pattern of virile manhood set by Curzon or Kitchener, here was Gandhi saying that the best man was a woman. When Mira behn could not fulfill her adult responsibilities as the admiral's daughter, there was Gandhi, so childlike in his manners he was compared to Charlie Chaplin and even Mickey Mouse. Gandhi could speak English fluently, he could voice the West, but it was another

West he expressed, or something between India and the West, where misfits like Mira and Andrews found a sphere of action and a place for themselves.

That sphere and place still exist: anyone can reenter it, by reading Gandhi's correspondence to Mira or to Andrews. Those letters detail a long instruction, largely by example, showing them there is another way to live and to be. Gandhi dashed off his letters hastily without thought to style, in transit, on trains, anywhere— all totaled, a post office nightmare mounting into the thousands, possibly ten thousands. In those letters, Gandhi steps down from the leader's podium because he prefers the role of servant. He is the male who longs to assume womanly duties such as nursing and mothering. He makes matters of great policy secondary to the welfare of the person to whom he is writing. In the letters, the grim seriousness of things must take a backseat to humor. So gentle and unobtrusive were these "moral lessons" that Mira and Andrews, reading Gandhi's letters, were scarcely conscious that almost all the assumptions of their upbringing were being contradicted. In prison Mira surrendered the right to have visitors in exchange for the right to receive his letters. After all, many prisoners receive visitors, while Gandhi's letters were for her, as they were for Andrews, the key unlocking the door of a lonelier imprisonment.

One letter to Charlie Andrews must stand here, as a sample of hundreds that, equally suitably, could have been selected. It begins, typically, with Gandhi fretting about his correspondent's health and, typically, with Gandhi joking. When Andrews tore the envelope open, the first line he read was, "My Dear Charlie, I shall be good this time and not accuse you of crimes against the laws of God and man regarding health." Gandhi then continued his lesson in the good manners of the affections:

> But there is no doubt you need a curator euphemistically called a nurse. And how I should like to occupy that post! If you cannot have a nurse like me, who would make love to

you but at the same time enforce strict obedience to doctor's orders, you need a wife who would see that you had your food properly served, you never went out without the abdominal bandage and who would not allow you to over-worry yourself. . . . Not being able to nurse you myself I can only fret.

Just as he had been Mira's father and Manu's mother, so he would be Andrew's wife. The oddity of the proposition is exceeded only by its enormity: here was someone who would be to each person he knew a chaste, platonic spouse or spiritual nearest of kin.

Was Gandhi the West that the West has forgotten? In his letters he often appeared a figure of white flannel-like softness, calling for an unseasonable, sweeter version of humanity. As such, he evoked for many Europeans the shadows of long-forgotten ancestors—the ancient ruler-sage, the medieval Franciscan saint, the New England moral experimenters. And as such he posed, in an Indian dhoti, as an anachronistic conscience for the modern world.

Conclusion
At the End of the World

In the year 1912, and continuing into 1913, a philosopher was traveling across Asia. The grant that financed the trip, the Albert Kahn Traveling Fellowship, mandated that at journey's end he turn in a report of his activities. It was beneath the dignity of the philosophical mind, though, simply to record, first this, then that. Instead our philosopher refined his impressions into an inquiry into the very nature of civilization. His report, published as *An Essay on the Civilizations of India, China, and Japan*, is forgotten today, but possibly it should not be: its lucidity and masterly generalizations make it, as his traveling companion said, "within its limits a masterpiece." The philosopher did not merely surmount, he exploited his personal, often peevish reactions to reach a deeper level of understanding, in a way believed impossible—and perhaps even undesirable—to do today. The little book has long been out of print, its few readers long dead, and if the philosopher is remembered at all, it is because his young traveling companion later wrote a far better-known work, entitled *A Passage to India*.

Yes, the philosopher was E. M. Forster's friend and mentor, Goldsworthy Lowes Dickinson. "Dickinson could be ever so gay and ridiculous, laughing and talking at once, making everyone laugh," so Forster recalled, "shooting out little glints of nonsense like flying fish." Goldie Dickinson amused his companions in India, but the country did not return the favor by amusing him. He recoiled before India; its intellectual and physical messiness suffocated him; and only as he neared the Chinese border did he feel he could breathe freely again. But what did personal reactions matter to a philosopher, except as clues to some larger impersonal truth? Dickinson mined his own responses for insight as he described the English in India. "Of all the western nations the English are the least capable of appreciating the qualities of Indian civilization and the most capable of appreciating its defects." So Dickinson described not only his own deficiencies but also that larger historical irony whereby English values came to roost precariously on a social substratum in many ways their antithesis.

Dickinson's *Essay on the Civilizations* is most memorable for its thesis. There is no East and West, he argued in 1913, no Europe versus Asia. "A Chinese, after all, is not so unlike an Englishman, and a Japanese not so unlike a Frenchman." However, Dickinson marked a single exception to the seamless whole that the modern world was becoming: "The real antithesis is not between East and West, but between India and the rest of the world." Only India is different; only India unspools some other possibility fantastically. India is the odd man out of the global citizenry, Dickinson held, because religion, religion, religion everywhere had transported the land to somewhere nearly extraterrestrial. All other countries were located on planet Earth, in present time, in specific material conditions—which were so much "maya" or secondary reality in India, where what was most important had migrated over the mountaintops into the clouds.

What did his Indian readers make of this distinction, India versus all the rest. At the time there was one pundit particularly qualified to judge Dickinson's extravagant thesis. Sri Aurobindo, because of his travels and English education, could evaluate and, because of his superpatriotism, would surely rebut Dickinson's segregating

India into its own pejorative category. Yet when Aurobindo, who read everything, read *An Essay on the Civilizations*, he concurred: Dickinson was correct. Tourists and gurus since then, far less learned than Dickinson or Aurobindo, continue to evoke (ad nauseum) the idea of India's dark exceptionalism. But Dickinson's backward, religiously obsessed country seems another place than contemporary India, filled with cities and computers and cinemas, with engines and intellectuals and industrialization. And yet as recently as 1996 the *Wall Street Journal* ran a feature article explaining why marketing strategies that worked so neatly in China or Japan failed in India. One Indian marketing guru, whom the *Wall Street Journal* profiled, instructed his European and American executive-clients to repeat a mantra over and over: "India is different. India, different. India . . . different."

꘏

In 1914, the year after Dickinson's tour, two people formed a partnership intended to demonstrate, among other things, that any such dichotomy as Dickinson's was flatly wrong. A woman, Mirra Alfassa Richard, and a man, Akroyd A. Ghose, together attempted an India-West synthesis strange and unprecedented, though they dropped hints that all previous history had prepared the stage for their experiment.

Sailing for Pondicherry in 1914, Madame Richard was on a private expedition to locate a new and different way of life in the unknown. Her ship going to India and Dickinson's returning from there might nearly have crossed, say, somewhere in the Arabian Sea, and metaphorically "ships that pass in the night" is a suitable image, for truly they were traveling in opposite directions. For all his curiosity about other civilizations, Dickinson was English to the bone; for all his philosophic exploration of other mentalities, he believed European-style rationality would reign everywhere in the future. But although a sophisticated Parisian, Mirra Richard (1878–1973) had other elements in her background, Turkish and Egyptian, and had lived in North Africa, and she felt she never entirely belonged in western Europe. An early interest in the occult had drawn her, even as a girl, to faraway, dreamlike lands. *Occult* is a word now covered in a fin de siècle dust of marginality and quaintness, but a century ago many were the bright minds— Yeats, Jung, William James, and this young parisienne—who considered scientific exploration and occult explorations equal gateways to the coming era. In contrast to the philosopher Dickinson, who descended in India into a backward land the furthest point from home, Mirra Richard thus ventured there into the land of the future, which conceivably might make for her a home evermore.

She gave herself over to India fully, unlike other figures in this book who did so only in part. What they did in the shade for a few or more years she acted out in the open over the long haul. Their limited experiment of an Indo-European fusion conducted with mixed result she determined to carry to its final conclusion. During his half year in India, E. M. Forster investigated different kinds of human interaction than he had known in England, but Mirra Richard spent over a half century living and creating such interactions herself. Annie Besant combined spiritual beliefs and social actions to shape a new sort of public arena, but she never severed herself from western definitions of "spiritual" and "social" to do so, as Mirra Richard did. Isherwood explored how Hinduism might profit a secular westerner, and so did she—only not from the safety of a galaxy away in Los Angeles.

In traveling to India, Mirra Richard declared she was in quest of "*something else,* a 'third position'" different from the possibilities that either India or Europe offered. She was the first inhabitant of the new third position, and her loyalties resided neither on the subcontinent nor on the European landmass. While other westerners, during their stays in India, had as their ultimate reference point, their polar star for navigation, either India (Forster, Besant, Mira behn) or their homeland in the West (Curzon, Naipaul, Isherwood), Mirra Richard's pointed to a vague destination that was neither India nor Europe. Her third position represented a merger of Curzon's material reforms and Besant's spiritualized politics, of Naipaul's search for Enlightenment values and Isherwood's for religious tradition—a blend that would make a breakthrough never known or tried on any continent before.

There was little reason to expect that Pondicherry would fulfill her foolish hopes. She appeared to be simply accompanying her husband, Paul Richard, who had some minor political business to transact there. Pondicherry, a tiny sliver of French territory in southeast India, was an unlikely goal for a seeker of any kind in 1914, since it possessed no famous temples, no schools of venerable learning, no celebrated holy men, no pilgrimage sites. In the dry season, much of its surrounding area was red baked clay and sand, and Mirra Richard had every reason to suppose she had landed on barren soil.

In 1914, she was exactly the age Mary Curzon had been when she died, but at thirty-six Mirra Richard was vibrantly alive, avid for new experiences, and eager to be at the center of things. She was a handsome woman, striking in her heavy makeup and high fashion, and she had a not unsympathetic but inconsequential husband in tow. She pined for some greater spiritual marriage: she was the western bride, representing a new West that had shed its aggression and hyper-rationalism, but who—or, more likely, what—could possibly be the groom?

If only European cultural traditions or, say, French or English literature had interested Madame Richard more, Pondicherry could have procured for her the perfect preceptor, one of England's most brilliant graduates, Akroyd Ghose (1872–1950). He had swept all the relevant academic prizes during his terms at Cambridge (at Forster's King's College) while in his spare hours he composed not merely English but Latin and Greek poetry as well. He read Dante's *Commedia* and Goethe in the original, as diversions while he mastered European languages and literature ranging from ancient Greek to contemporary French. Why was such a worldly cognoscente residing in the backwater of Pondicherry? Well, Akroyd Ghose might be an Indian—he *was* an Indian, definitely—but his upbringing had obliterated his nationality.

Ghose's father, a physician trained in England who believed success was spelled *B-r-i-t-i-s-h*, had made sure his son grew up innocent and ignorant of Indian ways. As a boy Akroyd had learned no Indian tongue, and English was his first (and for many years his only) language. When at age seven he was sent to England for schooling, the father instructed that Akroyd not "make the acquaintance of any Indian or undergo any Indian influence." The good doctor rethought these instructions and added, to be on the safe side, that his son learn nothing about any religion whatsoever. The boy grew to adulthood without returning for a single visit to India. Thirteen years later, in 1893, a ship was at last bringing Akroyd back from England, when Dr. Ghose learned that it had sunk in midvoyage. Utterly despondent, he died of "heartbreak" before finding out the report was erroneous, and the son upon whom he had expended such stoical love stepped, quite well, upon Indian shores.

Metaphorically, however, the fatal news possessed a grain of truth: the son he had envisioned, the successful British facsimile, was dead—or in the process of dying. Before leaving England, Akroyd had effortlessly passed all the examinations for the British foreign service, except the riding test, thus voiding on a technicality the career his father had destined him for. Missing taking the riding test was his protest against an upbringing that had been too cold and lonely to capture his heart as it had captivated his mind. Despite knowing all of western culture, he returned to India feeling cheated and blank in regard to some part of himself. Once back, in quick succession he mastered Bengali, Marathi, Gujarati, and Sanskrit as well as the cultural traditions his father had tabooed. From England's brightest (Indian) son he changed into its fiercest opponent. As the new century began, Ghose remade himself into no Gandhi-style pacifist but a revolutionary firebrand determined to eject from India the England that had once been all he knew.

The British charged the young revolutionary with sedition in 1908, and though they failed to convict him, they succeeded anyway in vitiating his opposition. During his year-long internment awaiting trial, he devoted himself to yoga and spiritual exercises and lost his taste for political activity. Politics, he now felt, had confined him to an arena of rhetoric and action that he had learned in England and was all too western. Yoga, Hindu spirituality, moved him out into the open, into a sphere upon which the conqueror had scarcely left a trace. After his release from the Alipur jail in Calcutta, he put himself beyond British influence (and danger) by sailing for the French enclave of Pondicherry. When he had returned from England, he had dropped the English "Akroyd," and now he dispensed with the "Ghose" and became known only by a version of his middle name: Aurobindo. Disciples were slow in coming; he was not yet the *Sri* Aurobindo whom some would venerate as little, if any, less than god. But by 1914, Pondicherry possessed Divinity's best-kept secret, a seer who might correspond, after all, to the one Mirra Richard had so long fantasized.

Fortunate it was—to jump ahead of our story—that his religious vocation and Mirra Richard's husband prevented their ever marrying. They would have been the too-odd couple, he the Indian the West had made and she the European lapping up since childhood eastern mysticism—everything reversed, crisscrossed, the opposite of how it was supposed to be. What could such a union have possibly produced?

※

As Mirra Richard gazed out her window in Pondichéry, particularly in November, she might have wondered where in the world she had come to. At that time of year irregular depressions over the Bay of Bengal cause a second, unpredictable monsoon to sweep that segment of the Indian coast. The dull November sky blends into the leaden gray sea to make a cloudy gray blur, and rains with no intention of stopping all but erase the contours of the *ville blanche*—that geometric grid of neatly planned streets— which the French had imposed on Indian soil. Several days of such rains can make Pondichéry feel to its drenched inhabitants like the soggy end of the world. As ends of the world go, Pondichéry's is a sweet, gentle version, compared to the Götterdämmerungs of famine and ethnic warfare elsewhere. It just appears that here, in the tiny colony, the European idea of progress has run out of steam, or ceased building in the middle of construction.

As Madame Richard gazed out the window, she observed the outermost reaches of one of Europe's two great empires fraying into the sea. And she daydreamed that she and her new spiritual consort, Aurobindo, would build a different kind of empire, beyond anything the French had attempted. Like the earlier Pilgrims in the remote Massachusetts wilderness, she determined to establish in this province beyond the provinces the center of a new world. Incredibly enough, she and Aurobindo did put Pondicherry on the map of global culture. For every book written about the French in India—to take one measure—there are probably a hundred written about Aurobindo and Madame Richard. These volumes praise (for they are almost all hagiography, disguised or blatant) a Frenchwoman's and an Indian man's ability to leave nationality, race, ideology, and petty gender considerations behind to create a utopia on earth.

And what do all those many books report of Mirra Richard and Aurobindo *doing*? If their activities are compared with the stupendous agendas of Curzon or Besant, really not very much at all. Their great work, as with most guru-teachers, was simply the creation of their personalities. As with many other gurus, in the communal world of action they merely started an ashram, a kind of full-time Sunday school where devotees came for religious instruction. But Mirra Richard and Aurobindo were gurus with a difference, and their ashram quietly parted company with anything India had ever known. The great saints of modern India, from Ramakrishna to Ramana Maharshi, knew nearly nothing of the West, whereas Aurobindo and Mirra Richard together knew more than almost any westerner did. Although other ashrams have started religious schools, Mirra Richard could thus begin possibly the most progressive *secular* school in India at that time. Far from restricting themselves to spiritual transformation, they wanted to transform the earth, and Mirra Richard did that *literally* when she set up a utopian experiment that turned desert into green garden and to which people from a hundred countries flocked. From a western standpoint, this mixture of India and Europe, of religion and social action, was then so amazing that figures as diverse as Aldous Huxley, the explorer-soldier Sir Francis Younghusband, and the Latin American poet Gabriela Mistral clamored for Aurobindo to receive the Nobel Prize. From a traditional Indian standpoint, their achievement was so remarkable that devotees bow down now at Aurobindo and Richard's grave, worshipping the saints, possibly the deities, of the religion of the future. This unprecedented combination— Nobel Prize nominations and religious prostrations—may indicate that Madame Richard did realize a "third position" after all, in defiance of skeptical philosophers like Dickinson who trumpeted that India was off in a religious dreamworld of its own, irrelevant to the West.

Mirra Richard and Aurobindo consciously intended their union to symbolize, to epitomize this "third position" of India and the West together, catalyzing a better future for humankind. When Woodrow Wilson's daughter lived in Pondichéry during the 1930s and '40s, she corresponded with Henry Ford, to entice him to the Aurobindo ashram, promising Aurobindo would satisfy Ford's insatiable curiosity about his previous reincarnations. But various commitments kept postponing the automaker's arrival, and then Margaret Wilson died, and not long thereafter Ford himself did. For the next twenty-five years, Mirra Richard dreamed of that meeting—Ford's money saying hello to Aurobindo's wisdom. In her mind it symbolized a greater marriage, materially dynamic America the groom and visionary India the bride, the international couple whose child would be the balanced "third position" that an always unbalanced, ever polarized world had in all the long centuries never known.

✷

Aurobindo died only in 1950, and Mirra Richard even more recently, in 1973, and they both lived public lives surrounded by witnesses. Oddly, though, what really went on between them during their lifetimes remains largely unknown. Their biographies float in a sea of sentimental print, where not one objective drop, no critical word, surfaces anywhere. "The greatest pity it is," Ashis Nandy, one of India's leading sociologists, observed, "that no independent scholar ever thought to interview Sri Aurobindo. Aurobindo's first language was English, he knew European thought, and he could have explained what he was up to to any audience." Nandy was struck by the fact that "all sorts of non-Buddhists interview the Dalai Lama on every subject, with the result that Tibetan Buddhism went overnight from being unknown to world-respected. By contrast, to Aurobindo only the devotee came, who asked the easy question, and never the disinterested inquirer, to ask the difficult one."

Ashis Nandy's neighbor, flying on a United Nations mission, was exchanging the usual pleasantries with the man in the next seat. Eventually the stranger asked Nandy's neighbor where he was from. He answered India.

"Oh, isn't that nice. That is so nice," the man blathered. "India is such a nice country. My mother went there and became a goddess."

"Really!" Nandy's neighbor exclaimed. "How did that happen?"

"I couldn't say. I actually don't know much about it."

The man on the flight was Mirra and Paul Richard's son. Just as the English schoolboy Akroyd remade himself into the guru Sri Aurobindo, so Mirra Richard disposed of her old identity. She converted herself into "the Mother"—the title holy women in India assume. Ironically, as the Mother, she largely ceased being her own son's mother. (Likewise, when Ghose earlier changed into Aurobindo, he discarded his devoted wife. Shedding the cocoon of one's mundane identity can involve, evidently, an abrupt and notuncruel metamorphosis.) As the Mother, she became with Aurobindo little short of divine; for disciples, in fact, not short at all. Satyajit Ray filmed a comedy, *Devi* (1960), about a man who worships his daughter-in-law as a goddess, much to her chagrin. Mirra Richard suffered her apotheosis more gracefully, as a lesson for others to do the same.

But beneath the Authorized Version of her life, murkiness reigns. What happened for instance to Paul Richard, Mirra's husband, who shared all her occult and spiritual interests? It was he who, on an earlier visit to Pondichéry in 1910, learned about Aurobindo and became his first western disciple. Thus Paul Richard set in motion the fateful drama. And then: poof. No Stalinist history ever more completely erased a person from the photograph or deleted him from the record. K. S. Srinivas Iyengar wrote an 800-page biography of the Mother, at a certain point in which Paul Richard simply disappears, heard of no more. In traditional Indian narrative, this lacuna is not problematic: Paul Richard's duty was to evaporate. Sri Aurobindo and the Mother were fated to join forces, and fate momentarily availed itself of a Monsieur Richard. Afterward, the good monsieur's duty done, he holds no more interest.

In prosaic terms, a curious triangle evidently formed in Pondichéry, and as the unwanted leg of it, Paul hobbled off, first to the Himalayas and then back to France. In his absence, Aurobindo and the Mother began . . . in fact, it is not clear exactly what they did begin. Obviously it could be labeled some sort of an "affair," but no disciple has ever suspected for a second it was the dirty, illicit affair ordinary paramours have. Aurobindo and the Mother were soaring high above the ordinary. Grandiosity, as Madame Blavatsky's and even Annie Besant's stories revealed, is an occupational hazard in their line of work; nor did Aurobindo and the Mother stand apart from the manufacture of the mythology that metamorphosed them. Delivering a radio address to celebrate India's Independence in 1947, Aurobindo pointed out that Independence Day and his birthday falling on the same day was no mere coincidence. "You know how the Christians have a way of saying 'love in Christ'?" the Mother would ask, and then reassure her disciples it was similarly acceptable to say "love in the Mother." Such sotto voce megalomania was modesty itself, though, compared to the claims each posited on the other's behalf. The higher gods descend to listen, Aurobindo stated, whenever the Mother plays the organ. "Since the beginning of earthly history," the Mother explained, "Sri Aurobindo has always presided over the great earthly transformations, under one form or another, under one name or another."

But if Mirra Richard was a Blavatsky-like prophetess on Sunday, Tuesday might find her a Forsterian humanist liberal, Wednesday a Curzon empire builder, and on Friday even a Naipaul-like skeptic. The Mother's activities in Pondichéry resemble Yamoussoukro, in Naipaul's description of the goings-on there, where magic and superstition possess the night but are forgotten in the morning's light. Whenever a wild Blavatsky-type seeker actually approached the Mother, wishing to take a supernatural nosedive into infinity, she would sweetly reason him back to levelheadedness. She despised miracles-are-my-calling-card yogis; she rejected the magic-lantern show of superstition. The Mother and Aurobindo both had excellent modern educations, they knew history, and they placed their efforts within a historical context. When the Mother later founded her experimental city, she listed as its cardinal rule "NO RELIGIONS." Religious mentality had characterized one stage in the historical development of consciousness, and the Mother's city would furnish a propitious place for the next stage. The Mother used an occult or otherworldly interest to underwrite western-style, utilitarian, humanitarian projects in the here and now. As in Annie Besant's translation of the Gita, Hindu spirituality was suddenly preoccupied with remaking *this* world.

The Mother was tempted away from her sensible, practical humanitarianism, however, by her need to create her "third position." It was like irresistible, forbidden fruit for her—the possibility of creating a new dispensation that would combine India and the West and simultaneously supersede them. The Mother and Aurobindo thus took two antithetical notions—Hindu transcendence and western historicism—ideas that cancel each other out, and they yoked them together as the basis of their program. On the one hand, they borrowed from ancient Indian Yoga, which holds that whatever happens in time is repetitive, painful, and of limited reality; on the other, they appropriated recent trends in European philosophy, which stressed historical conditions as shaping everything that matters. It was historical perspective, especially its extreme form of social evolution, that the British used to justify their ruling their little Indian brothers (no longer brothers, in fact, but a less-evolved, quasi-negroid species). And this pernicious evolutionary thinking was exactly what Aurobindo and the Mother smuggled into Indian philosophy.

Were they playing into the hands of the colonialists, who justified their rule in India by claiming they had brought the necessary torch of progress to the subcontinent? Perhaps not. Aurobindo and the Mother were in one way shrewder than Gandhi. Gandhi opposed western progress with the idea of eternal unchanging Truth, but no sooner had Gandhi died than India forgot about his Truth and demanded only progress and more progress. The Mother and Aurobindo ducked the insidious debate about whether the Indians were ready to take the torch of advance in their own shaky hands (as Besant or Forster said) or whether they still needed to copy western models (Curzon's or Naipaul's position). The Mother and Aurobindo defanged evolutionary progress by spiritualizing the idea of progress instead of futilely rejecting it. They adopted Social Darwinism not to differentiate among the races but to characterize the history of human consciousness as a whole. Once human consciousness, and not manufacturing or military superiority, was the measure, then the Social Darwinism debate entirely changed. Aurobindo gave that debate a whole different twist when he proposed that the human species itself could evolve into something like a race of Christs or Buddhas—if only we could direct the course of evolution consciously. Aurobindo's manifesto, "*Man is a transitional being; he is not final,*" indirectly rebuked the Europeans, who, hubris-mad, supposed themselves the final products of history.

But how would the next human transition be accomplished? How, for that matter, do you steer the course of evolution consciously? In a discussion evening at the Pondichéry ashram during the early 1920s, such questions were put to Aurobindo. He answered with a comic gesture, a burlesque imitation of complete ignorance, throwing his hands comically into the air. "I have *no idea.*" When the laughter died down, he added quietly, "No one has tried it before."

❊

But then, in a secret and decades-long experiment, Aurobindo and the Mother did try it. On November 24, 1926, Aurobindo retired to his rooms, rarely making public appearances, delegating all outside affairs to the Mother's charge. This was the "experiment" (a favorite word of theirs)—to see whether a "superior person," if undistracted and pursuing no other aim, could consciously effect the next turn in human evolution. Aurobindo and the Mother maintained that what they were attempting paralleled "a new [European] science called psycho-analysis." But western psychiatry in the '20s took as its starting point the neurotic patient. Aurobindo's experiment began, instead, with one of the most accomplished people on the planet—a psychiatry for the well. Aurobindo could have been an important official under the Raj; alternatively, he could have led the revolution against the British. (After Gandhi consolidated his authority, he offered Aurobindo all his power, if he would come out of retirement.) Instead Aurobindo chose to stay behind closed doors, to raise the workings of consciousness to a new stage.

And did he? His disciples say yes; others don't know what to say. Freud's achievement was rendering his "new science" into a common language that could become part of the common debate. Aurobindo's sixty-eight published volumes (he was doing something in that room alone) indulge in a personal, eccentric terminology that appeals to the converted but, for others, obscures to the point of inconclusiveness his rarefied experiment. Reports leaked out about Aurobindo's fasting for twenty-three days, while walking up and down the room in eight-hour stretches. Stories circulated about his nights without sleep, his writing from six in the evening till six in the morning and then continuing on the next day as though he'd just risen from a deep rest. "Food and sleep are no longer [for Aurobindo and the Mother] the unique and all-absorbing source of the renewal of energy," one disciple said. But devotees say that sort of thing; beyond the devotees, the reputation of Aurobindo trails off, a fabulous but faint whisper, like those rumors of Himalayan yogis who do feats beyond belief. Suppose all we knew of Einstein was that he had fiddled with some numbers and formulas in a closed room, and he had never published the result. Aurobindo, a man conceivably of equivalent mental powers, conjoined the best of western education and Indian spirituality in his room. His disciples say, a new Superman, and most others say, Who?

Whatever advances Aurobindo made, it was thus left to the Mother to propagate in the common, everyday realm. Their arrangement in Pondichéry resembles that situation at Adyar, where Leadbeater handled the spiritual and Annie the practical end of Theosophy—except Aurobindo was hardly Leadbeater's showboat flimflam (nor was the Mother the Besantian Locomotive Express). If the arrangement reverses western stereotypes about gender roles, it may conform to certain Indian ones about the passive, spiritual male and the active, practical female. The god Shiva had his consort Parvati to direct his energies outward, though hardly into such up-to-date projects as the Mother now began to initiate.

Originally a traditional, males-only establishment, Aurobindo's ashram in Pondichéry opened its door first to women aspirants, then to families, and on December 2, 1943, the Mother took the bold step of starting a school. She set up not a religious school to propagate their teachings, but a secular, modern one, to teach students to think for themselves. As early as 1910 Aurobindo had stated, when such views were bold pedagogy,

> The first principle of true teaching is that nothing can be taught. The teacher is not an instructor or task-master, he is a helper and guide. ... He does not impart knowledge to him [the student], he shows him how to acquire knowledge for himself.

With little or no knowledge of Dewey or Montessori, the Mother concocted her own progressive school—one that offered courses from sculpture to judo, intended to educate the whole child. Examinations, grades, and diplomas belonged to education's *ancien régime* and had no place in her school. Born a Victorian, the Mother became the enemy of Victorian education. Even into the 1960s, she would burst into the classroom declaring, we'll do away with fixed schedules and organize everything around subjects. Better, we'll do away with subjects and organize everything around students' interests. Similar revolts in pedagogy were upsetting Berkeley and Paris and Berlin colleges at the time, but the Mother wasn't in touch with Berkeley or Berlin. She was a woman isolated for half a century at the world's edge, conjuring out of her octogenarian brain education à la mode. When some teachers complained that one boy did nothing but daydream and look out the window at girls, the Mother answered: very proper for someone his age, leave him alone. Left alone, the students tended to develop, according to their temperaments, sturdy practical skills they devoted to public projects or Forsterian artistic sensibilities upon which no nuance was lost. The Mother's ashram school produced, in its modest way, some of the most impressive graduates in India. But the Mother tended not to think modestly. In 1952 she renamed the ashram school, grandly, the Sri Aurobindo International Center for Education, declaring it was destined to become "the greatest seat of knowledge upon earth."

And even that would be insufficient. Her cherished Aurobindo had not written sixty volumes and in his own body emanated the next step in evolution merely to start a new schoolhouse. In the 1960s, in her ninth decade, the Mother realized that if she were to inaugurate the next step in evolution on earth, it was now or never. She boldly changed tenses: her vision expressed fifty years before, she rewrote, using present- instead of future-tense verbs:

> A new light breaks upon the earth,
> A new world is born. . . .

She determined to create something even greater than Curzon or Annie Besant had fantasized—a practical utopia where human evolution can continue: "a place," as she described it, "where men can live away from all national rivalries, social conventions, self-contradictory moralities, and contending religions." On February 29, 1968, the Mother rechristened two thousand acres outside Pondicherry "Auroville," the so-called prototypical City of the Future. The soils from scores of nations were ceremonially mixed in a symbolic urn, and the United Nations formally recognized the project.

No before-and-after picture could juxtapose a starker contrast than those denuded, hard-soil acres *before*—flatness and dryness and barrenness everywhere—and the garden community, green and flourishing, a quarter century *after*. Reams of World Bank money have poured into desolate locales elsewhere, affecting little transformation; in Auroville, with relatively little cash infusion but many idealists' labor, as bleak a spot as exists on earth was made to blossom with a million trees and bushes. And if this transformation could take place in Auroville, in overpopulated, soil-impoverished India, then surely it could succeed anywhere.

Should development experts be paying attention? The Indian minister of agriculture, upon visiting Auroville, praised its agronomic practices and technical expertise, but added, "These things have been tried before. Of course they never last." Auroville as a viable model has brought in a hung jury almost since its inception, and nowhere is opinion more divided than between the Aurovilleans themselves and the Aurobindo ashram in Pondichéry. The ashram, ascetic and predominantly Indian, and Auroville, permissive and mostly western, can appear like the two children of the Mother-Aurobindo marriage. And they have coexisted in deadly animosity the way only siblings can. They float like opposing dreams—the Mother's versus Mirra Richard's—the religious dream of a divine destination versus the Enlightenment dream of having it on earth. Once upon a time the Mother's agendas had seemed all of a piece when she was alive in body to contain them. That body brought together in a "third position" ambitions as different as Curzon's and Besant's for politics, and Forster's and Naipaul's for the self, and Isherwood's and Martin Luther King Jr.'s for religion, but after the Mother died those sets of opposites, those western antonyms, broke apart and went their separate ways.

For half a century, though, Mirra Richard had known the happiness that Annie Besant tasted for only one fleeting, sweet moment in 1917, when as president of both the Indian National Congress and the Theosophical Society she brought spirit and politics, East and West, into a semblance of balance. Mirra Richard's story suggests that not only Annie Besant but every figure in this book might have attained his heart's desire in India, had he been content to enact that desire upon a small enough stage. V. S. Naipaul was disappointed not to locate western civilization in an Indian mirror, whereas in the Mother's tiny corner in Pondichéry, India and Europe did reflect each other. On the most miniature scale conceivable, she even accomplished what Curzon imagined his great Empire achieving—spreading education, converting underutilized areas to productivity, the different races all mingling together. But Curzon ended with his viceroyalty soured and his molten ambition disappointed—a fate Richard was safe from because a side of her was content, as E. M. Forster was, simply to live among Indians. Perhaps, most of all, she resembles Christopher Isherwood, experiencing the great good fortune of finding the ideal teacher, one's precious guru. But Isherwood was always sneaking off to satisfy his emotional, erotic side, while the Mother converted her pious teacher into her spiritual lover.

In her days of glory, so legendary a time they might not have happened in time, heaven and earth, work and prayer, East and West, were all one—just as, their disciples claim, Aurobindo and the Mother became spiritually one. And Mirra Richard achieved her synthesis, her work, in defiance of the European highbrows like Dickinson who argued that "the contrast is that between India and the rest of the world." Forster in his Indian costume or Naipaul with his Indian heritage attempted an Indian-western fusion at the personal level of their own identity; Curzon and Besant attempted such a fusion politically through changing social institutions and altering communal living arrangements; still others, say, Isherwood, melded East-West religious ideas about the universe. What each did in his or her particular area, the Mother and Aurobindo essayed across the board: the personal *and* the political *and* the religious all came to play a part in their unprecedented partnership in Pondichéry.

They are venerated today primarily as guru-teachers or religious saints, but Aurobindo's career began in revolutionary agitation and the Mother's ended by founding a new city. Religion became politics: their spiritual vision, they believed, had to prove itself by improving material conditions and enhancing communal harmony, or else it had failed. The political became the personal: even as they built at the ashram and in Auroville scale models for better communal living, the Mother and Aurobindo breathed a deliciously close, erotic intimacy (even if unconsummated) more intense than most married couples enjoy. Their liaison, at once intimate, social, and religious, gave them a heady autonomy over a province at once small (for Aurobindo, no larger than a room) and infinite, without borders; their latitude in reimagining the possible—even the next step in human evolution!—makes creative novelists like Forster and Isherwood seem positively prosaic, leaden-footed by comparison. The Mother's and Aurobindo's imaginations were so unbounded that their far-fetched "experiments" belong today less to history than to mythology. No one else dared go so far: they shed as so many useless rags their upbringing, their spouses, and even their names, and in doing so, the problems that once troubled Akroyd Ghose and Mirra Richard melted curatively in the air. The marriage that could never take place between them became, ironically, the most fruitful marriage of all.

Alas, however, the memory (at least outside India) of that remarkable pair has also dissolved in air. Any good library in the West possesses hundreds of books about Aurobindo and the Mother, but hardly one written after the 1970s. Why was their glory so transient? Quite possibly because when Mirra Richard donned the heavy Indian robes of the Mother, their hem inadvertently tripped her, and she toppled from her new third position over into an older position, one that was too fixed, too religious, too Hindu, for what she envisioned. The prophetess of the City of the Future became—with a hubris that would have done Lord Curzon credit—the priestess of a religion of the past.

No sooner did Mirra Richard pass away in 1973 than "religion" began to swallow her remains whole. Like Mrs. Moore in *A Passage to India*, she became the "idol" of a posthumous local cult and an idiosyncratic, talented individual both shrunk and bloated into an amorphous quasi-deity. On November 17, the Mother's *Mahasamadhi* day (the day she entered unbroken nirvana or, as we'd say, died), the streets outside the ashram are thronged, block after block, with sweet, silent pilgrims, and Pondichéry is then Jerusalem, Mecca, Bodhgaya. They stand patiently, waiting their turn to bow before the earthly ashes of the Holy—and not that fallible, warmhearted, energetic woman the ashram school graduates once knew. India, it's said, has suffered many conquerors and foreign influences but eventually absorbed them all. It suffered the Mughals, and it suffered Curzon with his dream of Empire, and it suffered even Naipaul with his ersatz legends and real bitterness about India. And so it suffered a stylish Frenchwoman, her thoughts abuzz with *fin de siècle* occultism and idealistic reforms, who sailed for Pondicherry in 1914, and today is. . . . "My mother went to India and became a goddess," the man on the plane related, "though I can't tell you much about it."

The November monsoon, which once drenched Mirra Richard and sent her hurrying for cover, passes, and December brightens into one of the most pleasant times to be in South India. The sun comes out, and Pondichéry no longer looks like the soggy, gray end of the world but a moderately prosperous Indian town with a bustling population of nearly half a million. The French influence is decaying, most noticeable now in the cheap price of beer and alcohol there. *Perhaps* it was once the site of a drama of high stakes—like Annie Besant's Adyar—but today Pondichéry seems a town ordinary enough. "The wind bloweth and the wind listeth": that biblical phrase for the mystery of impermanence is probably in nobody's mind as the breeze from the Bay of Bengal picks up and cools the townspeople moving in its soft circuits.

❈

Fifty years after Dickinson journeyed to the Orient, and ten years before the Mother entered her *Mahasamadhi*, a symposium took place that might have pricked both their interests. Oxford University Press published its proceedings under the title *The Glass Curtain between Asia and the West* (alluding to the more infamous Iron Curtain). The contributors to *The Glass Curtain*, such as Arnold Toynbee, no longer elicit high regard; its insights about lingering geocultural difference seem dated now, like an old newspaper. But the dedication to the volume remains memorable. Its Indian editor dedicated it to his young son Pico, in the hopes that he would mature into a world without even transparent barriers. Formerly when History was capitalized and personified, He or She was known to be inordinately fond of irony; in that respect it has not changed. For little Pico did grow up and discover, lo and behold, no insurmountable regional differences—and was he chagrined. Pico Iyer's *Video Night in Kathmandu* (1988) castigates

American or European tourists who fancy themselves explorers penetrating the wilds of Bali or Burma, when what they are encountering is the refuse of their own civilization dumped elsewhere. Pico Iyer's *Video Night* makes anyone today who still thinks in terms of India versus the West, as Dickinson did, or who attempts an eastern-western synthesis, as the Mother did, seem a mind troubled by mental retardation.

This present book is published shortly before the year 2000, but it may require an ultimate Millennium before folks stop thinking in terms of West versus East. Or, for that matter, before they stop setting up as opposites "traditional" versus "modern," "natural" versus "supernatural," "masculine" versus "feminine," "practical" versus "idealistic," and so on. Boundaries realign and technologies make obsolete, but ordinary human thought continues to think in terms of *this* versus *that*, to define something by its dissimilarity to something else. But the test of a first-rate mind, F. Scott Fitzgerald suggested, is whether it can hold two contradictory ideas simultaneously—and still function. This book is the story of first-rate intelligences who went to India and yoked contradictory ideas and fabricated "third positions" there, in the hopes of shaping a better-functioning future.

Sometimes those marriages of opposites, like Curzon's between realpolitik and idealism—or the Mother's between evolution and Yoga—were so mind-boggling that eyewitnesses had either to bow down before or ignore them. Dickinson's *Essay on the Civilizations* is a brilliant and convincing argument that some things cannot be combined, most of all a positivistic approach to knowledge and a religious sentiment of faith. Yet off to the side, escaping his attention, was his companion Forster doing just that in India, immersing his secular intellect in an almost medieval milieu of mystics and wayward pilgrims. In that marriage of incongruities, Forster achieved the great event of his life. Curzon, Mirra Richard, and Forster each makes a kind of signpost—as does Besant's occultism *plus* revolutionary politics, and Isherwood's hedonism *plus* a guru, and Yeats's Balzac *plus* Patanjali—showing that things once thought to lie in opposite directions might be found side by side along the same route. The figures in this book, curiously, all deciphered this far-fetched signpost in India. Why was that?

In easier places—in California, say, or on a lucky vacation—what one wanted to happen may be exactly what happens. Such a paradisaical fulfillment of desire inevitably proves fleeting, and many from Dickinson to Naipaul believed it could never happen at all in India, not with its castes and classes and poverty and difficulties. Desire, whether sexual like Forster's or sublimated like Mira behn's, did not meet fulfillment in India but detours, roadblocks, setbacks. "When obstacles cease to occur in my plans," Forster wrote, "it will be the surest proof that I have lost the East." Obstacles were in fact what most travelers encountered in India—on majestic scale in Curzon's instance, in poverty for the '60s hippies—hard things they had to deal with, one after another, and somehow to master.

But in the very unidyllic act of mastering, of finding their way when there seemed no way, a few of these travelers gained a different experience of fulfillment. India, like an old train changing course unannounced, detoured them around many of the limiting axioms, the musty assumptions of cultural modernity. It traversed familiar distinctions and left their old definitions behind, accidentally solving for them an age-old conundrum: How do you obtain the needed thing when you don't even know what to ask for? How arrive at a clarification beyond where your limited knowledge can direct you? As Annie Besant's itinerary of expectations got shredded in India, and events worked out differently from Mirra Richard's anticipation and with more difficulty than Forster foresaw, things often turned out ironically and oddly better. And thus encouraged and chastened, our travelers wended their way home to Europe or America—after a month, as Martin Luther King Jr. did, or after decades in Mira behn's case—though never again to "home" as a child would think of it.

Epilogue
Trying to Remember the Twentieth Century

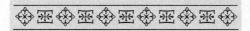

Envision, far away from India, a contemporary couple in their apartment in New York or Paris, its furnishings sparse and tasteful, aesthetically marred only by too much gadgetry, computers, fax, VCR. Far below them in the city thousands of lights flicker on in the dusk and transfigure the familiar with a momentary wonder. Let the man be, say, a psychologist at the university and she, oh, an economist for the World Bank. They look modernity directly in the face: the modern as viewed in the mirror of itself. Novelists from André Gide to Norman Rush have enjoyed whisking up such à la mode couples and dragging them through Third World mud and mosquitoes, and occasionally even to India, to test how fashionable outlooks alter at those "outposts of progress." And isn't that something like the perspective Emerson recommended? Look directly at something and you'll see the obvious, he said; but out of the corner of your eye, on the periphery of vision, you may catch the unexpected.

Certainly the modern consensus about identity, politics, and religion often shifted into a new focus when the travelers of our story stepped across the Indian perimeters. Once in India, if someone like Curzon or Naipaul clutched fast to the textbook definitions, he often defined himself into an untenable corner. But if he damned the old dictionaries (and etiquette books), as Forster and Besant tended to do, and conceded that down just might be up and religion politics, sometimes he opened up an acceptable living space unnoticed before. Modernity has been likened to an architect's logically planned, well-ordered house—everything in its place—eating going on in the dining nook, sleeping in the bedroom, entertaining in the den. But life can have other arrangements, many a traveler discovered in India: when there was no living room, it can in fact be cozy to entertain in the bedchamber.

Metaphors apart, *Father India* is a book about the world as it is but seen through a different lens. In the universities, such lens grinding is under way: everything is environmental economics or psychological anthropology or socio-linguistics, mixing and regrouping disciplines, as if the monolithic approaches and clear-cut divisions of an older understanding will no longer serve. And so, too, India and the West get mixed and reunderstood in new ways.

At the beginning of the twentieth century, nothing could have intoxicated Mrs. Besant or Morgan Forster more than their prospective trips to India. There, amid the oppressive heat and poverty, would unfold before them the ultimate adventure. Though they prided themselves on being realists, they were undertaking a quasi-enchanted travel to the far horizons of the possible, to the last station-stop of the imaginable. Now, by contrast, anyone can fly to India (or almost anywhere else) in less than a day, but like the time in transit, the possibilities upon arrival have also shrunk. As the century wore on, for Isherwood or Naipaul the India that extended their perimeters of vision was less a geographical place and more an internal transformation—a voyage outward and inward simultaneously. The ambition of this book has been to provide the excitement of both types of journey.

Interpreting the Interpreters

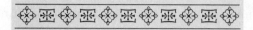

The travels and stays in India told of in this book, if construed as a single historic process, hardly conform to the old stereotypes of passive India and aggressive West. Perhaps a brief word should be added here about those earlier understandings—specifically "Romanticism" and "Orientalism"—once used to describe the West's encounter with India.

In Romantic works the West was an importer from India. Instead of procuring spices and silks, romancers imported poetic imagery and religious costumes (which, however, never changed or challenged anything essential in western society). "Thou by the Indian Ganges's side," ran Marvell's famous lines, "Should rubies find." In more recent Orientalist (or, more accurately, anti-Orientalist scholarship), the West is shown exporting to India—and the worst exports imaginable. Political domination; inappropriate development models; demeaning scholarly misinterpretation: such, according to anti-Orientalists, were the white man's gifts, or burdens, for India. Rare was the interpreter, Romanticist or anti-Orientalist, who saw western-Indian interactions in a chemical combination that fired unexpectedly in both directions simultaneously.

Romanticism chronologically precedes Orientalism, of course. Ever since Marco Polo, western reports of India, when not simply rationales for exploitation, exuded the perfumes of romantic effusion. That Romanticism of rubies and rajahs (and later the Raj) attained a new level of sophistication with the gradual discovery of religion. Indian religions, the various forms of "Hinduism," progressed over three centuries of western interpretation from an anthropological collage of voodoo beliefs to a religion older and somehow even more religious than Christianity. Nietzsche declared, for example, the *Laws of Manu* "a work which is spiritual and superior beyond comparison, which even to name in one breath with the Bible would be a sin against the Holy Ghost." This Romanticism was somewhat innocent, respectful, and if nothing else, charming.

Early in the twentieth century, however, a reaction set in that found such Romanticism anything but charming or innocent. Western critics of western colonialism cried a loud mea culpa (or rather *sua culpa*, since invariably it was other western interpreters, not the one writing, who were to blame). In his prophetic book *War in the Air* (1905), H. G. Wells faulted the British for belittling India through "a considerable literature expressing contempt for the subject races [i.e., Indians] and render[ing] it freely accessible to them." After World War I all the "great uncles" of English literature (as Mulk Raj Anand dubbed them)—George Bernard Shaw, Arnold Bennett, Joseph Conrad, John Galsworthy, E. M. Forster, and Wells himself—were damning the British imperial adventure. As for imperialism's intellectual expression and its literary exponents such as Kipling, was it not just a trifle cheeky, the critics demanded, to inform your colonial subject he was an inferior human being and then expect him to thank you for that information?

By the late 1960s the muckraking of the great uncles had entered the academy and practically defined a field of study. In 1978 a professor at Columbia University, Edward Said, summarized these arguments in an enormously influential book,

Orientalism. In contrast to the Enlightenment view where knowledge furnished the antidote to corrupting power, Said argued (borrowing from Michel Foucault) that the state of knowledge merely replicated the structure of power and perpetuated it. Applying Foucault's model to the Middle East, Said charged those Europeans who wrote about the Levant less with describing it than furnishing a rationale for dominating it. Although *Orientalism* restricted itself to the Arab and Islamic world, scholars of South Asia subsequently tailored Said's argument, with a cut here and an alteration there, to fit the poor humiliated Indians as well.

For the next decade every academic, if respectable, denounced Orientalism (the practice, not Said's book). The simplest western travelers were unmasked as imperialists in poor disguise; the most nonchalant travelogues, as devious arguments establishing western observers' superiority. So what that Annie Besant championed Indian Home Rule and went to prison for doing so: she was really recasting Indian politics in narrow European terms that ensured the English, whom she superficially opposed, would prevail. So what that J. B. S. Haldane took out Indian citizenship and developed "Gandhian," nonviolent biological research: he was imposing western scientific rationality upon indigenous ways of knowing. Such arguments sound, twenty years later, a bit dated or simplistic. More recent critiques have shown the cruder adaptions of *Orientalism* to the Indian scene to be flawed in many instances. Said and Foucault were not wrong that knowledge and power are necessarily related—the great uncles knew that—but the relationship can take more complicated forms than the term "western hegemonic discourse" repeated over and over suggested. Said's critics (James Clifford, Ernest Gellner, Dennis Potter, Aijaz Ahmad, et al.) indirectly pose a question that was once nearly unthinkable in academic circles: as colonialism began its retreat, did a more fruitful post-Romanticist, post-Orientalist encounter between India and the West become possible? (In response to his critics, Said asked this question himself, in an essay, "The Coming End of the Age of Orientalism," appended to a reissue of the 1978 volume.)

Appendix

Lord Curzon at the beginning of the twentieth century and V. S. Naipaul at the end are Orientalism's stock villains—the bad boys of European imperial hubris. Most figures in this book, though, expressed views not dissimilar to Said's, yet the more they lamented Orientalism, ironically, the more they seemed to inch beyond it. Forster acknowledged that colonialism had bequeathed an "irremediable bitterness" walling off Englishman from Indian, and his *A Passage to India* closes with the impossibility of friendship between them. Forster himself, however, had numerous close Indian friends, and in a maharajah's court he participated in the public sphere more fully than he had in England. Proselytizing Christianity was bound to oppress Indians, Isherwood believed, just as it oppressed him. Yet via India and Hinduism Isherwood reinterpreted what religion was, which paradoxically enabled him to tolerate even Christianity. Neither Romanticism's exotic India nor the anti-Orientalist's ravaging imperialism quite allows for this complicated encounter or for the unexpected to happen.

Oddly, though, Foucault, who furnished the theory behind *Orientalism*, did leave hypothetical space where the unexpected might happen and even happen redemptively. In his last books (*The Use of Pleasure* and *The Care of the Self*), Foucault proposed that, although the omniscient, omnipotent establishment monopolized power/knowledge in the present, it did not possess a monopoly for all time. There was a "surplus" of other meanings beyond those that society prescribed at any particular moment. An individual with a willingness to experiment might, if nimble, stumble upon evocative other possibilities. India (or any other civilization), if conceived as something simultaneously geographical and intellectual, both an outward and inward location, might embody or symbolize that surplus of meaning for westerners (exactly as the West did for certain Indians). Scholarship derivative of Foucault usually postulates the perpetuation of social blinders, whereas Foucault showed those blinders potentially falling away. Similarly, second-rate works that copy *Orientalism* describe in the corridor between cultures a one-way and brutal traffic. But the intercultural corridor that Yeats, Besant, Mirra Richard, and Isherwood stepped into ran west to east and east to west simultaneously. Rather, the corridor didn't budge, but they moved through it, their beings in flux and their senses receptive to contrary impressions.

Selected Bibliography

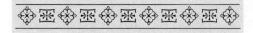

Ackerley, J. R. *Hindoo Holiday: An Indian Journal*. New York: Viking Press, 1960.

Alter, Joseph S. "Gandhi's Body, Gandhi's Truth: Nonviolence and the Biomoral Imperative of Public Health." *The Journal of Asian Studies* 55, no. 2 (May 1996): 301–22.

Ahmad, Aijaz. *In Theory: Classes, Nation, Literatures*. Verso: London, 1992.

Appadurai, Arjun. "Disjuncture and Difference in the Global Cultural Economy." *Public Culture* 2, no. 2 (spring 1990): 1–24.

Appelwhite, James. "A Visit with V. S. Naipaul." *Raritan* 10, no. 10 (summer 1990): 48–54.

Aronson, Alex. *Europe Looks at India: A Study in Cultural Relations*. Calcutta: Riddhi-India, 1946.

Ashe, Geoffrey. *Gandhi*. New York: Stein and Day, 1968.

Attenborough, Richard. *In Search of Gandhi*. Piscataway, New Jersey: New Century Publishers, 1982.

Ballhatchet, Kenneth. *Race, Sex, and Class under the Raj: Imperial Attitudes and Policies, 1793–1905*. New York: St. Martin's Press, 1980.

Batchelor, Stephen. *The Awakening of the West: The Encounter of Buddhism and Western Culture*. Berkeley, Cal.: Parallax Press, 1994.

Beauman, Nicola. *E. M. Forster*. New York: Knopf, 1994.

Besant, Annie. *An Autobiography*. London: T. Fisher Unwin, 1893.

——. *The Case for India: Presidential Address to the Indian National Congress*. Los Angeles: Theosophical Publishing House, 1918.

——. *Hindu Ideals*. Benares, India: Theosophical Society, 1904.

Besterman, Theodore. *Mrs Annie Besant: A Modern Prophet*. London: Kegan Paul, 1934.

Bingham, Nigel. "The Novelist V. S. Naipaul Talks to Nigel Bingham about His Childhood in Trinidad." *The Listener* 88 (September 7, 1972): 306–7.

Blavatsky, H. P. *The Secret Doctrine*. London: Theosophical Publishing House, 1893.

Breckenridge, Carol A., and Peter Van der Veer, eds. *Orientalism and the Postcolonial Predicament: Perspectives on South Asia*. Philadelphia: University of Pennsylvania Press, 1993.

Brégeon, Janine. *Le Margousier*. Paris: Flammarion, 1984.

Brown, Judith. *Gandhi: Prisoner of Hope*. New Haven: Yale University Press, 1989.

Buruma, Ian. "Indian Love Call." *The New York Review of Books* (September 22, 1994): 27–28.

———. "Signs of Life." *The New York Review of Books* (February 14, 1991): 3–5.

Cannadine, David. "Lord Curzon as Ceremonial Impresario," in *Aspects of Aristocracy: Grandeur and Decline in Modern Britain*. New Haven: Yale University Press, 1994.

Case, Margaret H., ed. *Heinrich Zimmer: Coming into His Own*. Princeton: Princeton University Press, 1994.

Chatterjee, Partha. *The Nation and Its Fragments: Colonial and Postcolonial Histories*. Princeton: Princeton University Press, 1993.

Chaudhuri, Nirad. *The Continent of Circe*. New York: Oxford University Press, 1966.

———. "Passage to and from India." *Encounter* (June 1954): 19–24.

Choudhuri, Manmohan, and Ramjee Singh, eds. *Mahatma Gandhi: 125 Years*. Varanasi: Sarva Seva Sangh Prakashan, 1995.

Clark, Ronald. *JBS: The Life and Work of J. B. S. Haldane*. New York: Coward-McCann, 1969.

Clifford, James. *Routes: Travel and Translation in the Late Twentieth Century*. Cambridge: Harvard University Press, 1997.

———. *The Predicament of Culture: Twentieth-Century Ethnography, Literature, and Art*. Cambridge: Harvard University Press, 1988.

Cortázar, Julio. "Advice for Tourists," in *Around the Day in Eighty Worlds*. Trans. Thomas Christensen. San Francisco: North Point Press, 1986.

Cousins, James H., ed. *The Annie Besant Centenary Book, 1847–1947*. Madras: The Besant Centenary Celebrations Committee, 1947.

Coward, H. *Jung and Eastern Thought*. Albany: State University of New York Press, 1985.

Curzon, George Nathaniel. *British Government in India: The Story of the Viceroys and Government Houses*. 2 vols. London: Cassell and Co., 1925.

———. *Leaves from a Viceroy's Notebooks and Other Papers*. London: Macmillan, 1926.

———. *Lord Curzon in India: A Selection from His Speeches as Viceroy and Governor General of India*. London: Macmillan and Co., 1906.

———. *The Place of India in the Empire*. London: J. Murray, 1909.

——. *A Viceroy's India: Leaves from Lord Curzon's Notebooks.* Ed. by Peter King. London: Sidgewick and Jackson, 1986.

Dalrymple, William. *City of Djinns: A Year in Delhi.* New Delhi: Indus, 1993.

Das, G. K. *E. M. Forster's India.* Totowa, New Jersey: Rowman and Littlefield, 1977.

Das, Veena, ed. *Mirrors of Violence: Communities, Riots, and Survivors in South Asia.* New Delhi: Oxford University Press, 1990.

Devi, Maitreya. *It Does Not Die: A Romance.* Chicago: University of Chicago Press, 1994.

Dickinson, G. Lowes. *An Essay on the Civilizations of India, China, and Japan.* London: J. M. Dent and Sons, 1914.

Dinnage, Rosemary. *Annie Besant.* Penguin Books, 1986.

Dilks, David. *Curzon in India,* vol. 1, *Achievement.* London: Rupert Hart-Davis, 1969.

——. *Curzon in India,* vol. 2, *Frustration.* New York: Taplinger, 1970.

Drommamraju, Krishna. *Haldane: The Life and Work of J. B. S. Haldane.* Aberdeen, U.K.: Aberdeen University Press, 1985.

Dumont, Louis. *Homo Hierarchus.* Trans. Mark Saintsbury. London: Paladin, 1970.

——. *Religion/Politics and History in India.* Paris: Mouton Publishers, 1970.

Dunaway, David King, ed. *Aldous Huxley Recollected: An Oral History.* New York: Carroll and Graf Publishers, Inc., 1995.

——. *Huxley in Hollywood.* London: Bloomsbury, 1986.

Edwardes, Michael. *High Noon of Empire: India under Curzon.* London: Eyre and Spottiswoode, 1965.

Einstein, Albert. "Mahatma Gandhi," in *Out of My Later Years.* New York: Philosophical Library, 1950.

Eliade, Mircea. *Bengal Nights.* Chicago: University of Chicago Press, 1994.

Elwin, Verrier. *The Tribal World of Verrier Elwin.* London: Oxford University Press, 1964.

Fields, Rick. *How the Swans Came to the Lake: A Narrative History of Buddhism in America.* Boston: Shambhala, 1992.

Finney, Brian. *Christopher Isherwood: A Critical Biography.* New York: Oxford University Press, 1979.

Forster, E. M. *Abinger Harvest.* New York: Harcourt, Brace and Company, 1936.

——. *A Passage to India.* New York: Harcourt, Brace and World, 1924.

——. *Goldsworthy Lowes Dickinson.* New York: Harcourt, Brace and Company, 1934.

——. ["Kanaya"]: unpublished manuscript of Forster's relation to this barber in Dewas. Cambridge: King's College Library, 1921.

——. *Only Connect: Letters to Indian Friends.* New Delhi: Arnold-Heinemann, 1979.

——. *Selected Letters of E. M. Forster,* vol. 2, *1921–1970.* Edited by Mary Lago and P. N. Furbank. Cambridge: Harvard University Press, 1985.

——. *The Hill of Devi.* New York: Harcourt, Brace and Company, 1953.

——. *Two Cheers for Democracy.* New York: Harcourt, Brace and Company, 1951.

Frank, Katherine. "Mr. Rushdie and Mrs. Gandhi." *Biography* 19, no. 3 (summer 1996): 245–57.

Freedman, Ralph. *Hermann Hesse: Pilgrim of Crisis.* New York: Pantheon, 1975.

Fryer, Jonathon. *Eye of the Camera: A Life of Christopher Isherwood.* London: Allison and Busby, 1993.

——. *Isherwood.* Garden City, New York: Doubleday and Co., 1978.

Furbank, P. N. *E. M. Forster: A Life.* New York: Harcourt Brace Jovanovich, 1977, 1978.

Gandhi, M. K. *An Autobiography, or The Story of My Experiments with Truth.* Ahmedabad: Narvajivan Publishing House, 1927.

——. *The Collected Writings of Mahatma Gandhi.* 97 vols. Ahmedabad: Narvajivan Publishing House, 1958–1994.

Gilmour, David. *Curzon.* London: John Murray, 1994.

Ginsberg, Allen. *Indian Journals: March 1962–May 1963.* San Francisco: City Lights Books, 1970.

Glenn, Jerome Clayton. *Linking the Future: Findhorn, Auroville, Arcosanti.* Cambridge, Mass.: Hexiad Project, 1979.

Godwin, Jocelyn. *The Theosophical Enlightenment.* Albany: State University of New York Press, 1994.

Goradia, Nayana. *Lord Curzon: The Last of the British Moghuls.* Delhi: Oxford University Press, 1993.

Gorra, Michael. *After Empire: Scott, Naipaul, Rushdie.* Chicago: University of Chicago Press, 1997.

Gowda, H. H. Anniah, ed. *A Garland for E. M. Forster.* Mysore: The Literary Half-Yearly, 1969.

Green, Martin. *Children of the Sun: A Narrative of "Decadence" in England after 1918.* New York: Basic Books, 1976.

——. *Gandhi: Voice of a New Age Revolution.* New York: Continuum, 1993.

Halbfass, Wilhelm. *India and Europe: An Essay in Understanding.* Albany: State University of New York Press, 1988.

Hamilton, Ian. "Without a Place: An Interview with V. S. Naipaul." *Savacou* 9/10 (1974): 120–26.

Hamner, Robert D., ed. *Critical Perspectives on V. S. Naipaul.* Washington, D.C.: Three Continents Press, 1977.

——. *V. S. Naipaul.* New York: Twayne Publishers, 1973.

Hardwick, Elizabeth. "Meeting V. S. Naipaul." *New York Times Book Review* (May 13, 1979): 1, 36.

Hawley, John Stratton. "Naming Hinduism." *Wilson Quarterly* (summer 1991): 20–34.

Heilbrun, Carolyn. *Christopher Isherwood*. New York: Columbia University Press, 1970.

Hesse, Hermann, and Romain Rolland. *Correspondence, Diary Entries, 1915–1940*. London: Oswald Wolff, 1978.

Hogan, Patricia Colm, and Lalita Pandit, eds. *Literary India: Comparative Studies in Aesthetics, Colonialism, and Culture*. Albany, New York: SUNY Press, 1995.

Horsman, Mathew, and Andrew Marshall. *After the Nation-State: Citizens, Tribalism, and the New World Disorder*. London: HarperCollins, 1994.

Hughes, Peter. *V. S. Naipaul*. London: Routledge, 1988.

Huxley, Aldous. *Jesting Pilate: Travels through India, Burma, Malaya, China, and America*. New York: Paragon House, 1991 (orig. pub., 1926).

———. *The Perennial Philosophy*. New York: Harper and Row, 1970.

Inden, Ronald. *Imagining India*. Oxford: Blackwell Publishers, 1990.

Ingram, Catherine. *In the Footsteps of Gandhi: Conversations with Spiritual Social Activists*. Berkeley: Parallax Press, 1990.

Isherwood, Christopher. *Christopher and His Kind*. New York: Farrar, Straus, 1976.

———. *Lions and Shadows*. New York: New Directions, 1947.

———. *A Meeting by the River*. New York: Farrar, Straus, 1967.

———. *My Guru and His Disciple*. New York: Farrar, Straus, 1980.

———. *Ramakrishna and His Disciples*. Hollywood: Vedanta Society, 1965.

———, ed. *Vedanta for Modern Man*. Hollywood: Vedanta Society, 1951.

———, ed. *Vedanta for the Western World*. Hollywood: Vedanta Press, 1971.

Iyer, Raghavan Narasimhan, ed. *The Glass Curtain between Asia and Europe: A Symposium on the Historical Encounters and the Changing Attitudes of the Peoples of the East and West*. London: Oxford University Press, 1965.

Iyer, S. Subramanya, et al. *Annie Besant: Servant of Humanity*. Madras: New India, 1924.

Jarvis, Kelvin. *V. S. Naipaul: A Selective Bibliography with Annotations, 1957–1987*. Metuchen, New Jersey: The Scarecrow Press, 1989.

Jhabvala, Ruth Prawer. *An Experience of India*. New York: W. W. Norton, 1972.

Judd, Denis. *Balfour and the British Empire*. New York: St. Martin's Press, 1968.

Jung, Carl. *Memories, Dreams, Reflections*. Ed. Aniela Jaffé. Trans. Richard and Clara Winston. New York: Pantheon Books, 1963.

———. *Psychology and the East*. Princeton: Princeton University Press, 1978.

Kakar, Sudhir. "Encounters of the Psychological Kind: Freud, Jung, and India." *The Psychoanalytic Study of Society* 19 (1994): 263–72.

———. "Western Science, Eastern Minds." *Wilson Quarterly* (winter 1991): 109–16.

Kapur, Sudarshan. *Raising up a Prophet: The African-American Encounter with Gandhi*. Boston: Beacon Press, 1992.

Kedourie, Elie. *The Crossman Confession and Other Essays in Politics, History, and Religion*. London: Mansell, 1984.

Kemp, Peter. "Severed from Rootlessness." *Times Literary Supplement* (August 7, 1987): 838–39.

Kepel, Gilles. *The Revenge of God: The Resurgence of Islam, Christianity, and Judaism in the Modern World*. University Park: Penn State University Press, 1994.

Khilnani, Sunil. *The Idea of India*. New York: Farrar, Straus and Giroux, 1997.

King, Bruce. *V. S. Naipaul*. New York: St. Martin's Press, 1993.

King, Francis. *Christopher Isherwood*. Essex: Longman Group, Ltd., 1976.

King, Martin Luther, Jr. *A Testament of Hope: The Essential Writings of Martin Luther King, Jr.* Ed. James M. Washington. San Francisco: Harper & Row, 1986.

King, Peter. *The Viceroy's Fall: How Kitchener Destroyed Curzon*. London: Sidgewick and Jackson, 1986.

Koestler, Arthur. *The Lotus and the Robot*. New York: Macmillan, 1961.

Kuehn, Robert E., ed. *Aldous Huxley: A Collection of Critical Essays*. Englewood Cliffs, New Jersey: Prentice-Hall, 1974.

Lambert, Angela. *Unquiet Souls: A Social History of the Illustrious, Irreverent, Intimate Group of British Aristocrats Known as the Souls*. New York: Harper and Row, 1984.

Lehman, John. *Christopher Isherwood: A Personal Memoir*. New York: Henry Holt, 1987.

Leslie, Shane. *Studies in Sublime Failure*. London: Ernest Benn Limited, 1932.

Levy, Jacques E. *Cesar Chavez: Autobiography of La Causa*. New York: W. W. Norton, 1975.

Lloyd, Sarah. *An Indian Attachment*. New York: William Morrow and Company, 1984.

"M." *The Gospel of Sri Ramakrishna*. Trans. Swami Nikhilanana. New York: Ramakrishna-Vivekananda Center, 1974.

Madan, T. N., ed. *Religion in India*. Delhi: Oxford University Press, 1992.

Mandela, Nelson. "Gandhi, the Prisoner: A Comparison," in *Mahatma Gandhi: 125 Years*. Ed. B. R. Nanda. New Delhi: Wiley Eastern Limited, 1995.

Masson, Jeffery M. *My Father's Guru: A Journey through Spirituality and Disillusion*. Reading, Mass.: Addison-Wesley, 1993.

Maugham, Somerset. *The Gentleman in the Parlour: A Record of a Journey from Rangoon to Haiphong*. New York: Paragon House, 1989.

——. *The Razor's Edge*. London: William Heinemann, 1944.

McDermott, Robert, ed. *The Essential Aurobindo*. New York: Schocken Books, 1973.

Meade, Marion. *Madame Blavatsky: The Woman behind the Myth.* New York: G. P. Putnam's Sons, 1980.

Mehta, Ved. *Mahatma Gandhi and His Apostles.* New York: Penguin, 1977.

Medwick, Catherine. "Life, Literature, and Politics: An Interview with V. S. Naipaul." *Vogue* (August 1981): 129–30.

Merton, Thomas. *The Asian Journals of Thomas Merton.* New York: New Directions, 1975.

Metcalf, Thomas R. *The New Cambridge History of India,* vol. 3, pt. 4, *Ideologies of the Raj.* Cambridge: Cambridge University Press, 1995.

Michaux, Henri. *A Barbarian in Asia.* Trans. Sylvia Beach. New York: New Directions, 1949.

Michener, Charles. "The Dark Visions of V. S. Naipaul." *Newsweek* (November 16, 1981): 104–11.

Mitter, Partha. *Art and Nationalism in Colonial India, 1850–1922: Occidental Orientations.* Cambridge: Cambridge University Press, 1995.

Monier-Williams, Monier. *Hinduism.* Delhi: Rare Books, 1971.

Mosley, Leonard. *Curzon: The End of an Epoch.* London: Readers Union; Longmans, Green & Co. 1961.

The Mother. *The Mother on Herself.* Pondicherry: Sri Aurobindo Ashram, 1977.

Motwani, Kewal. *Three Great Sages: Sri Aurobindo, Dr. Annie Besant, J. Krishnamurti.* Madras: Ganesh and Co., 1951.

Mount, Ferdinand. "No Home for Mr. Biswas." *The Spectator* 252 (May 5, 1984): 21–3.

Mulgan, Geoff. *Politics in an Anti-Political Age.* London: Policy Press, 1994.

Mudal. "Woodrow Wilson." *Mother India* 15, no. 2 (August 1963): 61–63.

Muthana, I. M. *Mother Besant and Mahatma Gandhi.* Tamil Nadu: Thenpulam Publishers, 1986.

Myrdal, Gunnar. *The Political Element in the Development of Economic Theory.* New Brunswick: Transaction Publishers, [1954] 1990.

Naipaul, Shiva. *An Unfinished Journey.* New York: Viking, 1982.

Naipaul, V. S. *An Area of Darkness.* New York: Macmillan, 1965.

——. *Finding the Center.* New York: Knopf, 1984.

——. *India: A Million Mutinies Now.* New York: Viking, 1991.

——. *India: A Wounded Civilization.* New York: Knopf, 1977.

——. "One Out of Many." *In a Free State.* New York: Knopf, 1971.

——. *The Overcrowded Barracoon.* New York: Knopf, 1973.

——. "Our Universal Civilization." *New York Review of Books* (January 31, 1991): 22–25.

Nanda, B. R., ed. *Mahatma Gandhi: 125 Years.* New Delhi: Wiley Eastern Limited, 1995.

Nandy, Ashis. *The Intimate Enemy: Loss and Recovery of Self under Colonialism.* Delhi: Oxford University Press, 1983.

——. *The Savage Freud: And Other Essays on Possible and Retrievable Selves.* Princeton: Princeton University Press, 1995.

——. *Traditions, Tyranny and Utopias: Essays in the Politics of Awareness.* Delhi: Oxford University Press, 1987.

Narasaimaiah, C. D., ed. *Gandhi and the West.* Mysore: University of Mysore, 1969.

Natwar-Singh, K., ed. *E. M. Forster: A Tribute.* New York: Harcourt, Brace and World, 1964.

Nethercot, Arthur H. *The First Five Lives of Annie Besant.* Chicago: University of Chicago Press, 1961.

——. *The Last Four Lives of Annie Besant.* Chicago: University of Chicago Press, 1963.

Nicolson, Harold. *Curzon: The Last Phase 1919–1925. A Study in Post-War Diplomacy.* Boston: Houghton Mifflin Company, 1934.

——. *Some People.* London: Constable and Company, 1927.

Nicolson, Nigel. *Mary Curzon.* New York: Harper and Row, 1977.

Nightingale, Peggy. *Journey through Darkness: The Writing of V. S. Naipaul.* St. Lucia: University of Queensland, 1987.

O'Malley, L. S. S., ed. *Modern India and the West: A Study of Their Interactions.* London: Oxford, 1941.

Page, Norman. *E. M. Forster.* New York: St. Martin's Press, 1987.

Pandit, M. P., ed. *Memorable Moments with the Mother.* Pondicherry: Pipti Publications, 1975.

——. *Sri Aurobindo and the Mother.* Pondicherry: Pipti Publications, 1975.

Parekh, Bhikhu. *Colonialism, Tradition, and Reform: An Analysis of Gandhi's Political Discourse.* New Delhi: Sage Publications, 1989.

——. *Gandhi's Political Philosophy: A Critical Examination.* London: Macmillan, 1989.

Parker, Peter. *Ackerley: A Life of J. R. Ackerley.* New York: Farrar, Straus and Giroux, 1989.

Parry, Benita. *Delusions and Discoveries: Studies of India in the British Imagination, 1880–1930.* London: Allan Lane/Penguin Press, 1972.

Paxton, Nancy L. "Complicity and Resistance in the Writings of Flora Annie Steel and Annie Besant," in *Western Women and Imperialism: Complicity and Resistance.* Ed. Nupur Chaudarhuri and Margaret Strobel. Bloomington: Indiana University Press, 1992.

Porter, Dennis. *Haunted Journeys: Desire and Transgression in European Travel Writing.* Princeton: Princeton University Press, 1991.

Pratt, Mary Louise. *Imperial Eyes: Travel Writing and Transculturation.* London: Routledge, 1991.

Radhakrishnan, S., ed. *Mahatma Gandhi: 100 Years.* New Delhi: Gandhi Peace Foundation, 1968.

Rai, Sudha. *V. S. Naipaul: A Study in Expatriate Sensibility.* Atlantic Highlands, New Jersey: Humanities Press, 1982.

Ramachandran, G., and T. K. Mahadevan, eds. *Gandhi: His Relevance for Our Times.* Bombay: Bharatiya Vidya Bhavan, 1964.

Rampersad, Arnold. "V. S. Naipaul in the South." *Raritan* 10, no. 10 (summer 1990): 24–47.

Reynolds, Reginald. *To Live in Mankind: A Quest for Gandhi.* London: Andre Deutsch, 1951.

Robb, David D. "Christopher Isherwood and Vedanta: A Study of Twentieth-Century Religious Conversion." Honolulu: Unpublished Thesis, University of Hawaii Library, 1976.

Rushdie, Salman. *Imaginary Homelands: Essays and Criticism, 1981–1991.* London: Granta Books, 1991.

Said, Edward W. "East Isn't East: The Impending End of the Age of Orientalism." *Times Literary Supplement* (February 3, 1995): 3–6.

———. "Expectations of Inferiority." *New Statesman* 102 (October 16, 1981): 21–22.

———. *Orientalism.* New York: Vintage Books, 1978.

Scott, Paul. *My Appointment with the Muse: Essays, 1961–75.* Ed. Shelley C. Reece. London: Heinemann, 1986.

———. *The Raj Quartet.* New York: William Morrow and Co., 1976.

Sethna, K. D. "The First Americans in the Sri Aurobindo Ashram." *Mother India* 28, no. 7 (July 1976): 599–602.

Shahane, Vasant A., ed. *Approaches to E. M. Forster.* New Delhi: Arnold-Heinemann, 1981.

Shaw, George Bernard. "Mrs. Besant's Passage through Fabian Socialism," in *The Annie Besant Centenary Book, 1847–1947,* ed. James H. Cousins. Madras: The Besant Centenary Celebrations Committee, 1947.

Shenker, Israel. "V. S. Naipaul, Man without a Society." *New York Times Book Review* (October 17, 1971): 4, 22.

Singhi, Narenda K. *Towards a Theory of Alternative Society.* Jaipur: Rawat Publications, 1987.

Slade, Madeleine [Mira behn]. *The Spirit's Pilgrimage.* New York: Coward-McCann, 1960.

Stallworthy, Jon. *Louis MacNeice.* New York: W. W. Norton, 1995.

Stallybrass, Oliver, ed. *Aspects of E. M. Forster.* New York: Harcourt, Brace, and World, 1969.

Stape, J. H., ed. *E. M. Forster: Interviews and Recollections.* New York: St. Martin's Press, 1993.

Stokes, Eric. "The High-Caste Defector." *Times Literary Supplement* (October 21, 1977): 1229.

Storr, Anthony. *Feet of Clay: Saints, Sinners, and Madmen: A Study of Gurus.* New York: The Free Press, 1996.

Tambiah, Stanley Jevarala. *Culture, Thought, and Social Action: An Anthropological Perspective.* Cambridge: Harvard University Press, 1985.

———. *Magic, Science, Religion, and the Scope of Rationality.* New York: Cambridge University Press, 1990.

Theroux, Paul. *V. S. Naipaul: An Introduction to His Work.* New York: Africana Publishing Corporation, 1972.

Tillet, Gregory. *The Elder Brother: A Biography of Charles Webster Leadbeater.* London: Routledge and Kegan Paul, 1982.

Tillis, Malcolm, and Cynthia Giles, eds. *Turning East: New Lives in India: Twenty Westerners and Their Spiritual Quests.* New York: Paragon House, 1989.

Tinker, Hugh. *The Ordeal of Love: C. F. Andrews and India.* Delhi: Oxford University Press, 1979.

Towers, Robert. "India's Long Night." *New York Review of Books,* 24 (July 14, 1977): 6–12.

Trilling, Lionel. *E. M. Forster.* New York: New Directions, 1964.

Wade, Stephen. *Christopher Isherwood.* New York: St. Martin's Press, 1991.

Washington, Peter. *Madame Blavatsky's Baboon: A History of the Mystics, Mediums, and Misfits Who Brought Spiritualism to America.* New York: Schocken Books, 1995.

Watt, Donald, ed. *Aldous Huxley: The Critical Heritage.* London: Routledge and Kegan Paul, 1975.

West, Geoffrey. *The Life of Annie Besant.* London: Gerald Howe, 1929.

Walsh, William. *V. S. Naipaul.* Edinburgh: Oliver and Boyd, 1973.

Weber, Max. *The Religion of India: The Sociology of Hinduism and Buddhism.* Trans. and ed. Hans H. Gerth and Don Martindale. Glencoe: Free Press, 1958.

Wellock, Wilfred. *Off the Beaten Track: Adventures in the Art of Living.* Varanasi: Sarva Seva Sangh Prakashan, 1963.

Williams, Gertrude Marvin. *The Passionate Pilgrim: A Life of Annie Besant.* New York: Coward-McCann, 1931.

Winkler, Ken. *A Thousand Journeys: The Biography of Lama Anagarika Govinda.* Longsmead, England: Element, 1990.

Wood, Heather. *Third-Class Ticket.* London: Routledge and Kegan Paul, 1980.

Wurgaft, Lewis D. *The Imperial Imagination: Magic and Myth in Kipling's India.* Middletown, Connecticut: Wesleyan University Press, 1981.

Yatiswarananda, Swami. *Adventures in Religious Life.* Madras: Sri Ramakrishna Math, 1975.

Yale, John, ed. *What Vedanta Means to Me: A Symposium.* New York: Doubleday, 1960.

Yourcenar, Marguerite. "On Some Erotic and Mystic Themes of the *Gita-Govinda,*" in *That Mighty Sculptor, Time.* Trans. Walter Kasier. New York: Farrar, Straus and Giroux, 1992.

ACKNOWLEDGMENTS

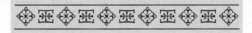

I thank, before anyone else, two people without whose vision and help this book would simply not exist: my agent, Molly Friedrich, and my editor, Terry Karten. People now lament that publishing is in a deplorable and desperate condition, but that is only because it's in a desperate and deplorable condition. However, as long as people like Molly Friedrich and Terry Karten work in publishing, one cannot deplore wholesale nor despair entirely.

Four other great souls assisted in the birth. The godfather of this book, Jay Tolson, has editorially improved more contemporary writing than perhaps any other person now alive in America, and he often proved smarter about this book than its own author. If the book has a godfather, then its godmother was Eloise Goreau in Princeton, who applied her crystalline logic and unsurpassed knowledge of the intricacies of English to reading draft after draft of the book. Two people who gave equally brilliant and indispensable help at an earlier stage were Bish Sanyal and Lee Siegal.

This book was written in the shade of several institutions. Chief among these was the East-West Center in Honolulu, one of the liveliest and most civil places in the whole history of civilization.

Acknowledgments

The two program heads with whom I worked, Larry Smith and Geoff White, should be cloned and made head of every program everywhere, and then the world would run perfectly. At the East-West Center, I enjoyed the friendship and encouragement also of Jeanne Yamamoto, Judy Ledgerwood, Dru Gladney and Mary Hammond, Dick and Romi Morse, Grant Otoshi, Shahjehan Khan, and especially, Wimal Dissanayake. The East-West Center, through which thousands of people from every Asian country have passed, has done more to build up goodwill for America and support for American interests in Asia and the Pacific than any other U.S. pro-grams—indeed, than all of them combined—have done. The recent severe Congressional budget cuts that have undermined the East-West Center reveal an almost suicidal lack of vision of the world beyond Washington.

This book also owes a debt and a deep appreciation to the fol-lowing organizations and people:

The Woodrow Wilson International Center for Scholars in Washington, and especially to Mary Brown Bullock, former head of the Asia program, Jim Morris, George Seay, Lindsay Collins, and Susan Nugent; and to my colleagues at the *WQ,* Jim Carman (who shamanically dispelled all computer quandaries), Steve Lagerfeld, and Bob Landers.

The American Institute of Indian Studies, and especially to Kaye Hill in Chicago and L. S. Suri in Delhi, who showed a competence and consideration that went beyond the call of duty or else pro-vide a better definition of duty.

The *Institut Français de Pondichéry,* and especially to François Hollier and Dominic Goodall.

The Sri Aurobindo Ashram, and to Prashant Khanna, Peter Heehs, and that human exemplar, Shaupon Boshu.

The École Française d'Extrême-Orient, and to Madame L'Hernault and to Jean Deloche.

The Vedanta Society (in Hollywood and Santa Barbara), and espe-cially to Jnana, Udaisane, Vivekeprana, Shraddhaprana, and Shopa (Katherine McGregor).

Acknowledgments

The Theosophical Society, and its unfailing hospitality at Adyar, and to Conrad Jameson whose humor, depth of humanity, and vision might inspire anyone to become a Theosophist.

The Center for the Study of Developing Societies, and to Ashis Nandy.

And to Klaus Rötzer, of the École Française, for showing how one should live in India and everywhere.

To the following individuals, many thanks for their assistance, knowledge, and encouragement: Anne (in Auroville), Don Bachardy, Karen Birdsong, Carla Borden, Nona Boren, Chris Candland, Diane Davis, Wendy Doniger, John Kenneth Galbraith, Ramu Gandhi, Sumit Ganguly, Susan Ginsburg, David Ginsburg, Nancy Goldring, Francis Gouda, Richard Grove, Max Holland, Laura Huxley, Sondra Luther, Sudhir Kakar, Katie Morris, Glenn Paige, Phil Paine, Debra Pughe, Tappan Raychauduri, G. Sundari, Khushwant Singh, Ashley Tatum, Karma Lekshe Tsomo, and Kathryn Weathersby.

INDEX

Index

Index

Macaulay, Thomas, 12, 17, 43
MacNeice, Louis, 7–8
Mahatma Gandhi (Rolland), 259
Maine, Henry, 13
Mandela, Nelson, 18, 189, 236
Mann, Thomas, 204
Manu, 243–244
Mao Zedong, 166, 191
Marco Polo, 295
Marriage
  child, 14–15, 16
  suttee and, 14–15, 16
Marryat, Ellen, 72–73
Marx, Karl, 24, 50, 179, 191, 239
Masood, Syed Ross, 129–130
Materialism, 25–26, 64, 180–181, 195–196, 238, 251
Maugham, Somerset, 199, 202, 210, 218
Maurice (Forster), 126, 138
Mayo, Katherine, 150
Mays, Benjamin, 249
Meditation, 183–184, 185, 220, 221
Meeting by the River, A (Isherwood), 212, 218
Mescaline, 220–221
Miguel Street (Naipaul), 154, 174
Mill, James, 13
Mill, John Stuart, 23, 240
Million Mutinies Now, A (Naipaul), 165, 166–171, 173
Minelli, Liza, 199
Mira behn, 259–264, 265, 267–268, 272, 291. *See also* Slade, Madeleine (Mira behn)
Mr. Norris Changes Trains (Isherwood), 199
Mr. Stone and the Knights Companion (Naipaul), 155
Mistral, Gabriela, 277
Mokashi-Punekar, Shankar, 182
Monier-Williams, Monier, 186
Montessori, Maria, 5, 284
Montgomery bus boycott, 250–251, 252
Moore, G. E., 111
Mormonism, 85, 87
Mother India (Mayo), 150
Mountbatten, Lord, 242, 265
Mughal empire, 12, 42, 288
Müller, Max, 186

My Guru and His Disciple (Isherwood), 185, 207, 211, 222
Mystic Masseur, The (Naipaul), 154, 174

Naipaul, V. S., 7, 51, 100–103, 110–113, 147–176, 272–273, 280, 281, 286, 288, 291, 292, 297
  background, 150–156
  books, 100, 149–150, 154, 155, 157–158, 161–162, 163–174
  caste system and, 152, 158, 160
  in England, 150–151, 153–156
  father and, 155–156, 157–158, 164, 174
  Gandhi and, 227, 231, 240
  Hinduism and, 111, 152, 160, 169
  identity issues and, 101–102
  in India, 3, 4, 6, 100–102, 110–111, 147–150, 157–162, 164–170, 172–176
  in the Ivory Coast, 162–165
  marriage, 155
  in New York, 170–172, 174–175
  Trinidad and, 150–153, 155, 160, 161–162, 174
Nandy, Ashis, 266, 278
National Association for the Advancement of Colored People (NAACP), 247
Nationalism, 17, 42–46, 90–91, 152, 158, 238, 245, 257, 266
National Reformer (newspaper), 66–67, 68
National Secular Society, 61–64
Nazism, 199–200
Nehru, Jawaharlal, 18, 25, 42, 91, 152, 158, 188, 243, 245, 246, 251–252
Nehru, Motilal, 90
New Age movement, 75–76, 95
New India (newspaper), 80–81
Nietzsche, Friedrich, 250, 295
Nixon, Richard, 166
Nobili, Roberto de, 172

Occult Chemistry (Besant and Leadbeater), 83, 93
Occultism, 69, 93, 272. *See also* Theosophy/Theosophical Society

Index

Index